Kick the Tire
and Light the Fire

Lee Brewer

Illumina
PUBLISHING

First Edition

Illumina Publishing
P.O. Box 2643, Friday Harbor, WA 98250
www.illuminapublishing.com
360.378.6047

Cover design and interior layout by Bruce Conway

All photos, illustrations and paintings by Lee Brewer unless otherwise noted.

Printed in the U.S.A. on recycled paper

ISBN: 978-0-9818092-8-1

Library of Congress Control Number: 2009932772

Acknowledgements

To Brother Bob; role model and fighter pilot in WW II.
Grandaughter Barbara Zeurcher for her computer expertise.
Dr. John Geyman for his sage advice.

Special acknowledgments go to all those aviators
who have gone West without recording their stories.

p. 268	p. 126	p. 261	p. 255

Identification of front cover photos
by page numbers

p. 245	p. 156	p. 97	p. 108
p. 215	p. 137	p. 227	p. 110
p. 228	p. 63	p. 135	p. 67
p. 254	p. 265	p. 77	p. 259

CONTENTS

Kick the Tire and Light the Fire

PREFACE

I have written an autobiography of some 500 pages with more than 200 pictures, illustrations and drawings, but you won't see them all here. How come? It all started about five years ago when I found that my father had kept the 67 letters I'd written to him during my service in WW II.

Steven Ambrose wrote *Band of Brothers* about WW II in Europe. Then, on TV, he solicited diaries, oral histories, documents and other material pertaining to WW II in the Pacific, ostensibly to write a similar historical account about that theater of operations. Time was of the essence because WW II veterans were dying at the rate of about 1500 a day.

I called the phone number given on my TV screen and spoke to Steven's wife in Idaho. She asked me to send what I had to the Eisenhower Center at The University of New Orleans. I put my 67 letters on tape and sent them and some other documents to the Center. I had made copies of the 21 ninety minute tapes as a record for my family. Then a suggestion was made: "Why don't you start from the beginning, when you were born?" I did this; thus, an autobiography. However, my editor said I had enough material to write two books. He suggested that I write one about my aviation life and another for my family: the complete autobiography.

What follows is my life of flight, gleaned from most of the mundane material in my autobiography that may be of some interest only to my family. I would like to share my experiences of being airborne, beginning with 10 hours of dual instruction in a Piper J-3 Cub flying out of a large cow pasture in Pennsylvania in 1943. Between then and now (2009) lie 25 years of military flying including combat duty in two wars and post-retirement civilian flying.

There is no fiction in this work, that is, no attempt to create a story. Besides facts, I offer opinions and feelings, however, and I tend to avoid names except where they seem to lend credence to the facts.

There was a hiatus relative to flying between 1946 and 1951 except for Air Force Reserve duties. This period included obtaining a college degree, marrying, building a house and working at Boeing Aircraft Company.

Another hiatus occurred between the time I retired from the Air Force in 1968 and 1984. During this period I was raising two children by myself and building a house. First things first. Rather than leaving blank pages for these periods, I fill them in with some other of my activities that I trust will not put you to sleep. These activities involve three love affairs: foremost is my love of flight. A second is my love of beauty, my art world. The third is my love of sailing. All three of these are intertwined, as I will try to show.

Chapter One

Early Interest and Influences

Let's take a look at some of the changes since I was born in 1924. Just a few years before this date, women had no right to vote and radio hadn't been invented yet. Many people still believed that the world was flat, not round. Columbus sailed on the world; Magellan didn't really sail around the world, he sailed on the world. A retired sea captain, around 1894 decided to sail around the world by himself. His name was Joshua Slocum. It took about 4 years to complete the trip, gaining the distinction of being the first man to do this. As he progressed, he was met, greeted and hosted by many dignitaries. One of these was the Prime Minister of South Africa, Paul Kruger. Recounting some his adventures to the Prime Minister, he mentioned something about sailing around the world. The Prime Minister interrupted him and, in his view, corrected him, saying that he was sailing on the world; and there you have it, a chief of state in the late nineteenth century harboring a false view of the world.

In 1924, when I was born, the airplane was only 21 years old. The speed record for aircraft in 1924 was 267 miles an hour. Nobody had flown around the world yet. In September 1924, the first flight around the world took place with four U.S. Army planes fitted with floats. (They used wheels from time to time on the trip.) Of the four that started from Seattle, only one completed the trip. There were no helicopters then. Most cars when I was born were Model T Fords. The first coast to coast flight took place in 1924, averaging 84 miles an hour, and it took 27 hours. There were no aircraft carriers. Football players never wore face masks (except those that wore glasses) and there was no separate offensive and defensive teams; the platoon system had not been invented yet. The football player was called a "60 minute man", and a substitute would take his place only because of an injury. Linemen on the offensive were not permitted to use their hands. Basketball was supposed to be a no-contact game. We openly discriminated against blacks. There was a radio show called Amos and Andy, a comedy, that chronicled goings on in a black community, and when on stage, the featured white actors had blackened faces and white lips. There was also a singer and entertainer called Al Jolson that, at times while on stage, impersonated a black this way. Then there was a nursery story for kids called *Little Black Sambo*. As late as 1943 I was told by the driver I could not sit in the rear of a bus in Montgomery, Alabama.

In 1924, clear up to WW II, there was little or no color photography. If you wanted your portrait in color, a black and white print was treated with pigments: oil colors were applied with cotton on the end of a wooden stick like a match stick. I have a photo of myself taken in 1942 that is treated this way. There were no match books. You could tell the make of a car by the shape of its radiator; they were distinct from one another; nowadays, cars all look alike. Hydraulic brakes were not common until the late thirties; there were no power brakes, no power steering and airplanes had tail skids instead of tail wheels. Water didn't come in bottles, it came from the tap in the kitchen sink. There was no espresso, except perhaps in Europe. No polyester, no nylon, no orlon, no sulfa drugs or antibiotics, no plastic boats (they are called "fiberglass", but they are made of plastic called polyester, reinforced with glass fiber). There was no DDT, no nuclear power plants, no nuclear weapons, no band-aids, no contact lenses, no laundry detergent, just soap. When one wore a hole through a shoe, one cut a piece of cardboard and inserted it as we did when we were kids. Although a cobbler could apply a half-sole, that cost money which was rare or non-existent during the Depression. Of course, a cardboard insert didn't work too well in wet weather. When I was growing up, there was no television; my high school physics teacher said television would never be commercially feasible because it cost too much. There was no penicillin, no GPS, no frozen foods, no Xerox, no scanners, no Frisbees, no radar, no contraceptive pills, no ballpoint pens; they came along in 1939 and cost $15. There were no lasers, nor credit cards. There were no garbage disposals, no clothes dryers and no dishwashers. People used to get married first then live together and divorce was stigmatic. There were no gay rights, no computer dating, no dual careers, no day-care centers, and no same sex marriages. We expected to be governed by good judgment and common sense. Somehow we were imbued with a sense of right and wrong and to stand up and take responsibility for our actions. Serving our country was a privilege; living here was a bigger privilege. We thought fast foods were what people ate during lent; a draft dodger was one who closed the door when the wind blew. I never heard of broccoli nor Brussel sprouts. I never heard of FM radio, tape decks, electric typewriters, computers, CDs or DVDs, yogurt, or males wearing earrings. We listened to the President's speeches on the radio. Anything with the label "made in Japan" on it was junk, and "making-out" referred to how you did on your school exams. Pizza Hut, McDonalds and instant coffee were never heard of. There was no pizza in the United States except in isolated Italian communities; the appetite for pizza as we know it was brought back by our soldiers who had been stationed in Italy during WW II, just as Napoleon's troops brought croissants to France from Turkey.

For a nickel, you could buy an ice cream cone, a Coke or a ride on the streetcar. In Seattle, a kid could ride for 2 cents in the summertime, and get a transfer, a small piece of paper, which allowed him to continue his trip within a time limit at no extra cost. You could spend your nickel and mail one letter and two postcards. The 3 cent stamp was standard. The postman delivered your mail to your residence twice a day and once on Saturday. A new Chevrolet coupe sold for $600 (if you could afford one). Gas was about 15 cents a gallon.

When I was growing up, grass was something that was green and grew around the house; coke was a soft drink and a rocker was a chair. Rock was synonymous with the word stone. Stoned meant somebody was throwing rocks at you. Pot was a utensil that your mother cooked with. Hardware was sold in a hardware store and software wasn't even a word. Crack was a defect in something or the noise a whip made. This was the last generation to believe that a lady needed a husband to have a baby. When I was a kid, coins were made out of silver, except pennies and nickels, of course. My first job paid 10 cents an hour helping a neighbor who was building a sailboat. This was at the age thirteen; however, I got much more out of it because I learned the value of the work ethic and craftsmanship. In the last two summers I was in high school, I worked in a fish and chip shop where my mother worked; I earned the minimum wage: 25 cents an hour. My primary job was peeling potatoes.

After my high school graduation in 1942, my brother Bob and I worked in a sheet metal shop in the Seattle-Tacoma Shipyard. The war was going on. We were building destroyers for the Navy. My wage was a dollar and 25 cents an hour... a good wage at that time. When I went into the Army in March of 1943, my pay was $50.00 a month. This was quite a raise from the pre-war salary for a soldier who earned $21.00 a month. I remember, in basic training, looking at the tip of my rifle at "present arms" at retreat each evening and saying to myself, "I've earned another dollar 66 2/3 cents today."

In the depression, the milkman would bring milk to your door or you could buy it in a store. It came in glass bottles and the cream would be floating on top. This was nice if you had a separate use for the cream. There was no such thing as homogenized milk. If you didn't want the cream separated, you would put your finger on the cardboard cap on the top of the bottle and shake it briskly.

In 1935, an ordinary bicycle cost about $20.00, and in my case, I had to pay half. A one pound loaf of bread was 10 cents; a pound and a half loaf 15 cents. A tire for my Model A Ford cost $4.75 at Sears Roebuck Company in 1940. Gasoline was about 17 cents a gallon then. We were all brown-baggers when it came to school lunches. I remember my mother sending me to the butcher shop to buy a dime's worth of lunch meat for the next day's brown bag lunches for three boys. Of course, dollars in those days were different. Inflation has eaten up the value of the dollar.

My First Car, A $75 1930 Model A. Ford. Note rock parking brake

In 1940, the Washington State sales tax was only 3%. The State printed small coupons in the green color of dollar bills. Each represented a third of a cent, and these were circulated and used to pay the sales tax on what you bought. Later, since the paper was fragile and wore out quickly, tokens (we called them "hickeys") were circulated. These were about the size of a nickel and made of aluminum with a hole punched in the center. During the war, aluminum was in short supply, so they were replaced by plastic tokens. When sales taxes were raised, pennies took the tokens' place. Incidentally, the sales tax is a poor tax. Why? Because poor persons spend all their income to survive, thus, it is all taxed. The wealthy person doesn't have to spend all of his income so his surplus is not taxed. This discrimination against the poor is unjust, therefore, a sales tax is a poor tax. The reason we have sales tax is that it is easy to collect: the State has thousands of tax collectors (merchants who sell anything but food in Washington nowadays) that the State does not have to hire. So much for a view of the general milieu between my birth in 1924 and about December 7, 1941.

Allow me to begin again about 1924, by telling about the general aviation atmosphere that existed during my formative years in the late twenties and the depression-ridden thirties. I was reared in a city in which aviation was dominant. Seattle had, and still has, the Boeing Airplane Company. Although the corporate headquarters of Boeing are now in Chicago, Boeing's principal construction activity is still in Seattle and its environs. Growing up in Seattle meant that there often were articles in the three local newspapers about Boeing activities. I remember looking for these while checking on the daily comic strips. Besides this local influence, there was the general excitement of aviation itself nearly everywhere. These years are a part of 'The Golden Age of Aviation,' the era of development from the Wright brothers' success to the beginnings of WW II. Heavier-than air-aviation wasn't very old when I was born, thus it was new and exciting not only to youth but to much of the public. This excitement was perhaps augmented by the contrast of drab life during the depression.

In the third grade (1933) my art teacher, Miss Foss, had us make small books for a project. I still have mine, complete with the Boeing Airplane Company logo I drew and a dedication page to my mother. This book served as a photo album for airplane pictures I took while growing up, some of which I show here.

As a child, building models and drawing pictures of airplanes were as close to flying as I could get. Primarily, these models were not of the flying kind, but those of solid wood construction. One could buy a kit that had printed plans, balsa wood, glue (which was seldom enough), sometimes paint and a small piece of sandpaper. These cost money, of course, a commodity that was non-existent or in short supply as a youngster. There was no allowance until I was thirteen, then it was a quarter a week. It is difficult to understand this paucity of money until one has been where there is none or very little. As a child, however, growing up with a dearth of money, it was 'normal', that is, I didn't know the difference; that was the way it was.

There was a next door neighbor who provided a silver dollar for an all-day job of cutting his lawn with a push type reel mower, trimming the periphery with hand clippers on hands and knees, raking the cut grass and clippings together and taking them to a compost pile. This was a good deal. I knew what my pay would be each time if I passed the owner's inspection. This source only appeared about every two weeks in the summer and, of course, the grass didn't grow in Seattle's winter. I also mowed the lawn of the grade school principal when I was twelve. I'm not sure how I came by this job, but I later suspected that it was a consideration that there was no father in our home and Mom could use some help. My father ran off with a housekeeper in my mother's absence when I was twelve. My brothers were fourteen and seven at that time.

I suspect the same consideration was given when I was offered a job in the school lunchroom adding the cost of each pupil's meal and making change. A free lunch was my wage. My ego got a boost when I was chosen for this job, thinking I got it because my arithmetic was superior in adding and making change.

Picking wild blackberries and selling them door to door was a seasonal source of small change. I tried a newspaper route but that failed; no one wanted to pay their bills and I was too shy to insist.

Mrs. Brewer and the boys in their aviation helmets and fleece lined coats. Circa 1933

One windfall occurred when my brother Bob, Stan Griffiths and I built a boat and then a neighbor wanted to buy it. It wasn't much of a boat: slab-sided, assembled from purloined green lumber from a house-building site. The nails we used came from a wonderful place in Stan's basement. There was a large box of hardware there with nails, screws and other neat stuff. The nails were always bent and rusty; their source was apple boxes, as near as I could figure. There was no hardware or lumber store nearby, so I was surprised when I learned one could buy nails that were straight and shiny.

Our boat's seams were caulked with kapok from an old mattress. We tore tar from street joints and melted it in a tin can over a fire. The kapok was dipped in this and paid into the boat's seams. At the end of summer, the boat was stored on its side against Stan's house. It was there that the neighbor saw it and wanted to buy it. I remember four dollars being the price, but my brother said it was five. We apologized to the buyer because the boat had no thwarts (seats). He said that was all right by him. Momentarily we considered building some more boats to make some money, but changed our minds when passing by the neighbor's house. He was using it to mix concrete.

Growing up, we had many of these water related activities since we lived near the beach. There were, we considered, prime spots on the beach. To assure we would occupy these, we would rise early, go down to the beach and spread blankets on our choice spots, then go back home and go to bed. Thus, we had reservations. Sunbathing and girl watching were how we occupied a good deal of our time on the beach. We would roll driftwood logs into the water and play with them. When we were through playing with them, we would keep an eye on them and challenge other kids that tried to usurp them. Those of Japanese descent were always challenged. This was odd, because we went to high school with kids of Japanese descent and there was no prejudice there. I think these challenges were the result of the news of Japanese aggression and atrocities in China in and around 1937.

Freighters sometimes would jettison dunnage overboard. Nowadays, cargo is carried in containers. Prior to containers, much cargo was shipped in wooden crates that were individually built. When the cargo was offloaded, the lumber from the crates was dumped overboard. Imagine a bunch of toothpicks randomly intertwined, picked up as a mass and dumped overboard. That's what these dunnage piles looked like. We would row out to take a look to see if we could find some salvageable wood. You could climb on this mass looking for good wood and it would slowly rotate, depending on your position. This was dangerous.

Another thing we did as kids that was water related, was to build a diving helmet. We used a gas tank from an old junk car. Some old cars had the gas tanks on the exterior, not hidden inside. The cross section of the tank was oval in shape. We cut the tank so you could put your head up inside it, fitting it around the shoulders and down the back and chest. The metal edges were sharp so we took an old garden hose, slit it lengthwise and laced it around the edges. Next, we got a piece of yellow cedar from Denny, Stan's older brother, who was building a boat, and shaped it on his band saw. It was cut to fit on the curved surface of the tank. This made a frame to hold a piece of glass so the diver could see ahead. The glass was set in putty and bolted to the tank. Next, a galvanized pipefitting was soldered to the upper rear of the tank, now a helmet. This was the weakest part of the construction. Soldering was weak and would break loose. We had no means of brazing or welding to make it stronger. We attached a garden hose to the helmet for an air source, the other end of the hose was attached to a double barrel tire pump in Ian's row boat. The helmet had a tendency to float up because of the air in it, so you had to hold it down with one hand over the top of the helmet. The other hand was used to keep the diver on the bottom by grasping a rope that was fastened between two five gallon cans with sand in them. The water would rise inside the helmet just below your mouth. You had a good view of the surroundings. How deep? Maybe ten or fifteen feet. How long? A few minutes at most; the cold water of Elliot Bay was the limiting factor.

Ian owned a rowboat. We were up the Duwamish River in the boat near what is now South Center. We were on the bank, naked, having a mud fight. There were no houses there, but the railroad was close by. Along came a passenger train whose patron's had an interesting view. We waved, the passengers waved and we continued our mudslinging.

Another time with the rowboat on the Duwamish near the West Seattle Bridge, we saw a large steamer coming down the river and we had to row to get out of its way. As it went by, we looked up at the stern to read the ship's name. It said, "Stanley A.Griffiths, Boston." There were three of us in the rowboat: my brother Bob, myself and Stanley A. Griffiths. Quite a coincidence.

On the river, we would explore old wooden ships that were tied up at a shipbreaker's yard. We would climb aboard to look around, being very careful because the decks and ladders were very slippery. Incidentally, there were scores of these old wooden vessels on Lake Union waiting their turn at the ship breakers.

From Alki Beach, you could see tugboats pulling log rafts to lumber mills. I often wondered why the rafts were being towed in opposite directions. I suppose the source of the timber and the location of the sawmill dictated where the rafts would go. Rowing out to the slow moving rafts, we would take a tennis ball, tie up to a raft and play ball tag. This was dangerous because if you fell off a log or in between them, you might not be able to surface again.

In the evenings, sometimes we would fish off the walkway on the seaward side of the natatorium. We would get bait from the fish and chips shop and try to see what we could catch. Usually it was the mud shark, (the dogfish, or squalus.) We didn't like mud sharks because, after all, they were sharks and they would scare us when we saw them in the water with us. Catching one, we would cut off its tail to keep score, slit the belly and toss it back into the water. This would attract other sharks. The beach might be littered with these carcasses the next morning. One time, Ian remarked that he had another one on his line and began pulling it in hand overhand, then, all of a sudden, the line became taut and burned his hands trying to stop whatever he had caught. Eventually, he got it under control and led it around to the beach; it was too heavy to lift out of the water. It was a skate, a bottom fish roughly diamond shaped like a ray. It was quite large, perhaps four feet across and attracted several spectators on the beach. Among the spectators was a woman who owned the natatorium. She wanted to put the skate in the cold water pool in the natatorium. It didn't happen; we pushed it back into the water.

One time Bob and Ian rowed over to Bainbridge Island. On the beach there, they found an old Indian dugout canoe that had a hole in the bottom, apparently abandoned. They towed it to Alki and we went to work on it. On a midnight requisition, we got some canvas to cover the canoe. The hole was patched, the canoe painted and a small canvas deck was made on the bow. This canoe was made for inland waters, unlike the oceangoing vessels whale-hunting Indians used historically. It had very little freeboard, perhaps four or five inches with two persons in it. We had a lot of fun with this canoe, which we christened "Kickapoo." However, one time it could have been the end of two of us.

On a bright summer day, five of us in the rowboat and the canoe went over to Bainbridge Island and were eating our lunch on the shore when the sheriff came along. He recognized the canoe that he thought should not have been in our possession. He went for help. In the meantime, the weather had changed; a strong northeasterly wind had arisen. Under the circumstances, we decided to leave. Les and Ian got in the rowboat and  Bob, Stan and I got in the canoe, but it wouldn't float with three of us in it. The two lightest of us, Stan and myself set out in the canoe. Bob joined Les and Ian in the rowboat. Our destination was Alki, about three miles distant. We had to take the waves on the port quarter, otherwise, taking them on the bow or broadside would swamp us. We lost sight of the rowboat because it was running a little more crosswind. They took turns rowing and bailing and landed on the south side of Alki point. Fortunately, our heading took us close to where we wanted to go. Adrenaline was pumping. Sometimes water would slop over the side into the canoe, flow past me and funnel out of the canoe past Stan. As we approached shore, we changed heading to come close to some small boats anchored offshore. We did this in case we swamped, we might be able to swim to one of these boats. This change in heading put the waves more to our rear and as we got near shore, the boat swamped and down we went. I rolled out to one side and Stan rolled out the other. A few swimming strokes, and we could stand. We pulled the canoe up on the beach. The other three had landed OK and notified their parents that they were safe. Some were out looking for Stan and myself. This was a harrowing experience that could have ended in disaster... a close one.

We used the canoe for spear fishing. We took large nails and put them on the streetcar tracks. The trolley would flatten them out, and with some filing we could fashion a point. We mounted these on a broom handle or some similar haft. We could paddle slowly over the sandy bottom and spear small sole. I don't remember eating any of these, but I do remember burying some in the backyard.

We stepped a mast on the canoe, built an outrigger for stability and bent on a canvas sail. The canoe would go fast downwind and crosswind, but it would not sail on a beat upwind because it had neither keel nor other device to grip the water and counter leeway. Glenn and I would tow the canoe upwind along the beach to Duwamish Head, a good mile away and sail back home. Glenn would crawl out on the outrigger to keep us upright in a good breeze. Fun, fun, fun.

Back to making money in order to pursue my interest in aviation. There were only a few paths open toward flying that did not cost money. One of these was a program sponsored by the Richfield Oil Company. It published a weekly newspaper which was free for the taking if you passed by one of their gas stations. The featured fictitious character in the paper was a teenaged pilot named Jimmy Allen. His adventures stoked the fire of flight in me and some of my friends. For the asking, one could join Jimmy Allen's club and obtain a small pair of wings to wear. This was a good advertising ploy for the oil company, capitalizing on the general interest in aviation.

There was another club called "The Junior Birdmen of America." I don't recall if this had a sponsor or not. I do remember that some sort of cost was involved. This club had a better set of wings to which small bars could be attached if you attained goals that were offered, somewhat analogous to merit badges in the Boy Scouts.

At age twelve, I learned of a model-making contest sponsored by Frederick and Nelson's department store in Seattle. One had to go to the store and pick up a set of plans, build the model and, on an appointed day, bring the model to the store for judging. This was to be a solid model of the Douglas DC-3, the aircraft that revolutionized the air transport industry in the thirties. I made my model, painted it silver, put it in a paper sack, and took it downtown. I looked at the other entries spread out on a long table and never took my model out of the sack because mine didn't look like the rest of them. The reason mine differed was that the plans were half-scale; one was supposed to double the dimensions. Not being familiar with such things, I only doubled the length, but neither the width nor height. Actually, my creation was much more handsome because it looked like a modern jet fighter: long and slim with swept back wings. One day, I would fly this historic aircraft, the C-47 (military designation for the DC-3).

When I was thirteen, Denny Griffiths, Stan's older brother, was building a sailboat. He hired me to help. My wage was ten cents an hour. I don't think we had a minimum wage law at that time (1937). I will say that I gained much more than a dime an hour because I learned a good deal from Denny. He was sort of a father figure for me and instilled in me a work ethic and an appreciation of fine craftsmanship.

Incidentally, Denny sold this boat to Eddie Allen, Boeing's chief test pilot. Eddie Allen died in a crash testing the second protoype B-29 on February 18, 1943. Less than an hour after this accident, I passed by Fry's meat packing plant in Seattle where I saw the tail of his airplane sticking out of a wall. Later, I would go into combat in a B-29. One airplane in our unit had Eddie Allen's name painted on it as a memorial.

Now I had a little money to spend on models. Another thing I bought was reading material, principally WW I pulp magazines. Pulp magazines got their name for their rough, cheap paper. My Mom read those that dealt with the wild west; I bought those that dealt with the exploits of aviators in WW I: *G-8 and His Battle Aces* was one of these.

Here are some of the aviation pulp magazines, mostly of aerial action in WW-I that we read during the thirties. 'G-8 and his Battle Aces was my favorite.

Others were *Wings, Aces* and *Air Trails*. These magazines cost ten to twenty cents apiece and would circulate among friends and, of course, my brother. There was no library near where I might have found other flight material. However, I remember reading Lindbergh's book, *We* in the sixth grade This was his story of his solo Atlantic crossing in May 1927.

There was no knife at home sharp enough to whittle on soft balsa wood. The softer the wood, the sharper the edge must be. Razor blades were my cutting tools. I don't know where they came from, because there was no father in the house and neither my brother nor I were shaving yet. I would take a blade and break it in half along its long dimension, then break each half with pliers so each had a pointed angle. A piece of adhesive tape from the medicine cabinet in the bathroom served as insulation for my finger when I pushed the tool. Occasionally, I would come by a blade that had only one edge and a backing metal strip. This facilitated pushing the tool without the tape needed to protect the fingers. I couldn't break this blade to make a pointed tool, however. I built solid models of several WW I fighters, a Martin B-10 bomber, a Bell Airacuda, the DC -3 (as described above), a Sikorski amphibian and some of my own design. A flying model of a WW I Fokker D-8 I made was too heavy to fly well because I had painted it with some cheap black paint I'd found in the garage. So, I took it up on top of the roof, wound up its rubber band-powered propeller, doused it with kerosene, lit it afire, and launched it.

I made another gross error the first time I tried building a flying model. A kit was given to me by an uncle who was visiting. I immediately opened the kit and started to work. I followed the directions and spread the plans out and put a sheet of waxed paper over them (to keep balsa pieces from sticking to the paper plans when glue was applied). As the first step, I was to glue balsa strips on the images shown through the transparent waxed paper, making the framework of the fuselage's side. These pieces were held in place by straight pins until the glue dried. I understood the length and size of the framework joinery pieces, but didn't understand a thin line shown that looked like it fastened the extremities of the frame members together. Since it appeared only as a line and had no thickness, I assumed that it was a length of thread and glued one there. Proud of my work and my speed in building, I took my work downstairs to show my uncle. He was puzzled by the thread and pointed out that the line represented the cross-sectional view of the tissue paper covering of the airplane, not a thread.

As a kid, I heard that there were tiny gas engines that could be used to power flying models, but I never saw one. Also I heard that there were small gas engines that powered Maytag washing machines that could be used to power the 'bugs' (sometimes called 'soap-box racers') that we built. I never saw any of these engines either.

My models hung on threads in the bedroom I shared with my older brother. I don't recall any modeling done by Bob, but he was interested in the pulp literature that circulated, as well as the aviation activity going on around Seattle. Later, he would become a role model for me, being a fighter pilot in combat in the Pacific Theater of Operations in WW II.

Somehow I got interested in modeling boats; perhaps growing up on a beach in Seattle had an influence. I made a small model of the 'Queen Mary', a passenger liner. Next was a model of the cruiser 'U.S.S. Indianapolis'. Later, I would have an indirect relationship with this warship during WW II. Columbus' ship 'Santa Maria' was next. Then I saw a movie with Errol Flynn called *Captain Blood*. His ship was called 'Arabella.' I made a model of this in 1937and still have it. I won first prize, (a small 'loving cup') in a model contest with this boat. A neighbor, who had a small jewelry shop in downtown Seattle, learned of this and offered to engrave my name on the cup if I let him display my model in his shop window for a while. It seems all the airplane models disappeared with time, but two ship models survived.

Model of Captain Blood's 'Arabella'. Made when I was 13.

Model of the 'Bounty' I made at 15

The other was of the 'H.M.S. Bounty,' which I made at age fifteen. Unknown by me for many years, Mom kept these intact. So much for models and their financing.

At age twelve I had a one-time only experience. I made a parachute from some canvas and rope. I jumped off the garage roof with it . Of course it didn't work. A second time I was 'airborne' was when I fell about thirty feet from a young cedar tree in which my brother Bob and another boy and I were playing 'tag' in tree tops. There would be three other times when I considered making a 'nylon letdown,' but didn't have to...close ones.

A repeated adventure was to go to Boeing Field in the south part of Seattle. From where we lived on Alki Beach in West Seattle, we would catch a streetcar and ride it as far as First Avenue South (this cost only two cents for students in the summer), and then walk over to Sixth Avenue South, turn south and go through 'Georgetown,' thence to Boeing Field. Sometimes we would catch a rickety old bus on Sixth Avenue South and go through 'Georgetown.' At other times, we would ride our bicycles from Alki to Boeing Field. What would we do there? Primarily, gawk...fill our eyes with the real thing. We'd usually keep our hands in our pockets, knowing that this attracted less attention.

Boeing model 247

However, there were times when hangar doors were left open, which we interpreted to be welcoming gestures for visiting boys. Out of sight, we would be more curious and climb in and on airplanes. One machine I well remember was a Boeing 247 (all metal twin engine transport which came out in 1933, about the same time as the DC-3). I recall having to step over the main wing spar where it passed through the passenger cabin. I also recall stealing a souvenir from this airplane. It was a small sign which read 'OCCUPIED.' It was designed for passengers who would temporarily disembark at intermediate

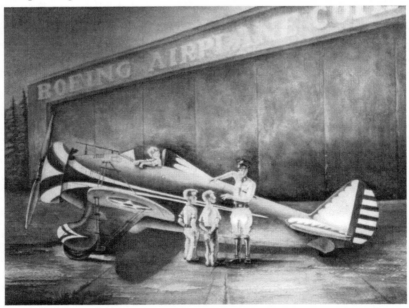

Watercolor of Lee, Stan and Bob with Boeing P-26 at Boeing Field, 1935. As the twig is bent, so grows the tree. All three of us became aviators.

stops. They would put the sign in their seat, thereby reserving that particular seat for the rest of the flight. This sign was on our bedroom wall for some time. Another machine I remember climbing into was a Kellet autogiro.

One visit in 1935 to Boeing Field particularly stands out. My brother Bob, Stan Griffiths and I saw three Boeing P-26s on the flight line. This was the first line fighter of the Army Air Corps at that time. We approached them with our hands in our pockets, gawking. A lieutenant came out of a hangar toward us and I thought we were going to catch a bit of hell; however, he asked us if we had any questions. Of course we did. We were quite impressed by him in his uniform, complete with tall leather boots, wings on his chest and swagger-stick in his hand. I was allowed to sit in the cockpit. It may be of interest to know that all three of us became aviators. "As the twig is bent, so grows the tree." The Boeing P-26 is an all time favorite of mine. I have made a watercolor painting of the experience we had that day.

When I was fourteen, one of our gang members, Ian Aitken, and I went out to Boeing Field in his father's 1929 Buick to look at airplanes. While we were gawking, a man came up to us and asked if we'd like to go for an airplane ride. The price was two dollars apiece. I didn't have any money, but Ian did. The pilot said we'd have to telephone home first to see if it was OK with our parents. We did this and off we went. I don't know what make of airplane it was. There were two seats in tandem, the pilot in front and both Ian and myself crammed in back. I was surprised to see things from the air that I didn't know existed; for example, a large water reservoir near the field. Another thing that surprised me was when we turned to land: the wing went down but I didn't fall in that direction; my weight was in the seat of my pants! Our flight was little more than a circuit around the field, but was impressive. Later, Ian also became an aviator.

There are several historical aviation events that took place in the thirties that I remember. I think I was about seven years old when Seattle was a-buzz about the first Pacific crossing from Japan to the United States. Clyde Pangborn and Hugh Herndon crashed in Wenatchee, Washington. They 'bellied-in' of necessity because they had intentionally jettisoned their landing gear to reduce drag and weight shortly after takeoff from a Japanese beach. Of course, there was no television then and radio stations made news broadcasts but once a day, usually in the evening. The 'buzz' was made by newshawkers trying to sell papers all over town including residential areas by voice, yelling, "EXTRA, EXTRA…READ ALL ABOUT IT."

In 1933, the Navy's dirigible 'Macon' visited Seattle. This was an impressive sight. My mother took a picture of it over Elliot Bay with her bellows-type Kodak. I have searched for this photo in my family without success. Later in that summer, the 'Macon' crashed in the sea off California. Only recently has the wreckage been found including that of a couple of 'Sparrow Hawk' fighters that it carried. I made a model of a 'Sparrow Hawk' after I had seen the 'Macon' over Seattle.

Airplane racing periodically made the news. The fastest machines were seaplanes, using the water as runways. There were no landing fields long enough to allow these aircraft to get up to flying speed. About 1934, I remember an Italian seaplane, a 'Macchi Castoldi,' setting the world speed record of 441 miles an hour. I had no inkling then that in the future I would fly more than twice that speed on a daily basis.

A boyhood hero of mine, one-eyed pioneering pilot Wiley Post and his passenger, humorist Will Rogers from Oklahoma, passed through Seattle on their way to Point Barrow, Alaska, in the summer of 1935. This made headline news, stuff for eleven year old boys to gobble up. Both were killed in an accident short of their goal in Alaska.

I remember seeing an article in the paper about the first flight of the Boeing P-26 and another around the same time about the XB-17's first flight at Boeing Field. There was a picture of this airplane on the front page of the paper with the caption, "A GIANT OF AN AIRPLANE" This airplane crashed later in Ohio because the pilot did not remove the elevator locks before takeoff. To keep the control surfaces from being flapped around and damaged by wind while parked, sometimes devices are put on them to secure them in place. A friend of mine committed the same error one time in a C-47 (DC-3) transport. He was the commander of a fighter squadron and was transporting all his pilots to another base. Shortly after takeoff,

Boeing P-26 'Peashooter' at Chino, California, an all-time favorite of mine.

he realized his error and cautiously made a circuit and managed to land safely. Needless to say, he was quite embarrassed

Later in 1937, the first B-17s were delivered to an operational unit in the Army Air Corps. Little did I foresee that the B-17 would be in my future.

Nineteen thirty-seven was full of aviation news. In May, the German airship 'Hindenburg' was destroyed by fire in New Jersey. There were dramatic pictures of this event in the papers and in the movie newsreels. Because of their spectacular nature, movie newsreels provided the images that radio could not.

Movies were very popular during the Depression. Perhaps they offered a temporary escape from the drab life that existed for many. Going to a movie theater usually had a program offering a cartoon, a newsreel, perhaps a chapter of an on-going serial drama (aimed at bringing you back the next week), and two major features. In my local theater, this cost ten cents for kids. Sometimes free dishes were given to patrons, hoping that they would come back several times in order to complete a set. Gas stations also did this at times during the Depression.

Visit to Boeing at age 13, 1937

On the second of July 1937, one of my heroes (heroines), Amelia Earhart, disappeared in the Pacific trying to circumnavigate the earth. This remains a mystery. Also in 1937, I remember a Russian airplane attempting to fly from Moscow over the pole to California. They ran into weather and maintenance problems and landed at Pearson Field in Vancouver, Washington. My future brother-in-law, Arthur Kennedy, was in the Army at Fort Vancouver at that time and was assigned to guard this airplane. He told me that the airplane had rusty nails in places where cotter pins would be expected. Recently, Arthur gave some photos to a museum at Pearson Field that he had taken of this airplane in 1937.

That year also saw the XB-15, a huge big brother of the B-17, debut and disappear from the news. I don't recall why it turned out to be a dud, but I vaguely remember that it didn't perform as expected. In the summer of 1938, the Boeing model 314 flying boat made its first flight off the water in Elliot Bay. This seaplane was brought down the Duwamish River from the Boeing plant and for several days made taxi runs on the bay west of downtown Seattle. I recall watching these from Alki Beach where we lived. School was out for the summer and we were at our usual habitat on the beach, girl-watching. Seeing the clipper takeoff was historic. Pan American Airways dubbed these aircraft 'Clippers', no doubt after the square riggers that plied the seas in the past.

Aviators and their feats were often printed in the papers. These grew to be my heroes. Those I remember are Eddie Rickenbacker, Jimmy Dolittle, Billy Mitchell, Amelia Earhart, Kingsford-Smith,

Myself, Mom and brother Bob

Brother-owners, Mom & chief potato peeler of the "Spud, fish & Chip Shop," Alki Beach, 1940

Clyde Pangborn, Howard Hughes, Howard Hawks, Roscoe Turner, Wiley Post and Charles Lindbergh. One that did not qualify for hero status was 'Wrong way Corrigan' who, in 1938, flew the Atlantic solo instead of heading for California, claiming that his compass was faulty.

Many of the pilots listed above gained fame by being the first to do things. A person whose name I don't recall, whom I met in Butte, Montana around 1964, had a 'first' claim. It was unheralded, but none the less, important to him and a fellow pilot. He told me that he and his friend were the first persons to take a horse up in an airplane. He

Earl Boyd, brother Bob, myself and Stan Griffiths about to take off for 'Army Day' at Fort Lewis, 45 miles south of Seattle, 20, April, 1941

said he had held a colt in his arms while his fellow pilot made a circuit of the field in Butte.

April 21st, 1941 was Army Day across the nation. The public was invited to attend celebrations at Army Posts. The nearest major post to Seattle was Fort Lewis, about 45 miles to the south. There would be military airplanes to see there. Four of us, my brother Bob, Stan Griffiths, Earl Boyd (a classmate of mine), and I decided to take in this event. Although we were old enough to drive, the only car available was my old Ford , which could only seat two. So, we went on bicycles.

We rode south on old highway 99 as far as north Tacoma the first day, about 30 miles. Earl had an aunt who lived there, so we slept in her back yard. The next morning we rode south 15 miles to Fort Lewis and took in the sights: trucks, tanks, artillery pieces and airplanes. A free meal was part of the attraction. It was little else than a plate of beans, however quite welcome. I took a couple of pictures of the airplanes, one of which had a large red ball painted on the fuselage aft of the rear cockpit. This was probably a squadron insignia, which was most likely changed following Pearl Harbor because that red

Visit to Fort Lewis, Army Day, April 21, 1941

'meat-ball' was the marking on Japanese warplanes in WW II. After we filled our bellies and eyes, we headed for home. We covered around 60 miles that day. Approaching West Seattle on Spokane Street, we had to decide whether to go the last couple of miles along the beach on the level to Alki, or go up Admiral Way (a steep hill), then downhill to Alki. I don't recall who made the decision, but it was a challenge to climb the hill after pedaling almost 60 miles. Our bicycles were one-speed machines, no gear shifting. Both Bob and I got bicycles for Christmas in 1935; his was red, mine was green. Colson was their trade name. They cost twenty dollars apiece. We knew they would be our Christmas presents because we each had to save one half their price, which wasn't easy.

In high school, there were many new things to occupy me. Athletics was one. Football and track, school politics and girls, even studies. The

Fifteen minutes of fame

father of one of my fellow football team mates ran a logging operation near Mt. Rainier. Early in the 1941 season he told us if we won the city championship he would have the team and their dates up to his camp for a logger's breakfast. That's where we were on the morning of Sunday, December 7th, 1941, when the Japanese attacked Pearl Harbor. We listened to the news on an automobile radio. The next day in school we heard the President ask Congress to declare war on Japan via radios in high school classrooms. These were very sobering times. Most of us were seventeen years old and looked future military service directly in the eye. There was no hiatus of interest in aviation for me between 1939-41. There were daily news reports of military air operations in the media, the Battle of Britain, for example.

At high school in a mechanical drawing class right after December 7th, we were tasked to make solid model airplanes. We painted them flat black. They were to be used in the service to train troops in aircraft identification. I recall one I made was a Japanese Aichi baku geki ki 99 fighter. Later, I would watch the Aichi aircraft plant disappear in Nagoya, Japan, as it was hit by some 400 two thousand pound bombs from my group of B-29s. A few days later we obliterated the Aichi aircraft engine works across the canal.

After high school graduation in June 1942, my immediate objective was to earn money for college. In September, it was on to college. The University of Washington required male students to take courses in ROTC (Reserve Officer Training Corps) for two years. This was a program begun by the Federal Government after the Civil War when it was realized that there had been a dearth of leadership in the military. The Morill Act, passed by Congress, offered land-grants to colleges and universities if they would provide the facilities for military leadership courses; the instructors would be provided by the military. I would be involved in this program later.

The University of Washington offered both a Navy and an Army ROTC program. Both Bob and I tried the Navy, hoping to get into flying training. I failed their physical examination. At that time, the Navy used some oxygen equipment that required holding a device in the mouth. My overbite was judged to be too great to accommodate this device. The Army had two branches in their ROTC: Infantry and Coast Artillery. I ended up in the Coast Artillery. In the meantime, Bob had volunteered for flight training in the Army Air Corps. It wasn't until 2005 that I learned Bob had failed the Navy physical too. He had a large, dark birthmark on his right buttock. Why this

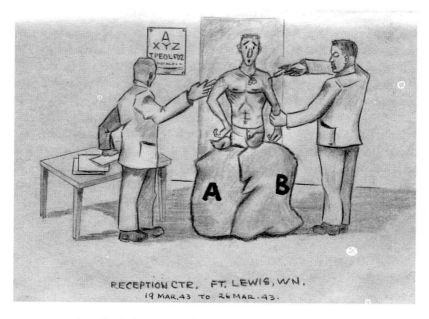

RECEPTION CTR, FT. LEWIS, WN.
19 MAR. 43 TO 26 MAR. 43.

was critical, I don't know. Perhaps such a mark was more prone to becoming cancerous. One of our gang, Ian, volunteered for Naval aviation and also failed their physical. He only had one testicle. He would be accepted if he underwent an operation (at his own expense) to determine if the second one was there, but hadn't descended. It would be removed if it were there. It was not there, so he passed the exam. Incidentally, since he was open, his appendix was removed. Ian, you recall, shared my first airplane ride at Boeing Field earlier. He became a Naval pilot, never leaving the country. His principal duty was ferrying airplanes here and there.

Bob left for pilot training in January of 1943. Another of our group, Stan Griffiths, left for pilot training about the same time. Since Bob and Stan were two years older, I presumed I'd have at least a year more before my draft number came up. I was wrong.

From here on I will quote verbatim from letters I wrote to my father during WW II. What better way to tell it like it was? Had I known what he did in 1936 (abandoning my mother with three kids during the Depression), these letters would probably not exist. I was not aware of the details of this until after the war (1946).

Please tolerate any errors in grammar or spelling you may find in my wartime letters; I entered the Army still eighteen years old. Also, there are racial slurs in my letters. These have no place in writing today, but deleting them here would alter the flavor of history. I tell it like it was. I will skip over much material in these letters to spare you of things that had no bearing on my progress toward getting airborne during the war. I will also annotate things in my letters that may be puzzling, for instance, the meaning of acronyms such as LOP (line of position).

Chapter Two

Training

There are many illustrations, photographs and sketches scattered herein, most of which have never been published before. I kept a small blank-paged journal during WW II in which I made sketches relative to my progress toward becoming airborne. These were made by an untrained artist, myself. This journal also has quotations that I liked and it served as a personal record of the individual bombing and mining missions I flew. I will quote verbatim from this source with some annotations.

Around the middle of January 1943, I was ordered to take physical examination to determine my classification for the draft.

Letter of 14 January, 1943: "After the physical there will be ten days before induction. The whole thing hits on like a ton of bricks. I guess they don't fool around long with it because I know of others who registered last June 30 when I did and they have just left since Christmas time. I went to the Navy recruiting station here and inquired [sic] about enlistment. All enlistment is frozen in all services except one part of the Navy. They take only 75 per week until February 1, that is, if one can pass the physical and the draft board will release him. Quite a mess. I don't know what to do."

Letter of 3 April 1943: "Here I am two weeks in the Army. We are on the go sixteen hours a day. I was at Fort Lewis for a week. This is Camp Callan, thirteen miles north of San Diego. I am in Antiaircraft Replacement Training, a branch of the Coast Artillery. The main reason of my being with the AA is probably because that is the branch of ROTC I had in school. We had a radio test, mechanical aptitude test and a general classification [IQ] test at Fort Lewis. We were graded from I to IV. I was graded I in all three, that's why I'm where I am. This is a school battalion, and we are all going to enlisted specialist schools or Officers' Candidate School. I am going to try my best to become an officer. We are here for basic training and schooling for thirteen weeks 'til about the Fourth of July, and if I'm lucky enough, I'll be sent to Camp Davis, North Carolina to Officer's Candidate School. We're in the best battalion, best battery and best platoon in the camp as far as officers' prospects go."

Annotation: I believe I adjusted quickly and well to regimented life. I seem to have had pride in my unit and was upbeat about the advancement possibilities. Our days were full and physical and we had no trouble sleeping. We ate well enough, but it always seemed to me that there wasn't enough. It was disturbing to see the supply sergeant tossing hot dogs to his pet dog. The hot dogs likely came from the mess hall. After I left the camp, I heard that the mess sergeant was arrested for taking food from the camp to a restaurant in La Jolla that his wife operated.

Letter of 17 April 1943: "Today was our big inspection day…every Saturday. Colonel said, "Mighty good." We just finished bayonet drill and are waiting to eat lunch. We were told we were the best outfit in camp. It will be Bob's birthday Monday…he'll be 21. It just doesn't seem that much time has elapsed since we were playing soldier."

Annotation: The mess hall required extra labor, and of course, a lot of it was available. We were put on a roster, taking turns working in the mess hall. One was designated as kitchen police (KP) or table waiter. My first term on KP, I was put to work peeling potatoes. The duty was from four in the morning until ten at night. Having peeled potatoes in a fish and chip shop two different summers when in high school, I was quite an expert at this. Once I had filled two large tubs with peeled potatoes, the mess sergeant came by and asked who had been helping me. I told him nobody had helped me. Then he told me if I filled a tub with peeled beets, I'd be through for the day. Peeling beets took a bit more time, but I got off early. Apparently, he didn't know peeling potatoes was my civilian occupation!

Letter of 15 May 1943: "This life is OK, but gets tougher every day, but if

Private Brewer, Coast Artillery Corps, Camp Callan, CA 1943. The badges are for marksmanship.

others can take it, I can too. I took the big math test for OCS this last Wednesday and don't know the results yet though. I surely hope I made it as it is quite important. For the past week we have been in quarantine for spinal meningitis, but it's all over now. During the

Lee with Coast Artillery

past week, here's [sic] some of the things we did, just as an example of what we do. Daily, we have infantry drill and gunner's instruction on our battalion's principal weapons, the 40mm AA guns and the AA .50 caliber machine guns. One day this week we fired .30 caliber machine guns at balloon targets. There is [sic] at least two hours daily devoted to physical hardening, and some of it's pretty exhausting. We had two hikes last week. One was about fifteen miles long and we simulated beach defense against landing Japs. The other hike was about twenty miles long and we split the battery and had maneuvers. Also, all yesterday I crawled up a gully in sand, mud and cactus on maneuvers. We have all this [sic] infantry tactics for physical hardening, AA defense, convoys, aircraft identification, first aid, etc. Next week we go through the infiltration course, which is a built-up battleground. We crawl for 450 yards through barbed wire, trenches, and all the time, .30 caliber machine guns chattering overhead four feet off the ground. Also booby traps blow up all around us. The next two weeks is the end of our basic and then we go to school for four weeks."

Annotation: All this fine training and we got paid for it too. A private was paid $50.00 per month. There was little to spend money on. The post had an exchange (PX) where one could buy shoe polish, shoe laces, razor blades, candy, shaving cream, soap, laundry soap and other sundries. Weak beer and soda pop were also available. The PX had a barber shop. A haircut cost 25 cents. The first one I had took one minute and 45 seconds. What has all this have to do with flying? My intention is to show how one could have gotten his nose out of the dirt and gain a position of trust in the most advanced bomber in combat in WW II. Bear with me.

Letter of 28 May 1943: "You said you were anxious to hear how I came out in the math exams. Well, I guess I did OK because I passed it. Last Monday we took the OCS physical examination and I passed everything but my teeth. So, on Tuesday they called me in and yanked two of them out. Next Monday we start to OCS Prep School here. This will last for four weeks. This period will take us up to about the Fourth of July and our training cycle will be completed here. If I'm still in that OCS group, I will be on my way to North Carolina. This is what I want. If I don't make it, I will be transferred to some "line outfit" in the states or I will be put on a banana boat going overseas. You can see how much going to OCS can mean and why I'm trying so much to get there. I know it seems sort of foolish to try to become an officer or even having aspirations of becoming one because I am only nineteen, but others have done it I guess. So far I've been able to take all they have handed out and [sic] come back for more, but there are a lot of fellows like myself that can't or won't take some of the physical hardening that we must go through."

Annotation: In my unit, there was a man who got sick each morning after we ran the obstacle course. On subsequent days, he sickened earlier until his illness hit him when the bugle sounded reveille in the morning. Adjustment by ailment, I believe. Another man in our barracks adjusted by hanging himself with two neckties... "I'm glad to hear that Bob got classified as a pilot as that is what he wanted."

Annotation: My brother Bob was two years my senior and naturally served as a role model for me through childhood and our teenage years. Now he was doing what I wanted to do. I was no longer following him; I was shunted into a different direction. I felt hung out to dry and a tinge of jealousy.

Letter of 4 June 1943: "We are going to school now eight and a half hours during the day and one and a quarter hours every night except Tuesday noon to Wednesday noon. This time is spent on an overnight bivouac and forced march. We made close to 22 miles yesterday and rose at 4:00 AM and we marched into camp. I am lucky to not get blisters as the others do. In fifteen minutes, I have to fall out to go down to school tonight…we march almost a mile to the building at a 'brace,' which is an exaggerated position of attention."

Letter of 20 June 1943: "Today is Sunday and we're in the middle of a rugged weekend. We are on alert. This means we are assigned to the defense of the camp from the east from possible attack by enemy aircraft. This isn't training or practice, it is a real situation. We are given live ammunition and ordered to use it if someone comes into our gun position zone and there is no answer when challenged. This Friday we were on alert (24 hours) and today we go on again. Tomorrow we have the last of our hikes...a 25 mile forced march to be done in seven and half hours with a total weight of 40 pounds. This includes our packs, bedding, rifle, gas mask, tin hats and bayonets and the rest of our full field equipment.

Right now, I have four blisters from our last hike. After the hike tomorrow, we're on bivouac the same night...by Tuesday morning there's going to be a lot of worn out guys around here.

It's now Tuesday, 6:15PM. That hike was a honey yesterday. Twenty five and a half miles in six and three quarter hours! But we did it with light packs instead of the full field pack. I added another blister to one of my feet, but each time we go, it seems I am in just a little better shape. I lost 8 pounds yesterday, and up to now, I've gained back five. All day today I spent digging holes to plant trees."

Annotation: The only casualty from our alert assignments was the bayonetting of a cow in the middle of the night when it failed to answer with the proper password when challenged.

An area near the recreation hall was surveyed, stakes put in the ground and strings stretched forming squares in line with equal spaces between them. Then we dug holes three feet deep in these squares whose sides had to be plumb and corners square. I expected concrete to be poured for a foundation...but no. Topsoil was brought in and a small tree was planted in each hole. This was Army landscaping.

Letter of 26 June 1943: "Well, tonight is Saturday night and this is the end of my twelfth training week here. By this time next week our basic training will have been completed. During next week we are going out on maneuvers and are going to combat the Marine Corps at Camp Pendleton up the coast.

I've found that I have passed the OCS prep course we had a couple of weeks ago and this was quite [a] relief as they don't usually let us know where we stand at all. I surely hope I go to Camp Davis when we leave here although one never knows. We keep hearing about the quotas being cut, and things like that keep me thinking just what is going to happen."

Letter of 14 July 1943: "About two weeks ago we [50 OCS men in our battery] were called down to appear before the board again. Why? We didn't know. When we got down there, they told us the purpose of the interview was to eliminate 95% of us, as the quotas had been cut. Formerly, an average of 50 men per month were taken from this camp, this is why my chances seemed so good. Now they take 5% of 50, or between two or three a month. They chose those with the most college education and over 21 years of age. I was let out with 46 other men. Of course I felt pretty lousy about this for a while, but I have two more pokers in the fire now. I still have my application in for AA OCS and am subject to call if they ever reach my name. This is ASTP (Army Specialized Training Program). Under this, I would go back to some college or university and take engineering, as I was at the U. of W. ASTP courses last from twelve weeks to two years, all the time giving college credits. I have taken the test for that and passed. The IQ requirement is 115, mine is 138 according to the Army, so I am eligible. The other opportunity is the Army Air Corps. I took their written exam and passed. I next go up to Santa Ana (80 miles) for a physical exam and then before a board here at camp. If I pass these two things, I will be in, and will be sent to preflight school such as Bob is in now. Anyhow, I'm going to be around here longer than I thought.

Annotation: There is evidence here of resiliency in the face of adversity. I was disappointed that the quota cut me off from officer training, but quickly found new goals to pursue. Now I had a chance to again follow in my brother's footsteps: to fly. What was the motivation (outside of flying) that caused me to seek advancement in the first place? Part of the motivation was that because I grew up with my older brother and his age group, I had been imbued with a need to be equal with them or left out. Another factor might be that since we were raised in a poverty situation during the Depression (in her later years, my mother told me that there were times when she didn't know where the next meal would come from) there was a motive to be something better. Although I didn't realize it, this may also have been the motive to excel in academics and athletics in my school years.

Letter of 6 August 1943: "First, I'll tell you how I stand with the Air Corps. I passed the physical OK and also appeared before the Aviation Cadet Board here last Monday. All I have to wait for now is my transfer and shipment. God only knows when this will be. Five fellows who got in the Air Corps a couple of months ago, that I went through training with, left a few days ago."

Annotation: While waiting to be shipped out, some of us were put to work constructing a demonstration area to show trainees what fox holes, slit trenches, tank traps and other earth works were. Picks and shovels, and later an 80 pound jack-hammer, were our tools.

Letter of 5 September 1943: "This is Mississippi. [I] may leave here either the seventh or the fifteenth; just taking tests here. We will go to college for five or six months, anywhere in the USA, wherever there is an opening."

Annotation: The Air Corps had a backlog of people waiting to get into flight training. To accommodate these large numbers, small colleges were used to stash away those waiting. Ostensibly, these colleges were to upgrade the educational level of those who would fly, thereby enhancing the efficiency of aircrews. My brother Bob attended such a school in Missouri.

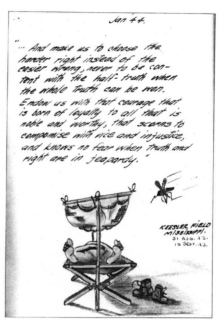

Letter of 11 September 1943: "Keesler Field, Mississippi. I am shipping out on Monday the thirteenth, destination unknown. I'm surely glad that I got my transfer to the Air Corps, as it offers a future, flying is definitely a thing of the future, and if I'd stayed in the outfit I was in, what could a knowledge of an antiaircraft gun do me? Although it's just like starting all over again after I have been in for six months and am eligible for my fifteen day furlough (if I were attached to a unit) but I'll have to give that up and expect no time off until such time as they pin my wings on me or wash me out. I know I can fly, they can wash me out only through a physical.

Letter of 28 September 1943: "I have been at this new place two weeks today, and it's by far the nicest spot I've been in. Slippery Rock is 50 miles north of Pittsburgh. This is the State Teachers' College and there are about 500 men in our detachment. There are civilian students on the campus also, about 200 girls. Here I will go to school from three to five months. Then I will go to Preflight at Nashville, Tennessee. We will get ten hours in the air while here. We took an examination at [sic] Mississippi on these five subjects: math, physics, history and geography (navigation, really), and English. They grade each of these sections separately and if one gets a sufficiently high score on one or more of these subjects, he 'screens out' of the subject. This means that he will probably not take those subjects for such long periods of time as the rest of his group. In the long run, this may mean he will leave here sooner than he is scheduled. I 'screened out' of all but the navigation, about which I never knew anything. I'm glad of this. It's not that I want to get out of here because I just got here and this is a nice place. It's just that I'd like to

Hangar flying without a hangar

advance as quickly as possible. The studies are fairly simple. Besides academics, we have military subjects and physical training. This Air Corps is the 'playboy' life alongside of some of the stuff we took in the Artillery…Here we keep our shoes shined and brass polished or we are 'gigged'…on maneuvers in California and the Mojave desert we were lucky if we could find a way to keep the bugs from falling into the fox holes we dug to sleep in… I probably shined my shoes once every two months or so. It makes me sore sometimes to hear some of the guys here from Brooklyn or North Carolina who have been in the Air Corps, not the Army, for almost two months and are squawking about not having any time off because they haven't been home for two months. Now, I think I had more free time here in a month than I had most of the spring and summer. I hope the Japs have some pretty poor soldiers, because most of the guys I've come in contact with from the East here aren't much to brag about."

Letter of 24 October 1943: "I got split up with my pals I came from California with [sic], but that's the Army for you. Discipline here is a little more rigid than I had before, but the physical exertion isn't as great and there is more free time on the average. All the college hours and credits I will get here will be transferred back to the University of Washington for me. If subjects were as tough here as I had last winter at home in college, there would be a lot of sleep lost."

Lettter of 12 October 1943: "We do practically the same thing every day, not much happens. Our studies are fairly simple. Our first four weeks are up now and I have 'screened out' of all subjects we were required to go through this training period of 4 to 5 months.

I have averaged a little over 97% in math, history, physics and navigation (which I am still taking) and three military subjects. I'll get to choose 'electives' or other subjects not required but offered, such as code or meteorology, which we will need later. I will leave here about the eighteenth."

Annotation: Stan Griffiths volunteered for pilot training about the same time as Bob did. I don't know the reason why, but he failed, 'washed-out' in the vernacular. This was a great disappointment for him and I had heartfelt sympathy for him. It was also a notice that the same thing could happen to me or Bob. Stan then took up Bombardier training.

Letter of 2 December 1943: "[I] had some tests recently: Navigation 100%, Civil Air Regulations 94%, meteorology 100% and 96%. We have to keep a flight log, or notebook, on what we do when we fly. I got all 100s on my six flights and [on] my drawings and notes."

Annotation: This flying was done in Piper Cubs out of a very large cow pasture north of the college. It was quite cold

Slippery Rock, PA

Final check from log book

and the airplanes had no heaters. We were told to wear our tennis shoes while flying in order to feel the rudder pedals better. Our feet were numb from the cold and we felt nothing. I still have my log book from these lessons.

"a merry heart doeth good like a medicine; but a broken spirit drieth the bones". *King Solomon.*

Nashville, TN

Christmas day 1943 was spent in Nashville, Tennessee. There were three classification centers in the country: Nashville, San Antonio and Santa Ana. Each had identical testing facilities to determine which kind of training the cadet was qualified to take.

Letter of 7 January 1944: "I am through with my tests here now, and all I do now is wait for the verdict. I put down for preference: pilot, navigator and bombardier training.

Letter of 12 January 1944: "My classification has come through this morning. We got the news and I'm going to become a navigator. I had my choice for pilot, navigator or bombardier because of qualifying for all. I had my preference for pilot first, navigator second and bombardier third. I talked to the officer of classification and he told me that I showed more aptitude for navigator. You are probably wondering why I didn't choose pilot training like Bob, right? There are a number of reasons and I think I have made the right choice. First, I received my highest scores in the test for navigation school rather than pilot or bombardier. Therefore navigation is the most logical one at which I would succeed. Second, today pilot washouts are 60 to 65%, while navigators is [sic] 5% and bombardiers is [sic] from two to 3%. There is no need to take unnecessary chances. Third, if I took pilot training and washed out, I'd kick myself mentally every time I thought of it for not taking what I was advised. Fourth, I have always liked drawing lines on a piece of paper, whether they were straight ones or not. I had dead reckoning in Pennsylvania and I think I'd like navigation. Fifth, flying I expect to do after the war will be for my own pleasure and enjoyment. We get some more flying in navigator's school, enough to have a license. Pilots will be a dime a dozen after the war and bombardiers will have no place after the war. Navigation is useful…we go to school and learn something. Sixth, I could probably do more good for the Army if I went where I could do the most good and where they want me. I hope I made the right decision. What do you think about it? Of course, if I were eliminated somewhere along the way, I always have the chance of taking one of these others for which I qualified, although it isn't a guarantee."

Annotation: The reasons for choosing navigation training instead of pilot training proved to be wise as you will see. However, some of my 'reasons' for not choosing pilot training are now seen by me to have been rationalizations. I always wanted to be a pilot, a goal I would achieve later. I don't know where the idea came from that navigators would get additional flying time to get a civil license.

Letter of 13 January 1944 (Montgomery, Alabama): "Here we are going through pre-flight school, which will last about nine weeks. I don't think I will regret having chosen navigation. Here I am already in my pre-pre flight whereas the others classified as pilots are still in Nashville, waiting. It seems the Corps has sufficient pilots now as evidenced by the fact they are bringing us navigators into a pilot's pre-flight school and are holding those who chose pilot training in reserve pools. Bob won't have to worry about any of this, as he is all set."

Letter of 5 February 1944: "Our school is through here in about six more weeks, about the middle of March. Studies aren't very hard and I think most of our time is wasted."

Letter of 27 March 1944 (Fort Myers, Florida): "I finished up with the pre-flight school at Maxwell Field about a week and a half early, and have been here at Buckingham Field for almost three weeks now. This is a flexible gunnery school here, the next to last phase of my navigator training. Advanced will be the last step after three more weeks here. There have been a lot of scares, as far as cadets go lately. Evidently the Air

Pre flight school

Corps is full, and the ground forces (infantry, etc.) need men. 38,000 were eliminated from cadet training last week all over the country in basic training centers. Nashville (where I was classified) closed up about a month ago, and today, we learned that my class is the last to go through gunnery here. There's one thing though, if I get thrown out of this like I did at Officers' Candidate School for the Artillery, I'll join the paratroopers before they put me in the infantry as a buck private. It's going to be a race against time anyhow af-

Quintessential aviation cadets with sabers, Maxwell Field, Alabama, 1944

ter working for something for over a year and when all the rest of the kids have made out so well."

"Gunnery is interesting here. There is certainly a lot to learn. We start out with .22s firing in a glorified shooting gallery and end up firing twin .50 caliber machine guns from turrets on Fortresses at 30,000 feet. Now we're shooing skeet with 12 gauge shotguns while traveling on a truck at 30 mph. Blindfolded, I know the 123 parts, by touch and name, of a .50 caliber gun."

"Here I have another Cadet Officer's job, only this time instead of having 40 or 50 men to look after, it's now 836!"

Annotation: Since the Air Corps was manufacturing so many Second Lieutenants, they invented a new rank, that of Flight Officer. Insignia was different, but the pay was the same. (Actually, it was greater if overseas). Ostensibly, the new rank would be given to those

who had mastered the technology related to their job, but didn't have the leadership skills to become a Second Lieutenant upon graduation. It was possible to advance from enlisted status to Flight Officer rank as our flight engineer did when we were in combat. Also, our co-pilot was promoted from Flight Officer to Second Lieutenant. All those in cadet training hoped to be commissioned as a lieutenant rather than be appointed as a Flight Officer. I embraced this idea, holding cadet leadership positions wherever I was. However, after establishing a record of this, when I came to navigation school, I decided to put all my effort into the course rather than play soldier.

Letter of 16 April 1944: "I have one more week here at Gunnery School, leaving the 23rd. This last week will be spent flying. I have been up on two missions this last week. We go up in B-17 Flying Fortresses for all different types of gunnery missions. Flights are four hours long and working in firing our guns at high altitude with oxygen wears you down as a hard day's work. It is interesting though; I use the navigator's equipment (while the pilot or instructor isn't around) instead of resting. There's certainly a lot to learn about this navigation business I can see before I start. I only hope that the 'tempus' will 'fugit' as it has lately…these weeks just fly by it seems. Graduation will come about the middle of September."

"Stan left Nebraska for the east coast, preparing to ship across to England with their brand new B-17G."

Annotation: Some of the B-17 pilots in Gunnery School were women. These were called WASPS (Womens' Air Service Pilots.) They

B-17. The plane we recieved aerial gunnery training in.

were civilians, but experienced aviators.

One day I saw one make a fine emergency landing. Her B-17 would not extend both main landing gears, only one, so she flew around to reduce the fuel load, and thus, the fire hazard. She came in, touched down perfectly on one extended gear and the tail wheel and kept the opposite wing up as speed decreased, then gently allowed the wing to touch which caused the airplane to make what we call a 'ground loop.' No one was hurt and there was a minimum amount of damage.

After each 'live' gunnery mission, the guns were to be cleared, that is, there were to be no cartridges left in the chambers because sometimes the heat generated from firing would cause the round to 'cook off.' Such was the case one time when one of the cadets failed to clear his gun. Before landing, the guns in the waist would be strapped to the floor of the airplane. This time a gun was stored without being cleared and it went off on its own. Unfortunately, the cadet was in the line of fire and lost both feet. His mutilated shoes hung from a nail in our briefing room as a reminder to handle the guns safely.

Letter of 4 May 1944: "Greetings from Georgia…moved again. Normally, the step after Gunnery School is Advanced Navigation, however, things aren't normal because advanced schools are crowded. That's why I am in a Navigator-Bombardier Pool here… a reserve for openings in Advanced. Minimum delay will be three weeks, although not definite. We attend classes here mainly to pass the time. There is one bright angle, however, they are so crowded here that they make a practice of sending 20 to 30% of a class home on furlough. Tomorrow, more definite news, but you cannot tell."

"Yea, through the valley of the Ruhr I fly, I will fear no evil for my .50 calibre are with me. My pilot and my copilot they comfort me, and my Navigator will never lead me astray – I hope."

Telegram of 11 May 1944: "WILL ARRIVE SEATTLE FRIDAY, SON."

Annotation: My furlough in Georgia granted me eighteen days, quite a few, but I had a long way to go. I bummed a ride on an airplane that was going to Shreveport, Louisiana, and

Waiting to get into Navigator's School, Moody Air Field, Valdosta, Georgia, 1944 then another in an AT-6, landing at Love Field, Dallas, Texas. At Dallas, there was no hitch-hiking allowed so I got on a bus for Seattle. Of the 18 days of furlough, I had only 4 days at home; the rest was traveling time. Commercial air transportation was almost non-existent during the war; only bus and train transportation were available. On the return trip from Seattle to Georgia, all five days and nights were spent in coaches with no place to lie down. Meals were eaten at stops. It was summer and the engines were coal burners. If you wanted to escape the heat, you opened a window. Then the soot, cinders and smoke would blow

Navigation cadet, Ellington Field, Houston, Texas

in…rather miserable. At a stop in Billings, Montana, I ate my first ever steak. It hung over the edges of a platter with French fries on top.

When I was at Love Field, Dallas, en route home on furlough, I was turning in my 'chute at the loft when a young lieutenant came through the door, his parachute all spilled out in his arms. He demanded to see the person who had packed his 'chute. The little old lady behind the counter extracted the inspection booklet from the tiny pocket on the 'chute and told the lieutenant she'd go get the packer. Another little old lady appeared and said she'd packed it. The lieutenant said he just wanted to shake her hand because he'd just jumped from his airplane and it had worked!

Letter of 17 July 1944: "Here I am in Texas! I finally got out of Georgia and into Advanced Navigation School. Tomorrow we are going to start classes. This is what I've been looking forward to for a long time and I'm glad I'm finally here, although I know the next few months aren't going to be a picnic. The trip over the weekend will be the last one I'll make as a cadet, the next time I'll either be a lieutenant or a private. Our course is to be sixteen weeks."

Annotation: Our school was at Ellington Field, near Houston.

Letter of 24 August 1944: "…classes all day long and in the evenings yet. We had a hurricane scare the past few days…evacuated

AT-18, C-60, Navigation Trainer

all the planes. [We] had to prepare for it by tying our buildings down fast. We fly another six hour mission tomorrow. Tough work I'll say right now. We have a big phase exam (one every three weeks) this Saturday again. I came out fourth highest of 538 in my class in our first exam, but the tests are really tough."

Annotation: Bob had graduated from Pilot School and was now overseas flying fighters. Stan was in England in a B-17 outfit going on some shuttle runs to the USSR, then to Italy and back to England.

Letter of 6 September 1944: "It seems quite a while since I came here to advanced when I try to reiterate all that has happened in the past few weeks. This is my eighth week now. By next Saturday we would [sic] be just half through with our sixteen week course. We're starting our celestial work now which will prove to be the most interesting phase I believe. I always did wonder how a man could find where he was in the middle of the ocean with just a little instrument and a bunch of tables. My last mission was a simulated combat mission in which the enemy was supposed to have invaded the southeast United States. We were to bomb a railroad bridge at Keesler Field, Mississippi, just where I was a year ago. [We] had a second phase exam a week ago and made out a little better this time, I was first with 94%."

Letter of 21 September 1944: "Last night our echelon had to go to the PX and start ordering our uniforms. Boy, those officers' clothes are nice. It certainly would be [a] shame to get this close to officer status and not make it, however, I'm still in good standing with my group. There are only about ten of my echelon of 48 who haven't flunked a flight mission, ground mission or phase exam or a number of them. So far, so good. There have been three washed out of my echelon so usually [the] percentage runs around 20%.

Letter of 15 October 1944: "We have only a couple of missions to fly now. Our last one was Friday, a night celestial from here up into Oklahoma and back [I] had pretty good results from it. It's sort of amazing to see how all this theory and stuff they teach us here on the ground really works. There are only two in my echelon who haven't flunked or haven't gotten unsatisfactory on some flight mission now. Can you picture me navigating about eight or ten hours at night from here over the Gulf to Havana, Cuba? This is to be the final big test, coming up next week. About a thousand miles with nothing but the stars and the water to look at."

Telegram of 8 November 1944: "WILL ARRIVE IN SEATTLE VIA AUTO THURSDAY AM."

Annotation: My graduation day was November 4. My new base would be Victorville Army Airfield, California. Some leave was granted and I headed home via auto that belonged to one of my fellow graduates. He and his wife had a 1941 sedan and were headed for Olympia, Washington. Another graduate from Spokane joined us. We drove nonstop; I got out at Enumclaw, Washington. Stan was home on leave and picked me up there. Between Houston and Enumclaw we had fourteen flat tires and four blowouts. Of course, tires were rationed during the war.

Graduation from Navigator's School, 4 Nov., 1944, 2nd Lieutenant, Army of the U.S.

It was night when we crossed the Rockies and my friend's wife was driving. I was sleeping but awoke hearing the wheels spinning. It was snowing heavily and we were sliding off the road. We tried to get the car back on the road but to no avail. Fortunately, a snow plow came by and pulled us back on the road. We followed him up over the pass, which was only about a half mile ahead. This was Eagle Pass, about 12,000 feet high. It was raining on the west side of the pass and we had no more weather problems.

Letter of 13 November 1944: "We haven't learned too much about our training here as yet, however, we are told it will be the eight week

Bombardier School. We have both B-17s and B-24s here and will be getting quite a bit of flying time in."

Letter of 28 November 1944: "We go to school about four hours in the AM and usually two hours plus physical training in the PM. No night classes. Quite different from the rigorous schedule we had in Texas. [We] could study, but we aren't allowed to take any notes in class and everything is kept in locked vaults, so all we learn must be absorbed in the classroom or through operating equipment. Note [the] clipping from tonight's paper about today's B-29 raid on Tokyo...especially the underlined part. These 'precision' instruments are radar, just what I'm learning here. On a

RADAR SCHOOL
VICTORVILLE, CALIF.
4 NOV 44 TO 6 JAN 45.

mission the other day, (brand new B-24s and sometimes B-17s) one leg was from San Diego to Los Angeles and we went right by my old Camp down there. [It] reminded me of the many times I had looked up at planes while there and thought what lucky devils they were flying up there...and here I was, just where I used to see them."

Annotation: We had a couple of days off at Christmas and I decided to go up to Mills College in Oakland to visit a girl from home

Our first jet, a P-59, masquerading as a propeller airplane. Around Christmas 1944, one made a pass at our BT-15 over Muroc Dry Lake, CA.

who was going to school there. I got
a ride in a BT-15 from Victorville
to Bakersfield and when passing
close to Muroc Army Air Field (now
Edwards Air Force Base), we were
'attacked' by an airplane that pulled
up alongside after making a pass at
us. I was astonished to see that the
plane had no propeller! It was a Bell
P-59, our first jet! The rest of my trip
was fruitless, spending much time
on buses."

2ⁿᵈ AiʀFoʀcE, LoiNcoLN, NEBRASKA.
6 JAN 45 TO 8 FEB 45.

Annotation: Stan was stationed
at Santa Ana and we spent a couple
of days together around Christmas.

Letter of 26 January 1945: "Nebraska. Here I am at the end of the
second day at my new base. My plane trip from Seattle to Omaha was
very smooth, covering the distance in twelve and a half hours. I don't
expect to be very long…perhaps two or three weeks. I'm going through
processing and the endless red tape the Army has. I will have no duty
here besides checking in each day until I'm shipped somewhere.
Nothing definite as to my assignment yet. I'm still hoping for twenty

Stan and Lee, Hollywood, January, 1945

SECOND AIR FORCE.
R.T.U., ALAMOGORDO, NEW MEXICO.
5 FEB 45 TO 11 APR. 45

nines, but I understand they're hard to get into from 'word of mouth' [news]. So, I won't be too disappointed if I don't get my wish."

Annotation: Lincoln, Nebraska was a routing pool. Those who had completed courses for aircrew jobs were sent here to be re-routed to bases that were set up to conduct Combat Crew Training.

Letter of 1 February 1945: "I guess that sketch of the planes I drew for you is going to come out as planned…I did the two of them (a P-47 and a B-29) to represent Bob and myself and, not with foresight, but rather sort of wishful thinking of how I might end up. It's going to be OK because this morning I was alerted for pending shipment to B-29s! Now I'll have the one big job I hoped for. I don't know where I will take my phase training in the twenty nines, but I'm sure we are leaving Lincoln the weekend sometime."

Letter of 6 February 1945: "Well, here I am in New Mexico… I certainly move around don't I? I left Lincoln last Saturday and after an uneventful train ride, I arrived here in Alamogordo, which is a small isolated town about 85 miles north of El Paso, Texas. I am here to go through Combat Crew Training. The class I am to join has already undergone some of this training. I will have nine weeks here, leaving the 11th

Staging Base,
Kearney, Nebraska.
11 APR 45. TO 19 APR 45.

of April. Who knows where I'll be two days later on my birthday? These twenty nines are beautiful ships and I'm so grateful that my assignment is with them. I flew this morning and we have completed all the requirements for

Ink drawing of the Port of Embarkation, Mather Field, Sacramento, CA

Combat Crew Training. The date to leave is still the 11th, however, there are rumors that it will be earlier. I have a good crew and get along fine with them. My pilot is a Cherokee Indian who can really handle these big birds. The class that finished ahead of us on March eleventh, just 11 days ago, is now on Saipan in the Marianas Islands."

Annotation: We flew some long distance missions in this training, some over 3,000 miles. One I recall had us dropping practice bombs on a sandy island called Freemason Island, just southeast of New

Tinian's two airfields: North Field in the foreground, the largest airfield in the world with four 8,600 foot runways, home of the 313 th Wing, in which my Group, the 504th belonged; The 509th Group that delivered the atomic bombs was also in the 313th• West Field, shown in the background was home for the 58th Wing. The 72nd Wing was on Saipan; an additional Wing was on Guam.

Orleans. These bombs matched the ballistics of some real ones and had a very small charge that would eject white powder so we could see where they hit. We would drop these one at a time for the sake of practice. When we dropped the first one, we noticed two men near their beached boat on the island. On our second pass, they were making waves in their boat, high tailing it out of there.

Our first encounter with the jet stream occurred a few times in this training. This phenomenon was unknown at this time. We just thought they were unusual high speed winds, around 200 miles an hour. These winds would have a profound effect on the tactics used in the Japan Air Offensive.

From Alamogordo we went by train to Kearny, Nebraska. It was

My B-29 crew. I am second from the right in the top rank. May, 1945

here that we picked up a new B-29 and flew it to Mather Field near Sacramento, California. From Mather, we flew to Hawaii, Kwajalein in the Marshall Islands and then to Saipan in the Marianas Islands. We left the airplane on Saipan and crossed the narrow channel to Tinian Island, our new home.

Letter of 5 May 1945: "I guess you know where the Maianas are. I am not allowed to encourage you to guess which one I'm on and it doesn't make any difference anyhow because they are much the same. There are still Japs on this island but they give litle or no trouble. From now on when you read about the 29 raids over the Nippon Empire in the papers, you can be sure some of them are mine."

Annotation: On Tinian, we were housed in a Quonset hut for newcomers. It was located on a corner of our Group's area. Outside, a few feet away was a machine gun nest which was manned around the clock by our infantry. We were told there were still some Nips around. This, plus the anticipation of going into combat shortly, elevated our anxiety. Also, not being scheduled for immediate duty increased anxiety. Noises outside our door awakened us one night, and we all reacted by grabbing our .45 pistols and flashlights. The noises continued, and on investigation, we found the source. It was a land crab. It was quite large, softball size, a big brother to the hermit crab which makes its home in an empty shell. The tension was relieved partially. Then, probably to further reduce tension, one guy tried to get the crab to come out of its shell by holding his cigarette lighter under it. That didn't work. Then another guy brought out a whiskey bottle and gave a shot to the crab; that worked. Apparently these crabs were quite athletic because our area and the sea were separated by a cliff of 200 feet.

So here we were, hot to trot, and nothing to do. Eat, sleep, write letters and wait. I was writing a letter with my back toward the center aisle down the middle of the hut. Our co-pilot was pacing up and down the length of the hut, talking all the time, apparently trying to quell some sort of anxiety. Periodically, he stopped behind me and peered over my shoulder to see what I was writing. This didn't set too well with me. Then he snapped a finger on the back of my head as he passed. I told him not to do that again. Then, when he did it a second time, I rose up, turned around and gave him what some call a 'forearm smash,' swinging the forearm horizontally, bent at the elbow; it is a body blow. He went over one cot and crashed on a second. I went back to my writing. I don't know if he felt it necessary to establish a pecking order at that time or if he was habitually obnoxious. Our relationship after that was cordial, but not friendly. We worked in separate places in the aircraft, so there was little contact. When not flying, you could choose your associates.

Annotation: Shortly after we arrived on Tinian, we happened to be down on the flight line when a B-29 on takeoff blew up. After the fire was out, we wandered toward the wreckage. Among the gawkers was the crew of a B-29 parked next to ours. One of the gunners of this crew was a loud-mouthed fellow who always seemed to have some wise remarks to say. True to color, he saw a GI (Government Issue) boot near the wreckage and said it looked like someone had his boot

blown off. Then he picked the boot up and realized a man's foot was still inside it. He dropped it and retched.

A few days after this happened, we got a jeep and decided to see some more of our island. We were warned not to go to the south end because all the Japanese hadn't been found yet, although each week the Army would comb the area looking for hidden enemies. Besides our base, North Field, there was another base in the middle of the island: West Field, which housed the 58th Wing. We decided to visit the 58th. The easten end of their runways terminated with a drop over a cliff. As we approached the cliff, a B-29 flew off the cliff only two or three hundred feet up. It started a left turn with the nose quite high, stalled and crashed not far from our jeep. We dismounted to see if we could rescue anyone. The fire was intense and the ammunition in the turrets began to cook off, sending bullets all over, so we retreated to a drainage ditch by our jeep; there wasn't anything we could do.

Chapter Three

Combat in World War II

The descriptions that follow are presented verbatim (with annotation for clarity) as recorded by me after each mission was flown. This was done in a small blank-page journal that I kept. This journal has sketches I made that have been used as illustrations in the major part of this work. A collection of quotations I gathered is also in this journal.

Please overlook faulty grammar and racial slurs. Racial slurs have no place in writing today. I tell it the way it was verbatim. To pass it on otherwise would omit the flavor of history. Realize also that these accounts were made as notes immediately after or even while still airborne as I copied material from my logs.

WW II B-29 Mission Number 1

May 16 and 17, 1945. Target was South Central Nagoya. A night-strike. Before takeoff, we watched a B-29 blowup with over 6000 gallons of gasoline aboard and a full bomb load of 37 M-17 incendiary bombs. I never saw such an explosion before in my life. The airplane was abandoned after engine fire on takeoff. All the crew bailed out over our field and no one was lost. Our takeoff was effected and we departed for Iwo Jima. Reaching Iwo, we headed for landfall on the south tip of Shiono Misaki peninsula, Japan, Island of Honshu. We went through a weak cold front north of Iwo. Landfall was made by radar. Overland, we headed for the IP (south tip of Biwa Ko). We were intercepted by an enemy night fighter, which evidently was clocking our speed and altitude for antiaircraft lights and batteries of flak guns, because he did not present any attacks. After IP, we turned on the bomb run as briefed. AFC on radar was out, making tuning very difficult. Direct radar bomb run was made. Flak was directed at us prior to and over target. Searchlights couldn't penetrate undercast. This was an incendiary attack, a fire blitz. The target was well lit up since we were in the last element of 500 aircraft. After target, we were intercepted by a Fireball, a Japanese rocket plane of short duration with a 1000 lb. warhead and a suicide pilot to guide it into the twenty nines.

We dove and picked up an IAS of 285 miles an hour and lost our attacker. Accurate but light flak was encountered at land's end near Hamamatsu Airfield. Course was set for Iwo Jima. Iwo was zero-zero. Arrived at base sweating out gasoline consumption. Arrived with only 400 gallons. Mission completed and a success... part of intensifying attacks to bring the Nips to their knees so soon after Germany's unconditional surrender.

I carried this clipping in my briefcase on my missions so I wouldn't have any hard feelings about bombing the enemy.

Annotation: one member of the crew that bailed out of the aircraft that was abandoned and exploded as described above, landed on the taxi strip in front of our aircraft as we were taxiing out for takeoff. We had to stop abruptly to keep from running over him. Upon takeoff, we passed over a large fire on the water, which I thought was another B-29, but it was jettisoned incendiary bombs from a B-29 that had some engine trouble on takeoff. Then, looking south there was a large fire on the 58th Wing's field on our island. Another large fire was on the 73rd Wing's field on Saipan. At that moment, I thought perhaps I was in the wrong outfit. Zero-zero means clouds down to the surface and no visibility. IAS means Indicated Air Speed. IP means Initial Point. Flak is antiaircraft shells exploding.

Letter of 30 May 1945: "Today is about the end of May…about this time last year I had just returned from furlough to Georgia and that seems a long time ago. I hardly think there's any chance of seeing Bob because there is some 1600 to 1800 nautical miles between us, although we are [at] about the same latitude. When his Group is finished in the Phillipines, they may move northward to Iwo Jima or Okinawa to fly cover for the B-29s. So far, we've had no cover, but the Nips have plenty of respect for our twelve guns. Thus far, we have flown on three strikes against the Jap mainland. One against Nagoya and two to Tokyo. Our CO (Commanding Officer), General LeMay, says that return trips to Tokyo won't be necessary because there is little left of the world's third largest

Tinian Cemetery; graves of those that died taking the island.

city. I agree. Our strikes at night (all three missions) were fire blitzes. I could see fires 200 nautical miles at sea. Looking down [when] over the targets was like looking into a blast furnace only there were miles and miles of this. I have a [sic] possibly 50 combat hours, so you can see how long the flights are."

WW II B-29 Mission Number 2

Target: Tokyo. May 23rd and 24th, 1945. A night incendiary attack. Landfall, course to IP, bomb run, breakaway and lands' end accomplished as usual by radar. Eight to ten tenths undercast over target area. Flak was encountered after landfall near Yokasuka and during the bomb run and on Chiba Peninsula near Kisarazu Airfield. No fighter attacks were pressed, although three Nip aircraft were seen. Malfunction of forward bomb bay caused 1/2 bombs not to fall on the MPI. Bombs later were salvoed over the water near Ohara after land's end, so as not to cause false fires that would detract from the accuracy of following crews. Crossed a cold front and a stationery front near Iwo Jima. One bomb kicked out of the rear bomb bay into the water near base. Gross weight at takeoff was 136,700 lbs., about maximum. We carried 38 E- 46 incendiary bombs. Six months to the day since the first B-29 attack on Japan. This was the largest strike of the war: Nine million pounds of incendiary bombs hit Tokyo. Fires could be seen 200 miles at sea. Time aloft was 1450 hours.

Annotation: MPI means Main Point of Impact. The B-29 was designed to have a gross weight of 120,000 pounds, however, you can see that we were exceeding that by quite a bit. To make our missions more effective, fuel was cut down to save weight for more bombs. In addition, toward the end of the war, guns, ammunition, and in some cases, even crewmembers were left on base so a greater weight of bombs could be carried.

The officers in our crew shared a Quonset hut with those of another crew whose aircraft ran out of fuel 70 miles north of base returning from a mission at night. They bailed out, but six of the twelve were lost, either drowned or victims of sharks.

Annotation: There was a variant model of the B-29 designated an F-13. The 'F' stood for 'Foto', or Photograph. The section immediately behind the bomb bays was outfitted with mounting rods, which supported several cameras used for reconnaissance. The bottom of

Washing machine I built on Tinian

this area was glassed-in to allow maximum view below the airplane. On one of our fire bombing raids on Tokyo in 1945, we employed all aircraft possible on a maximum effort mission. My crew was assigned an F-13 for that night. The radar operating equipment had been moved from behind the upper rear gun turret to the port side of the glassed-in area. That was where I sat that night. My view was impressive; it appeared I was sitting on a sheet of fire, mile after mile and still visible out to 200 miles at sea.

Annotation: The B-29 was designed to bomb from high altitude. Fighters that could match our altitudes would be short on fuel by the time they could intercept us. The B-29 was pressurized, insulated and heated. We were comfortable at 35 degrees below zero outside. However, we ran into problems at high altitudes. Bombing was inaccurate despite the famous Norden bombsight. We had no knowledge of the jet stream, a band of high speed winds that circled the Earth at high altitudes, often right over Japan. Heading upwind in 200 knots of wind, the B-29 would be a 'sitting duck' over the target for a long time. Heading downwind, there would be little time for the bombardier to do his thing. Flying crosswind, the correction for drift might exceed the Norden bombsight's capability (30 degrees). So the weather (wind) was an enemy.

Intelligence showed that a good deal of Japanese war industry was in the wood and paper Japanese houses. To defeat the weather and attack industry, most of our missions were at low (five to seven thousand feet), done at night to defeat anti-aircraft defenses. Fire bombs were used, very few high explosives. There were other higher altitude (18-20 thousand feet) high explosive missions flown in daylight, for example, hitting the Aichi aircraft factory in Nagoya with two thousand pounders. Low altitude strikes also saved fuel; the bombers didn't have to climb so high.

My group passing Fujiyama on the way to Tokyo. The image was on the cover of Life Magazine during the war.

WW II B-29 Mission Number 3

Second Tokyo mission. Target: Northwest Tokyo, 25th and 26th of May. Target was railroad marshalling yards and general industrial area two nautical miles west of Hirohito's imperial palace. Bomb load was 179 M 47 A2 incendiary bombs plus one photo flash bomb. Gross weight was 133,500 lbs. The mission completed total destruction of all Tokyo's industrial areas by B-29 strikes. Not much left of the world's third largest city. If the Nips were wise, they would give up right now. A few bursts of flak were encountered near Shizuoka on Suruga Wan, shortly after landfall. Landfall was 0045, 26th of May. Remainder of run to IP was undisturbed. IP (0111) to target, we were picked up by five search lights. CFC gunner dispensed RCM 'rope' by a camera hatch and the effects on lights were distraction to the rear and low. Flak was heavy to intense. 25 aircraft lost from the command, consisting of 5% of the striking force of 500 B-29s. We were picked up by gun-laying radar, most likely from the sixteen batteries of 64 heavy guns guarding the imperial palace. Just before bombs away, the pilot's fan-marker light flashed on (same frequency as some Jap radar.) Bombs away at 0116; on breakaway to the north, indicated airspeed was 302, true airspeed being 324 and ground speed was 349 knots or 391mph! Flak also encountered in North Tokyo and at Chosi Point. Near land's end, five balls of fire were seen; none pressed attacks. Two chased after us out to sea seven or eight minutes. Too fast for them. Fires seen 200 miles out to sea. Passed through a cold front at Iwo up and return. Probably won't return to Tokyo soon as there is little left to attack. Base at 0840 26th of May. Time aloft was 1410 hours.

Annotation: CFC means Central Fire Control; RCM means Radar Counter Measure.

WW II B-29 Mission Number 4

Target was Osaka. June 1, 1945. Form One time was 1550 hours. We carried 179 M-47 A2 incendiary bombs plus one cluster of twenty fragmentation bombs. Gross weight was 135,600 lbs. at takeoff. Takeoff was effected and heading set for assembly point north of Iwo Jima at Nashino Shima. In formation, we went to our reassembly point off Shikoku coast. Reassembling, we made landfall and approached inland by radar. Departure point and IP were made good. Some flak was observed on Amaji Island near our IP. IP turn was made and radar approach on target. Fifteen seconds before bombs away, flak hit us in number three engine and prop would not feather... fire got worse. Meanwhile, 20 to 25 Nip fighters were seen... 7 to 8 attacks made on us... tail gunner bagged one... radar shot out. About five minutes after bombs away, number three front bank of cylinders and prop siezed and spun off, hitting the prop on number four engine and breaking a foot or so off one of the prop blades. Number four was vibrating so badly we had to feather it. Two engines lost and 770 miles to Iwo Jima; altitude was 18,000 ft. Gradually we lost altitude until we were two hours out of target at 400 ft. We had jettisoned all the loose equipment and prepared to ditch. A buddy ship broke formation after number three fell off and flew with us. After 1/2 hour in ditching positions, we had gained some more altitude. We continued jettisoning equipment to lighten the aircraft. All the ammunition, cameras, gun sights, bombsight, flak suits and vests and mats, seats, radar units and miscellaneous equipment were jettisoned. We picked up altitude to 2600 ft. at about 20 ft. per minute. It looked like we could make Iwo then. Everyone held his breath when number one backfired twice at this time but it proved OK. Landing at Iwo, we blew out the inboard tire on the left [right] side and emergency brakes had to be used. Almost ran into a B-24 at the end of the runway then. Our engineer counted 67 flak and bullet holes on the underside only. Airplane was left at Iwo. We flew back to base in our buddy ship that had followed us from Osaka as he had to land for gas because of having to fly so low and slow to stay with us. Mission successful, airplane and nerves a wreck. Later, pilot, CFC gunner and myself awarded Purple Heart for minor wounds encountered on June 1, 1945.

Purple Heart, Tinian, Marianas Islands, June 1945

The B-29 may have been instrumental in increasing the general knowledge of flight. The high speed winds encountered at high altitudes was one of these. The B-29 was the first airplane to spend extended time in what became known as the 'jet stream.' Two hundred mile an hour winds were encountered by us both in training in the air offensive against Japan. The other phenomenon now known as the 'ground effect' was not established by measurement until after WW-II. A C-54 four engine transport lost power between Hawaii and California and the crew was astounded to witness that the aircraft seemed to gain lift proportional to their approach to the surface. They successfully landed in California. This prompted investigation and 'ground effect' was added to the flying lexicon. Pilots had noticed this 'floating' effect as touch downs were approached, but the phenomena had not been measured nor labeled yet.

Could this effect have been in operation when we prepared for ditching north of Iwo Jima on June 1, 1945? Generally, 'ground effect' comes noticeable at an altitude dependent on the aircraft's wingspan... about twice the wingspan. The B-29's wingspan was 141 feet. The lowest we descended that I noticed was to 400 feet as we were gradually forced down after having lost both engines on the right side over Osaka. When we had climbed back to 1200 feet, I asked our pilot what was happening. He said the lightening of the airplane by throwing all we could overboard and the fact that we had quit running around while doing this had allowed trimming the airplane better; burning gasoline also reduced our weight by at least 1320 pounds per hour.

As an airplane approaches the surface, the wing compresses the air underneath it making a denser medium, which then provides increased lift. Did this phenomenon aid in staying airborne instead of ditching on June 1, 1945?

Annotation: 'Form One' consists of paperwork that accompanies the aircraft. IP means Initial Point where the aircraft makes its final turn and heads for the target. 'Ditching' means putting the aircraft in the water. Flak suits and mats are canvas affairs with multiple pockets holding small pieces of steel to protect the crew from shrapnel and bullets. Losing two engines on the same side is much more serious than losing one on each side. 25% of our aircraft landed at Iwo with battle damage this mission. Feathering means turning the prop blades to streamline them so the airstream will not cause them to 'windmill.' In our case, the hydraulic line that enabled this to be done was destroyed, allowing the prop to 'windmill' faster and faster, eventually causing the engine to siezed, throwing the prop off which could slice the fuselage in two. When number three siezed, not only the prop came off but the whole front row of nine cylinders tore off the engine, breaking part of a prop blade off of number four engine as it went up and over the wing. Number four had to be feathered and shut down because of unbalanced vibration. When number three went by to the rear, the tail gunner mistook it for a fighter flying through the formation. The pilot replied, "Negative, that was number three." Shortly thereafter, we had no interphone contact with the tail gunner so I stepped through the aft pressure door and found him with his parachute on, gripping the sides of the open escape hatch, saying he was going to be the first one out. He obviously thought we were going down and responded by being ready to jump. I told him that the CFC gunner had been hit and didn't he think that the wounded man should go first. He agreed...then I told him that we needed him in the tail at his guns. He responded and went to his station. Several days later, the tail gunner came to visit me and asked if I'd told anyone about his behavior; I told him I hadn't, and this is the first time I've related this incident to

Our B-29 over Osaka. 1 June, 1945. Minutes before losing #3 and #4 engines.

anyone in sixty-four years. There's no shame in being scared; if you haven't been scared, you haven't lived.

Annotation: Please remember this text is mostly verbatim and if a few articles like 'the' and 'a' are missing, these accounts were jotted down in something like a notebook during wartime and are not presumed to be literary.

Letter of 6 June 1945: "I guess you know that Bob was decorated with the Air Medal, well, you have two sons who have been decorated now, only I didn't receive the Air Medal. You see, it all happened on June 1 on a mission over Osaka (Nips second largest city) and it seems I came back with a few scratches. I have been awarded the Purple Heart for wounds. It seems to me that I don't deserve such an honor, but the flight surgeon says that when the enemy draws American blood, it's ample reason for the award. I guarantee that this is the closest the Nips will ever to come to hitting me if I have to blast each one of the yellow runts first with a bomb. I'm going back to Osaka tomorrow and will drop you a note tomorrow night when we get back; this one's for revenge."

Letter of 25 June 1945: "This will be only a short reply to your letter...mainly to send a photo of my homely physiognomy. This was taken on 16 June after a brief pesentation ceremony in the building in the background in the picture.You can see from the picture that haircuts are at a premium. I do my own laundry. There are spots in the film or camera; I've lost no weight and I'm getting pretty brown under the sun here.

WW II B-29 Mission Number 5

June ninth. Target was Aichi engine and aircraft factory in south central Nagoya. Bomb load consisted of three 4 thousand-pound blockbusters. Takeoff was effected and heading set for Iwo Jima. Reaching Iwo, heading was altered to make good our assembly point off southeast edge of Shiono Misaki Peninsula near Owage. This was a daylight formation mission. 25 minutes were spent forming at the assembly point. We then made landfall and headed for the Bomber Command departure point and IP. Seven to eight Nip fighters were seen. Attacks varied from feints to aggressive attacks between IP, over target and land's end. Five to six fighters were seen. Flak was meager to moderate. Fuses were cut to our altitude but hit wide and behind, although two or three bursts were close enough to be heard. From land's end, we set heading for Iwo Jima and base. We arrived at base with ample 700 gallons of gasoline at 1642 K time. Time aloft was 1415 hours. This was a daylight formation high explosive mission. Later, in July, the Air Medal was awarded to our crew for the period of 16 May to 9 June.

WW II B-29 Mission Number 6

Target was Osaka. Total gasoline on board at takeoff was 6900 gallons. Bomb load consisted of 31 M-17 incendiary bombs. Takeoff was effected and heading set for Iwo Jima. We passed 85 nautical miles west of Iwo. We arrived at our assembly point south of Muroto Saki. It was 'socked-in' due to an extensive cold front lying off the Nip coast. We finally located our formation. However, number two prop governor was out and we could only get 21 in. of manifold pressure on number two. We could only get 39 in. manifold pressure on number three and four engines so we could not climb above the soup with the formation

The Aichi aircraft factory in Nagoya disappears after 160 four thousand bombs were applied. A couple of days later the aircraft engine works across the canal to the left disappeared in like manner.

with full power. The aircraft commander decided we didn't want to make the Osaka run singly with the aircraft dropping bombs from above us. With fuel running short, we went to the Bomber Command departure point on the easternmost tip of Shikoku Island and to the briefed IP by radar and chose a target of opportunity: Wakayama. We made a direct radar bomb run and release on the city. Land's end was effected at Shiono Misaki and we headed for Iwo and base. Over Iwo at 1305 K. Arrived at Tinian at 1652. Form One time was 1415 hours. No fighters seen; no flak seen. Solid cloud coverage from ground up to 21,000 ft. accredited for the lack of interception and enemy defenses. This was a scheduled daylight formation incendiary strike.

Annotation: the designation 'K' after the time refers to the local time in the Marianas Islands.

WW II B-29 Mission Number 7

Seventeenth and eighteenth of June. Target was Yokaichi. Night blitz. Takeoff was effected at 2019 K with bomb load of 178 M-47-A2 incendiary bombs. Gross weight was 135,785 lbs. Course was set for Iwo Jima. We went right up the Mariana Islands chain, followed up the Volcano Islands and Bonin Island chain. Landfall and initial point, being the same this time, were reached at 0306 K. We then headed on our bomb run. Yokaichi is located on the west edge of Ise Wan, or Nagoya Bay and is an important seaport with a deep harbor and many docks. There's a large oil and gasoline dump and refineries there (rather they were there). We could see the city of Hamamatsu on our right as we approached the Nip coast, ablaze from the 73rd Wing's strike there. There was much smoke and fire at our target. Approach, IP, bomb run and release accomplished by radar. Little ground defenses and no fighter defenses were encountered. A few searchlights were seen in the area. One searchlight at Nagoya blinked off and on and then went off. Venus coming up in the east was mistaken for a 'Baka' fireball interceptor until the gunners could be convinced it was a planet! Land's end was made by radar southwest of Uji Yamada. Abreast of Iwo at 0630 K. Base at 0932 K. Flight home uneventful, plenty of gasoline.

WW II B-29 Mission Number 8

19-20 June. Target was Fukuoka on northern Kyushu Island. Gross weight at takeoff was 137,000 lbs. Bomb load was 39 M-17 incendiary bombs. Takeoff was effected and heading set for Iwo Jima. Arrived at Iwo at 2024 K. We passed through a cold front northwest of Iwo. Turbulence was moderate. We dodged thunderstorms and heavy clouds in the front by radar. We hit our landfall some 38 miles south of the briefed point. Identification of point of landfall was made by radar as well as the approach inland to initial point, IP turn, approach to target, dodging known flak installations, bomb run and release, breakaway and land's end. Heading was set for Iwo Jima; arrived five nautical miles west of Iwo at 0435 K. Heading was then set for base. This was a night incendiary blitz strike with two wings of the Bomber Command striking Fukuoka. Total distance traveled was 2832 nautical miles or 3050 statute miles. Flak was seen over the target plus searchlights and much automatic weapons fire. No fighters were encountered. Arrived at base at 0816 K. Our longest trip (mission) so far. Time aloft was 1505 hours.

Letter of 28 June 1945: "I believe the rainy season has hit full force now. Water, mud, thunder, lightning and rain all the time. [I] had a letter from Bob the other day. He is still in the PIs [Philippine Islands]. (I believe you once thought he might be on Okinawa because

Our crew owed their lives to nearly 7000 Marines who took Iwo Jima. Without their heroic sacrifices our crippled B-29 wouldn't have had any place to land on 1 June, 1945.

of an APO [Army Post Office] change,) but he is still in the PIs. He's got some 90 missions and 270 [combat] hours now. I've nine missions and 144 [combat] hours. [A] rumor has it that we go home at 35 missions, however, [we] will have to wait and see.

[I] received your letter yesterday with a clipping in it. I am returning it if you want it. The story told in the clipping wasn't our [story], however, that incident happened on June 1, the same Osaka raid [that we got shot up in.] I saw that airplane hit the water and explode some four miles from us as we made our final approach to land at Iwo. I didn't know any of the crew; I believe it was from another Group."

Annotation: 'Victor' was our Group's call sign; 7 was the number painted on our airplane that we left on Iwo after having it all shot up. Passing through Iwo later, enroute on a mining mission, we traced the path of an armor-piercing machine gun bullet that had gone through the armor plate in front of our pilot, hit the elevator trim tab wheel (whose fragments had wounded our pilot,) then went through the armor plate behind our pilot and finally came to rest inside a broken glass jar that continued dried blood plasma which was to be used for blood transfusions. We retrieved the bullet and gave it to our pilot for a souvenir. Victor 7 was quite well patched up, but I don't know its eventual fate.

WW II B-29 Mission Number 9

6 June 1945. Target was the Aichi aircraft [engine] factory in southwest Nagoya. Bomb load consisted of seven 2000 pound bombs.

When we reached our assembly point southeast of Shiono Misaki, it was 'socked-in'. We couldn't find our squadron so we formed with seven B-29s of the 421st squadron. The leader was ten miles due east of the briefed course when we were halfway to the IP. At this point, we again ran into soup and the formation began to break up and we were then going to go in over the target alone. We still had ten tenths undercast as we set up a radar IP, twenty miles west of the target, made the radar controlled turn at the IP, approached the target and made a direct synchronous release by radar bombing. A few flak bursts were reported by the tail gunner in southeast Nagoya at breakaway and at Toyohashi at land's end. Both were low and meager. No fighters were seen. P-51s were supposed to cover us, but none were seen... too much weather. The trip to base was uneventful. Arrived at base at 1630. Time aloft was 1355 hours.

Annotation: 'direct synchronous run' means radar data are given to the bombardier who then enters it bit by bit into his Norden bombsight and the sight computes the proper release point. The impact of 441 one ton bombs makes a shock wave that is visible at the surface; it looks like a rapidly expanding circle, centered on the target.

Annotation: Relative to the letter above, when we arrived at Iwo Jima on just two engines on the same side after being hit by anti aircraft fire over Osaka, we were put in a 'stack'. A 'stack' was an orbit over the field, awaiting one's turn to land. First come, first served. In an airplane under us in the 'stack', the pilot was dead and the co-pilot was wounded three times. The bomb bay doors were jammed and the bombs were still on board. The co-pilot came over the island and had eight crewmen bailed out. He made another circuit, engaged the auto pilot to guide the B-29 away from the island, and bailed out with the remainder of his crew. A P-61 from Iwo had intercepted the B-29 and had led it to Iwo. After the airplane was abandoned, the pilot of the P-61 was ordered to shoot the B-29 down. The first burst of cannon and machine gun fire from the P-61 hit the left outboard engine and it caught fire. The power loss of the engine caused the B-29 to turn and swing back toward the island. The P-61 held its fire until it cleared the island again, then resumed firing. Altogether the P-61 poured 561 rounds of .50 caliber machine gun bullets and 320 rounds of 20mm. cannon shells into the B-29. It finally crashed into the sea.

This B-29 was more than a hazard to navigation over the airfield. If it had impacted on the only runway, other 'stacked' B-29s would have had no other place to land, including mine. Years later, in a magazine

SAKA got the incendiary treatment twice during the week under review -- first on 1 June and again on the 7th. Total results are 6.55 square miles of the city damaged. Of this, 3.15 square miles resulted from the 1 June mission and 3.4 from the 7 June strike. Total damage to the city is now 14.65 square miles.

Osaka is the second largest city in Japan, having had a population of 3,252,240 in 1940. Prior to the war it had the most important industrial concentration in the Far East but Tokyo recently has taken the lead as the manufacturing center of the Empire.

The city remains one of the principal centers of heavy industry. It is noted for its shipbuilding, iron and steel works, rolling stock works and non-ferrous metals enterprises, notably copper and aluminum. Other war materials produced are aircraft propellers and governors, munitions and ordnance, textiles, special steels, wire, electrical equipment, machines and machine tools and instruments.

RAILWAY HUB

An extensive system of railways hubs on Osaka, including the Tokaido main line, the Kansai line and numerous local electrical arteries.

Within the area are located numerous family factories and shadow plants, too small and too numerous to be selected as individual targets. In 1938 the whole city had some 15,000 factories. Osaka was the place where Japan first entered into modern industrialism and, except for the larger and newer installations, is mainly a conglomeration of home workshops and shack-like factories.

1 JUNE MISSION

On 1 June 509 B-29s were airborne against Osaka. The 58th supplied 119, the 73rd 153, 313th 119, 314th 118. Twenty nine aircraft did not bomb. Four hundred fifty seven dropped 2,683 tons of incendiaries on the primary target visually and by radar from 1036 to 1200 K at an average altitude of 19,794 feet.

Wing bombing totals are: 58th, 106 A/C, 650 tons; 73rd, 140 A/C, 904 tons; 313th, 108 A/C, 747 tons; 314th, 103 A/C, 481 tons. Ninety tons were dropped on targets of opportunity.

RESULTS

Damage assessment shows 3.26 square miles of damage,.11 of which is in the adjoining town of Amagasaki. Damage was caused to 11 numbered targets.

LOSSES

Ten aircraft were lost as follows: Two from the 73rd wing to AA; one each from the 58th and 73rd to accident; one ditching from the 73rd; two operational from the 314th and three from unknown causes from the 58th Wing. One aircraft of the 314th wing was abandoned over Iwo. This aircraft had been hit by flak over the target and the airplane commander had been killed. The elevator control had been jammed and the co-pilot wounded three times. The co-pilot brought the plane to Iwo, however, and the 10 men abandoned it and were rescued.

One hundred forty eight P-51s were airborne as escort but due to adverse weather conditions only 23 reached the target area. Twenty seven P-51s were lost because of the weather and one pilot rescued.

Enemy fighter opposition was moderate, with 90 making 150 to 175

called *True*, this story was embellished, purporting that the dead pilot was still flying the airplane and trying to land.

Extract from an intelligence report. This will give readers an idea of the typical day's work.

WW II B-29 Mission Number 10

28-29 June, 1945. Target was Moji near Yawata in the northernmost tip of Kyushu Island. Bomb load was 184 M-17-A2 incendiary napalm bombs (rubber-gasoline jelly type.) Landfall was made on Okino Shima Island at the extreme southwest tip of Shikoku. Heading was taken for the IP. A radar wind run was made on Okino Shima on the way to our IP and the new information given to the Bombardier. Two unidentified surface vessels were observed in Beppu Wan. One by left and tail gunners, the other by radar just before our IP. The IP made generally weak and unaggressive attacks. Several ineffective air-to-air phosphorus bombings were attempted.

Flak was generally moderate and inaccurate for the first part of the force but the accuracy increased for most following formations. Five planes are considered lost to flak and 26.8 percent of the aircraft over the targets sustained battle damage due to flak.

7 JUNE MISSION

On 7 June 449 aircraft were airborne in a strike against Osaka. Four hundred nine of them dropped 2,648 tons of incendiaries on the primary target by radar through 10/10 cloud. The wing totals are: 58th, 107 A/C, 681 tons; 73rd, 120 A/C, 784 tons; 313th, 77 A/C, 528 tons; 314th, 105 A/C, 654 tons. Nine targets of opportunity were bombed with 78.4 tons.

Mining Mission

Thirty one 313th Wing aircraft were airborne on the night of 7-8 June to lay mines in the eastern and western approaches to Shimonoseki Straits, Fukuoka and Karatsu.

Fifteen laid 108 1,000-pounders in the western approaches, seven laid 84 in the eastern approaches and four laid 48 at Fukuoka. Five jettisoned and returned early.

No enemy air opposition was encountered and no aircraft lost.

Enemy air opposition was light, 50 enemy fighters making 15-20 attacks. Flak was nil or meager to moderate and inaccurate due to the undercast.

Two B-29s were lost to unknown reasons. One of the 314th Wing was abandoned northwest of Guam. Eight of the crew were rescued. One of the 313th went down northwest of Tinian and six crew members were rescued.*

One hundred forty four P-51s were airborne from Iwo. B-29 crews reported seeing 40 to 60 of them in the target area and observed them destroy two enemy aircraft.

City area damaged in this mission totals 3.4 square miles. This raises the total city damage to 14.65 square miles, estimated to be 24 percent of the built-up portion of the city. (Secret)

XXI B.C. sets Bombing Record

The XXI Bomber Command established a new AAF record on 14 May with the greatest tonnage ever released on a single target in one mission -- 3,162 tons of incendiaries on Nagoya.

The previous AAF record was held by the 8th Air Force heavies, which dropped 2,923 tons on Cologne on 17 October 1944. It took 1,248 heavy bombers, attacking, to deliver the 2,923 tons about 325 miles, whereas only a third of that number, 471 B-29s, carried the 3,162 tons 1,350 miles to Nagoya. This record has since been broken several times by the XXI BomCom.

Another day's work.

good, radar heading for axis of attack was taken. Eleven miles from the target, the bomb bay doors were opened. As they opened, the bombs in the forward bomb bay fell away and also part of the aft load due to a mechanical malfunction of the release system. These bombs fell short of the target. A sharp climbing turn to the right was made as evasive action from flak. No fighters seen. Heading was taken to make good the briefed route to land's end. Since we still had bombs aboard, we decided to try to hit some small Nip town on our way out to land's end. Uwajima on Shikoku Island was selected. A direct synchronous radar run was made. Three large white explosions were observed after our bomb hits. Evidently we luckily struck an arsenal or munitions dump. Following aircraft on their way back from Moji observed the whole town in flames... destroyed. Land's end was made and return to base was uneventful. Time aloft was 1405 hours.

Annotation: Reconnaissance showed we'd hit some generators in Uwajima at the base of mountains. A lake above the town fed water through large pipes to the generators below.

WW II B-29 Mission Number 11

First and second of July. Target was Ube, port city on western Honshu. This was another night incendiary blitz. An industrially important city of 150,000, Ube has large coal mines under the harbor, steel mills and Japan's largest magnesium works. Bomb load was 40 E-46 aimable clusters of twenty bombs each. Takeoff was 'sweated out' because of no wind conditions and a maximum gross weight of 137,000 lbs. After the midpoint of Iwo Jima, we had stiff headwinds, arriving at the Bomber Command departure point at Okino Shima off the southwest of Shikoku at 0212. The IP was made good on northeast Kyushu by radar approach. Wind run was made by radar on Okino Shima. Bombing altitude was 10,800 ft. Indicated airspeed was 240 miles an hour. Bomb run and release by fixed angle was effected by radar as was breakaway and land's end. Excellent fires were observed in the target area. We may have trapped fifteen to 20,000 Nips working in the coal mines under the harbor. Return trip was quick because of tailwinds but uneventful. Time aloft was 1405 hours.

WW II B-29 Mission Number 12

Third and fourth of July. The target was the city of the Himeji. Night blitz attack. Target was 30 nautical miles west of Kobe, industrial and rail center. Bomb load was 184 M-17-A2 incendiary bombs. The trip to the mainland was uneventful, making landfall at 0054 1/2, Fourth of July. Landfall, turn control point, initial point, bomb run and release made by radar. AFC voltage out in radar making tuning very difficult. Over the target after bombs away we were attacked by one fighter, which the gunners said, pressed its attack to within 25 to 30 ft. of our empennage. I heard machine guns, thinking they were our tail gunner's, however, the fighter came in so quickly out of the dark, it wasn't seen until it opened fire, so we could bring no guns to bear on it. It was the fighter's guns I heard, showing how close it was! This was the only attack we had. Flak wasn't very heavy. Withdrawal and land's end accomplished by radar and trip to base was uneventful but quick because of good tailwinds.

Annotation: A 'wind run' is a maneuver observing a spot on the surface, either visually or by radar, on three different headings, checking wind drift on each heading then calculating the speed and the direction of the wind at your altitude. This information is given to the bombardier to refine his aiming as well as being used in navigation.

WW II B-29 Mission Number 13

Sixth of July. Target was Shimizu, industrial aluminum center of Japan and port city only 60 miles southwest of Tokyo. Reaching Iwo Jima after takeoff, the island chains were followed northward by radar to our Bomber Command departure point on O-Shima Island. Bomb load was 39 E-46 incendiary aimable clusters of twenty bombs each. Radar approach, run and release were made on the target, coming westward upwind across Suruga Wan. There was quite a bit of thunderstorm activity in the target and adjacent areas. Little flak was seen due to cloud coverage and much smoke. No enemy fighters or fireball 'Bakas' were seen.

Reconnaissance photos were posted on the bulliten boards as morale boosters for the troops.

Over the target, after bombs away, we ran into a smoke column rising from the fires set before us. Turbulence was the heaviest I've ever experienced. Strike altitude was 7500 ft. When we came out of the thermal, we were at 11,000 ft. altitude... gained 3500 ft. in about ten seconds! Break away and land's end effected by radar navigation and then we climbed to 21,000 ft. to return to base. Trip was quick but uneventful. Our quickest trip to and from the Empire...Form One time being only 1215 hours.

Letter of 16 July 1945: "[I] received your letter of 6 July yesterday. The reason I crossed out the word 'formation' on the clipping was because we do not fly these long distances in formation. Formation means fatigue for pilots who have to fly manually and also adjusting throttles to hold position is costly of precious fuel. On the daylight raids, we assemble at some point between Iwo Jima and the Nip coast, or just off the coast. A good navigation problem is to fly 1500 [nautical] miles to given coordinates over water within a small time limit. I am slowly building up confidence in my job. On night strikes, each airplane is on its own. [The] most danger at night is not from the enemy, but from other B-29s wheeling about in the same area."

WW II B-29 Mission Number 14

9 and 10 July. The target was Wakayama. A night incendiary attack. This city is located about 30 miles southwest of Osaka, Japan's second city. Wakayama was important as Osaka's harbor port as B-29 mining operations had bottled up the port facilities and shipping at Osaka. Bomb load was 40 AM-17 incendiary aimable clusters. Great fires were seen in the target area. Flak was moderate and meager. A few enemy aircraft were seen, however, we had no attacks pressed. Over the target, there was much smoke and turbulence. One B-29 was flipped completely over on its back, rolled right side up and was going in the opposite direction from which it came, being a couple of thousand feet higher...an Immelman turn! Fighters followed B-29s 200 miles to sea and made attacks near us. Some flak was sent up by Nip surface vessels near the coast. Return to base was uneventful.

This B-29 was hit by falling bombs from another B-29 at night; the circle with an E in it was our Group, the 504th in the 313" Wing. A picture of this B-29 is in General LeMay's book, "Mission with LeMay," captioned in error, saying, "Guam never looked so good," indicating the airplane was from Guam. It was from my unit on Tinian.

In late on the target. Thermal updraft from firestorms lifted our plane 3,500 feet in 10 seconds.

Time aloft was 1235 hours.

Annotation: I think Wakayama was the home of Yamaha pianos. It was common to talk of bombing the 'piano factory.'

Letter of 16 July 1945 continued: "I guess you know that Bob has moved again. I had a letter from him from his new base yesterday, however, I knew more than a week ago that he'd moved and also where he had moved to. Of course I cannot tell you his location and if you care to guess, don't associate his APO with your [guesses] of his new location. Security means a lot, as I know you know. I knew of his new location because I saw him in a newsreel in one of our movies! Perhaps I may be able to see him either on his base or in combat together over Nippon. I certainly hope so. In his letter, he wrote of having 300 [combat] hours and 100 missions. He expressed the hope that we could go home together sometime this year. To date I have some 217 combat hours and 14 missions to my credit. I guess I told you that I'd received the Air Medal recently. Actually, I've earned a cluster for it by now. Saw a shark while swimming the other day…guess I'll give up swimming for a while."

WW II B-29 Mission Number 15

16 & 17 July. Target was the city of Kuwana, ten miles southwest of Nagoya, an important industrial city because of having Japan's largest anti-friction bearing plants, steel works and harbor port facilities. We

carried M-17 bombs, 40 of them. We had large isolated and banks of thunderstorms about 200 miles off the Nip coast, much lightning and Saint Elmo's fire and the turbulence was moderate. We made our landfall on southeast Shiono Misaki, heading northward to our departure point and initial point on Biwa Ko. The target and adjacent countryside was 'socked-in' with nine to 10/10 undercast. Radar run and release was made and we broke away to the south down Ise Wan (Nagoya Bay). Land's end was made at the south end of the bay and our return to base was uneventful except for running through the weather again. Flak was light. No Nip fighters were seen by us this mission. Time aloft was 1315 hours.

WW II B-29 Mission Number 16

Heat of Blazing Jap City Hurls Bomb Back to B-29

GUAM, July 11.—(I.N.S.)—Thermal up-drafts from the terrific fires set in the Jap city of Wakayama reversed the laws of gravity and thrust a fused incendiary bomb back into the bomb-bay of a Super-fortress.

The amazing experience, during which the B-29 piloted by Maj. Robert H. Langdale of Houston, Tex., was flipped upside down, was related at 21st Bomber Command Headquarters tonight.

Heavy damage to three more Jap cities—Kofu, Shimizu and Chibu—was also revealed by headquarters after a study of reconnaissance photos. The cities were blasted in a raid by nearly 600 Superforts last Saturday.

RUNS INTO TROUBLE

Langdale's plane ran into trouble after dropping its fire bombs on Wakayama in yesterday's five-pronged raid on Honshu.

Huge fires set by B-29s which had preceded his bomber over the target sent thermal up-drafts of tremendous power surging sky-ward.

All the bombs had cleared the Superfort's bomb-bays when the crew was amazed to see one of them climb back into the bomb-bay. It tore off the door and damaged the horizontal stabilizer.

The next half-minute of action was so fantastic crewmen still do not quite believe it happened. The Superfort was flipped over on its back in a half-loop and its direction reversed completely.

EXTENSIVE DAMAGE

Extensive damage to three important military targets was also revealed by headquarters. The Chigusa ordnance and ammunition factory in the Nagoya arsenal district was 77 per cent wrecked; the Tachikawa army air arsenal more than 23 per cent destroyed and the Utsube oil refinery at Yokkaichi 50 per cent damaged.

Iwo Jima, won at such a heavy cost, again proved its worth today. Some 30 Superforts, returning from yesterday's five-way mission, made emergency landings on the tiny volcanic island.

Here is a Japanese fighter attack. At times, enemy fighters would follow us 200 miles out to sea from the mainland of Japan.

July 24, 1945. Target was the Aichi aircraft factory in south Nagoya. We carried seven 2000 pound bombs. A daylight formation strike, we reached our assembly point, found our squadron and headed inland for our IP on Biwa Ko. We had 10/10 undercast and bombed through the undercast. Moderate flak over Nagoya. At breakaway a formation of fighters was seen approaching. Ensuing attack seemed inevitable, but as they approached they were identified as P-51s!, the first fighter cover we'd ever had. This day was a bad one for the Nips. 600 B-29s started off the fireworks followed by three groups of P-51s and P-61 Black Widows from Iwo Jima hitting at low level. P-51s from Okinawa covered B-29 strikes against Kyushu. Targets were hit from Tokyo to Yawata. Meanwhile, some 1500 Naval planes from task force 38 of the third fleet generally raised hell in the inland sea area. In the evening, after the air strike drew to a close, units of task force 38 moved in under cover of darkness and shelled southern Honshu near Shiono Misaki. Trip back to base was uneventful."

Annotation: 'Biwa Ko' is mentioned in several of these mission accounts. This was a very large lake located not far from many of our major targets. The land-water contrasts made excellent points for exact navigation by radar, hence these were used for IPs (Initial Points) from which to begin bombing runs. A large city, Kyoto, was on this lake. I believe it was never bombed because it was the ancient capital and cultural center of Japan. As far as I know, we were never shot at near Kyoto. Perhaps there was a tacit understanding operating there.

WW II B-29 Mission Number 17

25-26 July. This was a mining mission to northern Honshu near Nanao Wan. The longest trip so far: a total of 2,956 nautical miles or 3,400 statute miles. Time aloft was 1550 hours.

Annotation: Bob's average flight was three hours long; mine was fifteen hours long. When one has been awarded a medal, a device called an 'Oak leaf Cluster' is awarded in lieu of another Air Medal if earned again. This device is attached to the ribbon of the medal.

WW II B-29 Mission Number 18

27-28 July. This was a 'Super Dumbo' mission. I flew with Captain Ferrell who was flying his 35th mission. Naval task force 38 was sighted by radar as we neared our rendezvous point with a U.S. submarine off the Nip coast 35 nautical miles southwest of Shiono Misaki. We arrived at the rendezvous at 0030 and located the submarine by radar through cloud decks below and circled 'till 0330. We had no calls for duty beyond standing by.

Annotation: This was part of the extensive Air-Sea Rescue Service carried out by the Twentieth Air Force and the Navy. Super Dumbos aided crippled planes coming off the mainland, directed subs or destroyers that were on duty to scenes of ditching or bailouts, conducted searches and gave air cover for Naval units of the Air-Sea Rescue Service which were flying right off the Jap coast or to aircraft that were on course back to Iwo Jima, Tinian, Saipan or Guam. Time aloft was 1515 hours.

Relative to the newsreel in which I saw Bob. I was really surprised seeing him on film. Later, Bob told me how this happened. He had just returned from a mission and had climbed out of his P-47 when a news reporter asked him if he would climb back in his airplane and dismount a second time. That's how he was filmed. The reporter said where this scene took place, thus, I learned where he'd moved to.

WW II B-29 Mission Number 19

29-30 July. This was another mining mission in the Shimanoseki Sraits area. Form One time was 1400 hours.

Annotation: We used to listen to 'Tokyo Rose', the Japanese

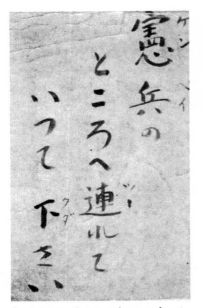

B-29s operated in China before they did in the Marianas Islands. So that the crews would be identified with Nationalist China, a chit printed on silk (like this one) and carried on one's person would identify one as an ally. Further identification was the number you see on the chit; it was registered with one's name with the League of Nations.

Carried on one's person in case of capture, it reads: "Take me to the military police, please." Memorized to this day: Kempei no tokoro e tsurete itte, kudesai. It was felt that survival chances were better in the hands of the military than in the civilian's.

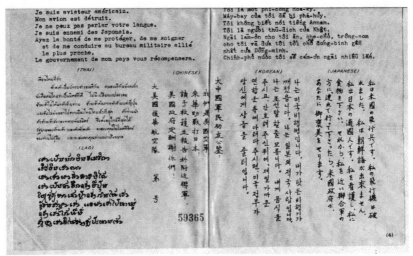

Reverse side of above chit. The numbers were registered with one's name in Geneva, Switzerland, with the League of Nations.

propaganda station for amusement. It was common for her to come on the air with, "Hello boys. I've had mine today. Have you had yours?" One time she addressed an officer in our Group and told him of the birth of his son in San Francisco before he received the news from home.

WW II B-29 Mission Number 20

1-2 August, 1945. Another mining mission in northern Honshu. Form One time was 1400 hours.

Annotation: While orbiting over the submarine as described in the 27-28 July mission above, a B-29 in some trouble on its way off the coast salvoed its bombs in the water. This was the procedure in case a B-29 couldn't drop its bombs on the primary target. The reason for this was to not start fires outside the target area because aircraft with malfunctioning radar would bomb on the fires set by others. In fact, the enemy would set fires in the countryside as lures, hoping to attract the bombs intended for our targets. When the B-29 salvoed its bombs in the water, they came uncomfortably close to the submarine on the surface below that was on stand-by for rescue service. The sub commander broke radio silence, uttered a few expletives and said he was diving. I watched the sub's image disappear from my radar screen.

Letter of 31 July 1945: "Today is payday again. [There is] not much use for money over here. Not counting my meals, I get along on $5.00 or so a month. To answer your questions, you figured correctly, between 28 June and 12 July I had five missions...how can I stand it? Well, that wasn't too bad. During six days, 24 July to 30 [July], out of those 144 hours, I spent 59 of them in the air. How's that? It's not too bad...true, one is very tired and we don't deserve any more rest than is absolutely necessary because we must keep up total war against the Nips. If we rest, the yellow bastards get a rest."

Letter of 1 August 1945: "Today is Air Force Day. There's going to be the biggest strike yet on Japan. It will be all over and a week old by the time you get this. [I'm] not going on this one, we've got some special work to do today. To date, I've got nineteen missions, 290 [combat] hours."

WW II B-29 Mission 21

5-6 August 1945. Another mining mission. Target was Rashin, Korea, eighty miles from Vladivostok, USSR. The longest flight. Aloft for 1845 hours, 3750 nautical call miles or 4312 statute miles.

Annotation: This was the day the atomic bomb was delivered to Hiroshima. We passed by there at a distance of 80 miles. One of our gunners recorded seeing a flash at 0815. I was sleeping. More about this later.

Letter of 18 August 1945: "I don't remember if I've written lately and told you all the news or not. First, Stan arrived on Tinian the second of August and I was sure glad to see him. What was more remarkable, however, was that he was assigned to my Wing, Group and even my squadron! He lives only about 100 ft. from me! How about that? [It is] really odd, considering all the other islands and outfits he could have been sent to.

The war is over. Stan didn't get any missions in over here and I'm glad he didn't have to. We didn't celebate war's end because we're saving that 'till we all get home. I had 22 missions, about 310 combat hours when the fifteenth of August came around with Japanese capitulation. Just about the first of August I was taken off my crew and given a staff position in my Wing. I hated to leave the crew, but it wasn't a matter of choice."

Annotation: You see Stan Griffith's name herein many times. He was in my brother Bob's school class, both being two years my senior. He was like a second older brother while I was growing up. I hold Stan in great esteem as a person and as a patriot. He volunteered for pilot training and failed, a great disappointment for him. Undaunted, he became a bombardier and flew a tour (35 combat missions) in B-17s in Europe. Returned to the States, he had a choice of becoming an instructor in a Bombardiers' School or returning overseas. He volunteered for combat training in B-29s and ended up in my unit on Tinian. We flew in the same formation on VJ Day over Tokyo. I still see him occasionally and respect him as a friend and fellow aviator.

Letter of 18 August 1945: "Did I tell you before that it's First Lieutenant now, since the 25th of July?"

Mission Number 22 VJ Day!

Letter of 3 September 1945: "Yesterday was VJ Day. While the surrender was being signed aboard the USS Missouri yesterday in Tokyo Bay, we were flying in formation [at 3800 feet] over Tokyo [and] over the Allied naval might in the Bay where I saw the Missouri, Yokohama Naval Base and then we broke out of formation and went in at 1200 feet and 'buzzed' Tokyo. What a messs. We had burned everything flat that wasn't built of stone. Stan was on our wing in the same formation and he took a picture of us in our B-29, Victor 64.

Yokohama was ashes... just ashes and rusted steel. The only green spot was the Emporor's Palace in the center of the city [Tokyo] and it was scorched on all sides. I could see Nips riding bicycles [and] digging clams in the tide flats. I saw smashed industry, black and rusted steel, abandoned. I saw the battleships Missouri,

VJ Day, Tokyo Bay, battleship Missouri on which surrender was made, 2 Sept, 1945. We over-flew this ceremony at 3800 feet in formation with hundreds of other B-29s in a show of force.

My B-29 (No. 64) over Tokyo Bay on VJ Day, 2 Sept., 1945. Picture taken by lifelong friend Stan Griffiths from his B-29.

Washington, Dakota, Tennessee and others; British battleships and cruisers, tens of U.S. cruisers and scores of U.S. and British destroyers and one Japanese battleship and several submarines in Yokasuka Naval Base. [The] weather was hazy, but Mount Fujiyama was in the distance. All in all, [it was] quite different from the other two times I was over what used to be the world's third largest city, Tokyo.

Letter of 12 September 1945: "Quite a surprise! Bob walked in on me the other day! A small world, isn't it? First Stan came and now a visit from Bob. Two years and seven months since Bob left home and I last saw him. He's looking fine, same as ever, (except [for] a poor excuse for a mustache). Stan, Bob and I played a touch football game yesterday; naturally, we've [sic] beat the tar out of the other side. [It was] the most fun I've had for a long time. I wouldn't have been more surprised if MacArthur had walked in the other day."

Letter Bob wrote to our father on 12 September 1945: "Are you wondering what I'm doing here? It was quite a surprise to Lee and Stan when I walked in on them. It was certainly swell to hear from them, when they said they were in the same Squadron. Anyway, I got leave from the Squadron and bummed my way in a B-29 from Okinawa to here. I've been knocking myself out ever since. The food and living conditions are something I'm not used to, and that, combined with their club here and fact that Lee and Stan are here is really swell. Yesterday, we just talked, played football and pitched some horseshoes, and then sat around the club last night drinking cokes and playing cards. Naturally, Lee, Stan and I beat [sic] the football game. Well, 'nuff for now."

Annotation: Bob hung around for 11 days. He was supposed to bum a ride from Okinawa to Manila, Philippine Islands, in order to board a ship for home. Stan, Bob and I caught a ride on a Navy aircraft to Guam, which is about 90 miles south of Tinian. There we visited Ira Scribner, a high school classmate of Stan's older brother, Denny. Ira was in the CBs (Naval Construction Battalion). Bob caught a ride to Manila and Stan and I flew back to Tinian in a C-47.

On Tinian, our Group, the 504th, was one of a couple that not only dropped bombs, but also laid mines. These were sown at night at low altitude by radar. The mines were of two sizes: 1500 and 2500 pounds. The mines, when dropped into the water, would sink to the bottom. Sophisticated devices that controlled each mine would then determine when it would become armed, that is, ready to explode. There were sensors that would measure the water pressure exerted by a ship, sometimes allowing the small ones to go by and then blowing up the big ones. Other sensors would count, perhaps allowing two ships to pass, but not the third. It was impossible for the enemy to sweep these mines, although our Navy did after the war using wooden vessels which had large generators and towed electrical cables whose signals disarmed them.

One B-29 would drop a string of mines and others would overlap and continue on a line until a harbor or strait was closed off. These were Naval mines, but the Navy didn't have the capability to sew up distant harbors without undue risk to their ships. These mines sank a tremendous amount of Japanese shipping. The enemy tried to clear some minefields by loading old hulks with lumber so they wouldn't sink and then run them back and forth through critical channels. I have a photo of one of these hulks taken from the air.

One time a reconnaissance airplane detected the Japanese unloading ships near the Shiminoseki Straits, putting the cargo on shallow daft barges, towing them along shore outside the minefield and reloading the cargo on other ships. This was an attempt to defeat our barrier. Then we were tasked to not only lay mines in the strait, but also in shallow water and up the beach into the brush.They could defeat these by gunfire and even discover the sensors in the mines, but they didn't know how the sensors were set on those lying on the bottom. A friend of mine, with whom I went to high school, spent most of the war at the University of Washingon in a Naval program. He was assigned to sweep mines after the war. He kidded me about finding mines in the bushes. I told him that was done on purpose, but he wouldn't believe me.

Returning from northern Korea the morning of August 6, 1945, we passed within 80 miles of Hiroshima at about 8:15 in the morning. One of our gunners saw a flash and noted the time. He gave this information to me and I entered it into my log. There were only supposed to be two other aircraft near Hiroshima besides the delivery aircraft, both of them involved in the drop. Apparently, they had forgotten about our mining mission. On our way back to our base, we often tuned in the Armed Forces Radio on Guam and listened to the news and music. This day there was startling news about an 'atomic' bomb at Hiroshima. I remember looking on my chart, locating Hiroshima and our course east of there. When we got back to base, the intelligence people got all excited about the notation in my log about the gunner seeing a flash at about 8:15.

Stan and I got a jeep and went out to the bomb dump and asked the sergeant in charge if we could take a look at an atomic bomb. He didn't know what we were talking about, so we went back to our unit and found out that there was another one down on the field, so we went down there. The Fat Man, which was delivered to Nagasaki three days later, was there in a pit, covered with a tarp and surrounded by many military police. Because the B-29 bomb bay doors were very low to the ground when open, some of the larger bombs that we carried had to be lowered into a pit, the airplane towed over the pit, and the bombs loaded that way. Such was the case with Fat Man, it being about 5 feet in diameter. Our Bomb Group, the 504th, and the 509th that delivered the atomic weapons, belonged to the same parent organization, the 313th Bomb Wing.

Incidentally, the Nagasaki bomb was originally slated to be delivered to Kokura, located on northern Kyushu. The delivery aircraft, named 'Bock's Car,' was to bomb only in visual conditions,

Atomic bomber *Enola Gay*, and accompanying bomber; the highly instrumented *Great Artiste*.

not through clouds. The target was obscured by clouds so the airplane circled, waiting for the clouds to clear. The second bomb bay on the bomber was fitted with an auxiliary fuel tank. Circling used much fuel (about 400 gallons an hour) and when the auxiliary fuel was tapped, the transfer pumps didn't work. Not only was the fuel unavailable, but now it was a liability because it could not be jettisoned and the weight of fuel added to the weight of the bomb meant that the airplane did not have enough fuel to fly to the nearest base which was on Okinawa. So, the bomb had to be dropped to reduce the weight. It could be dropped unarmed, that is, dropped as a non-nuclear device, a dud. However, at that moment, I believe this was 100% of our nuclear stockpile; it wasn't to be wasted.

The planned route to the secondary target, Nagasaki, was out over the sea, going south down Kyushu's west coast and then approaching Nagasaki from the sea which would give the best radar image of the target in case it had to be dropped through cloud cover. However, because of fuel shortage, the route to Nagasaki was taken directly over land. The aiming point was a 'Y' where two rivers joined in Nagasaki. There were broken clouds in the target area. The bombardier saw a 'Y' and visually dropped the weapon. He hit his aiming point, however, it was the wrong 'Y'; it was located in one of two valleys. Consequently, a portion of Nagasaki was spared somewhat because intervening hills between the two valleys acted like shielding.

The Nagasaki bomber, 'Bock's Car,' is in the Air Force Museum at Wright-Patterson Air Force Base at Dayton, Ohio. On the wall near the aircraft is a copy of the picture our B-29 'Victor 7' over Osaka, of which I have shown the original print elsewhere in this writing. The 'Enola Gay,' which delivered the weapon to Hiroshima, is in the Smithsonian Institution's Museum in Washington, D.C.

Let me get back to the night of 5-6 August 1945. We were laying mines in a Korean harbor called Rashin, way up north on the east coast of Korea, not far from Vladivostok, USSR. This night we were caught in searchlights. We reacted with our countermeasure of ejecting what we called 'rope'. We jammed their radar which was directing the lights. In Europe, strips of foil would be ejected from our bombers to jam enemy radar screens. The length of these was determined by the wave length of the enemy radar. Sometimes this was called 'chaff' or 'window.' Our 'rope' was foil, about ½ inch wide and about 200 feet long. There was a square piece of cardboard attached to a reel of 'rope' by a ribbon and each unit was encased in an unsealed cardboard box. The

Hiroshima (what was left of it)

slipstream would cause the box to fly open and the 'rope' would unreel and dangle from the square cardboard parachute. The 'rope' would expose an infinite number of flat surfaces to face the enemy radar, which used a multitude of wavelengths. One standard wavelength the Japanese used for gun-laying and search lights was 75 megacycles. This frequency lit a red light on the pilot's instrument panel. Normally, this indicated that the aircraft was over certain places in published letdowns in America, used widely in instrument flying. So, sometimes this light would come on, indicating enemy gun-laying or searchlight radar was in operation. Thus, it was a signal for one of the gunners to open the camera hatch in the rear of the airplane and throw some 'rope' out. This

Picture of my B-29 on the wall of the Air Force Museum, Dayton, Ohio next to the Nagasaki bomber Bock's Car

Nagasaki

worked well.

Because of such long distances between our base on Tinian and northern Japan and Korea (you recall that the Japanese occupied Korea for 40 years), we would load our mines on our base, fly to Iwo Jima, land with the mines on board, refuel, stay overnight and then launch our mining mission from there. I watched a mine drop out of a landing B-29 on Iwo Jima once; fortunately, it did not explode.

General LeMay, in his book, *Mission with Le May*, said, "during that short period [four and one half months] mines planted by the Wing [313th] were more destructive than any other weapon, accounting for about half the total tonnage disposed of…" Post war testimony of Japanese experts said that the mines parachuted by B-29s had an enormous share in choking off the Japanese supply routes at sea."

Our mining was so effective that, after the war, our Group , the 504th, was awarded a Presidential Unit Citation, which I didn't learn of until 1966!

There was a navigator in the other Wing on Tinian with whom I'd gone to high school. I visited him once and later learned he'd been lost on a mission. Those who had been appointed to gather up his personal belongings to be sent home brought some of his art goods to me to see if I wanted them. They thought it inappropriate to send every small thing to his survivors. That way, I got into oil painting. I still have some of my first efforts, rather crude for the most part. One is shown herein.

My first oil painting

Not too long before the end of the war, I was taken off my crew and transferred to Wing Headquarters. My job there was teaching. We had a course for newcomers about radar operations. The equipment we had in the B-29s used a PPI (Plan Position Indicator) which showed a map of the earth's surface beneath the airplane. It showed land masses, ships on the surface, airplanes below you and sometimes it could be tuned so it depicted runways on a field. We not only used it to fix our position, but also for bombing and laying mines. You could see through darkness and through clouds. We could see some clouds, especially those dense clouds associated with thunderstorms. Radar was used to navigate between the larger cumulonimbus clouds. It was quite versatile.

There was a secondary control for the autopilot near the radar controls. The pilot could transfer directional control of the aircraft to the radar operator who would refine the aircraft's heading when approaching bombing or mining targets. The secondary control could bank the airplane only; it had no conrol over altitude. If one had to make a more than shallow turn, the fuselage would rotate about its roll axis and the radar antenna would not be pointing straight down, thus, in changing direction, the radar would be blinded because it was not level. So, there was an art in doing this. Calculations in the head had to be made in order to judge how much turn should be made. My job in Wing was to relay all this information and more to incoming radar operators.

We even had a training aid, which was a large waterproof table

Surrender document required Japanese to place all aircraft in the open with propellers removed; note some with faulty landing gear, sitting cockeyed.

holding a few inches of water. Instead of radar, sound waves were used to bounce off and return from built-up objects under the water. The returning signals were then presented on a PPI oscilloscope just as the radar returns were presented aboard the airplane. We also had radar beacons whose coded signals could be received at great distances as aids to navigation.

The transfer to Wing level might be construed as a job promotion because the Wing Navigator had many from which to choose, however, that wasn't the whole story. Harking back to the first of June, when we got shot up so badly, in my letter to my father (which I related earlier), I mentioned being 'scratched' a bit and felt guilty about being awarded the Purple Heart. My injuries were more extensive than I knew at that time. While going by the upper rear turret to patch a shrapnel wound on the CFC (Central Fire Control) gunner's leg, something exploded inside the turret (I think it was a fighter's bullet[s] exploding ammunition in the turret), knocking me backwards, landing me on my derriere on a corner of a large box that contained survival gear. That hurt, and upon examination I found I was bleeding. I stuffed a roll of toilet paper in my crotch and went about my business. A few days after returning to our base, I was quite sore and went to see the

B-29s dropped supplies by parachute to Prisoner of War camps in Japan and Korea after the war. In the upper left you see a circle, the letters P.O.W. and an arrow showing which heading the B-29 should take on its run.

flight surgeon. He said I'd ruptured blood vessels in and around my anus. I managed to keep flying with my crew, then I got an infection. Outside the flight surgeon and my pilot, no one else knew of this. After all, getting knocked on your butt was nothing to brag about. The doctor located some bandages from the nurses that he thought were ideal for me: Kotex. I healed OK, but had trouble off and on for years with hemorrhoids. Kotex came in handy later while flying jet fighters because high G forces brought on more hemorrhoids. My pilot told Bob that he had put me in for the Bronze Star for leading the efforts to keep our airplane in the air after we were hit, but I never heard anything about that until Bob mentioned it years later.

An additional duty while on Tinian was being a censor. Your name would appear on the bulletin board assigning you this duty. Enlisted men were required to write their letters on one side of each page only and the envelopes were not to be sealed. The censor would pick up a bag of mail at the appointed place and time and isolate himself with a razor blade. The censor would open each letter, read it and cut out any portion that he deemed should not have been written. Guide lines were provided which specified what to censor, for example, false statements or classified information. The cut out portions were destroyed by the by the censor burning them. The letters were then sealed and a statement on the envelope made showing the letter had been censored and by whom. This notation was made on all envelopes whether any text had been cut out or not. I found that those who were the farthest removed from combat or other danger (for example, a cook or a clerk) wrote the most about being engaged with the enemy or suffering from hardships that didn't exist. Officers' mail was not censored.

Annotation: A B-29 from our outfit had engine trouble, and knowing that the enemy was about to capitulate, landed at a Japanese airfield on Kyushu. The troops there surrendered and treated the crew well enough that they were allowed to load up souvenirs from their stores. When the war ended, and the engine problem was taken care of, this crew returned to Tinian and sold much of their booty to others for souvenirs. This crew lived next door to ours, so I went over to see what their navigator had for sale. He said he only had a rifle left. He gave it to me. I cut the stock down a bit and used it to hunt deer in Montana, and eventually sold it in a garage sale in Friday Harbor around 1978.

There was some ill feeling for the Navy right after the war. As soon as the war was over, many ships steamed quickly back to the States to take part in celebrations. These included aircraft carriers, which could have carried thousands back home, but they didn't do this. I did have an opportunity to come back on a Navy vessel, an LST (Landing Ship Tank); they had many of these but not enough navigators to man them. I declined this chance.

One post war flight we made was a search mission. A C-47 transport aircraft was reported down west of our islands at a place called Parece Vela, which was just a group of reefs. Several B-29s flew search patterns; we found a pneumatic rubber life raft, which was empty. We circled the raft and called a PBY flying boat and notified them of what we had found. They homed-in on our broadcast signals, found us, landed on the sea, inspected the raft then machine gunned it so it would sink, then took off. No other trace of the aircraft was found.

Letter of 3 September 1945 (continued): "Our disposition here in the Marianas is unknown as to the future and lately I've been building a fence, painting, etc. when I'm not at my job in the Wing. A couple of Oak Leaf Clusters for my Air Medal ...I've been put in for the DFC which may come through. Enough. Yesterday will be quite a day to remember as well as others."

Letter of 21 October 1945: "Well, it's been a month since Bob left me here and a week ago Wednesday that Stan left Tinian for home, also today makes six months overseas for me. You asked me how long Bob spent with us: eleven days. I don't have many duties these days and since Stan left, it seems quite lonely at times. My crew is at Kwajelain, in the Marshall Islands, some 1500 miles southeast of here. I keep myself busy reading and painting. I am studying a book on astronomy, which is quite interesting. I'm painting (rather trying to paint) with some oil colors. Quite the thing.

At present, they're sending men home from here (enlisted men, 62-69 points and officers with 75 points). I have 66 points. I don't know when my turn will come for a ticket home, but it will be sooner or later, and in the meantime, something to look forward to. I wouldn't have anything to do immediately if I were home right now anyhow, and I'd just as soon be pulling down $10 a day here doing nothing."

Annotation: Finally in December, we got notification that we were to fly a B-29 back to the States. Since Stan had put in a tour of combat duty in Europe before coming to Tinian, he had sufficient points to go home earlier. The plane that we brought back to the States had some nose art on it, a scantily clad woman and a notation: 'Lucky Lady.' We had flown some missions in this aircraft back in the month of May. (There will be more about 'Lucky Lady' later in 2003). The route back from Tinian was via Kwajalein, in the Marshall Islands, in case we needed to land for some reason. Johnson Island, a speck of sand, was next, then on to Hawaii and California. We had a little trouble between Kwajalein and Johnson Island. We made position reports periodically on a long-range radio, but it failed. Consequently, we weren't able to make reports. When we arrived in Hawaii, we learned that two aircraft were out searching for us: a B-17 with a droppable boat and a PBY Catalina flying boat. The PBY found us in the traffic pattern at John Rogers Field in Honolulu. Incidentally, this was an odd flight with respect of the fact that we got there before we started. We had crossed the International Dateline and gained a day. It was the longest flight we'd ever made: about 21 hours. After the radio was repaired, we headed for Sacramento, California. We were briefed that if we had radio failure again, and were not more than halfway to Sacramento, that we were to return to Hawaii. After some 600 miles out, the radio failed again, so we had to turn around and go back to

Hawaii. The second try, we made it. Approaching San Francisco, we had some discussion about flying either over or under the Golden Gate Bridge. Not wanting to stretch our luck, we went over it as we were supposed to. We landed at Mather Field in Sacramento and taxied to the perimeter of the aerodrome and shut the airplane down.

Some of us got out and kissed the ground. I had another mission: we had a device on board that served as a toilet. If you used it, you'd clean it. Consequently, it was seldom if ever used. I really had some pressure on my bladder, so, after having kissed the ground, I walked into a wide, shallow drainage area behind the airplane and was busy relieving myself when I heard a public address system saying, "Ladies and gentlemen, this airplane has just returned from overseas with a combat crew". I looked over my shoulder and saw a bus full of civilians as well as an Army truck full of civilians stopped in front of our airplane. The base was having an open house for the public and this was part of it. I could have cared less, waved, and went about my business. I got home 5 days before Christmas.

In 2003, I was looking through a magazine I had subscribed to called *Aviation History*. In the rear of the magazine were many ads purveying aviation memorabilia. Looking at these, I was surprised to see a picture of the nose art that was on the aircraft that we brought back to the States from Tinian after the war. We had also flown some missions in this aircraft, 'Lucky Lady', during the war. The ad was

We flew some missions in this B-29 in May, 1945, and brought it home to the states in December 1945.

B-29 nose art

trying to sell the replicated image of 'Lucky Lady', reduced in size and hand-painted on aluminum so one could hang it on a wall at home or in an office. I sent an e mail message to the seller and also sent copies of photos I had of 'Lucky Lady.' He was surprised at this and asked if I had other nose art photos of B-29s. I have several, but most are not of the same quality. I did send one nice one I had, called 'Slave Girl'. It was received gratefully and he said if he used it in an ad, he would include a photo credit with my name.

Chapter Four

First Hiatus in Flying

Leaving 'Lucky Lady' and my crew, I turned in some of my gear at Mather Field and rode a train up to Portland, Oregon, where I was mustered out. From Portland I took a train to Seattle, arriving late at night at the King Street station and caught the last trackless trolley to Alki. I walked a couple of blocks with my baggage to home. Knocking on the door aroused no one so I walked around to the back of the house, reached through the window and grabbed my brother Glenn by the big toe and woke him up. He woke Mom and Bob up and we had a joyful reunion. I guess I was recognizable in spite of the mustache I had. Why a mustache? Well, when Bob came through Tinian on his way to Manila, he had one, so I grew one. I have a picture taken in a downtown bar of Ian, Stan, Bob and myself complete with mustaches. Mom said Bob looked like Robert Taylor and I looked like Errol Flynn.

We did some celebrating, sometimes on consecutive days. There was a time when Mom got Bob and me aside and said she was somewhat concerned about our celebrating. Perhaps she thought we were going to turn into alcoholics. We explained to her that the whoopee was temporary. Our house turned out to be sort of a headquarters for reunions with old friends that had just come home the from the service, talking about old times and also what had happened since we saw them last.

It wasn't too hard to find a date, and groups of us would go out to a roadhouse somewhere, dance, drink and have a good time. Getting around was a problem, of course; cars were not manufactured during the war and none of us had kept one that we had before the war. Back then, Bob had a '37 Chevrolet sedan which he sold to one of our friends who never went in the service because he had some malformations in his lower legs. He was generous about lending it to anybody if they had a date. Stan borrowed his father's car occasionally. I bought a 1932 Harley-Davidson motorcycle to get around on. It wasn't much of a

Post war celebration. Left to right: Ian Aitken, Stan Griffiths, my brother Bob and myself.

Post-war celebration left to right: Myself and date, Jack Southerland and Gloria Fink, Hugh Snow and Irene Couch, date and Ian Aitken, date and brother Bob, date and Gail Halliday.

machine, well worn out.

This has to do with the time from December 1945 to July 1951. Between these dates there was a hiatus relative to flying. It was a case of first things first. Now that the objective of defeating the enemy and being home among family and friends was achieved, the next thing to do was go back to school. Neither of my parents went to school beyond the eighth grade, so why did Bob and I aspire to a college education? For Glenn, our younger brother, it was natural for him to follow his brothers. For one thing, college was interrupted by the war, so it seemed a natural thing to do after war's end. Another factor was the 'GI Bill,' Congressional legislation that offered a subsidized opportunity for college. It was either this or look for employment for a living. Little thought was given by me to stay in the Air Corps, primarily because there were so many that wanted to stay in that it became a problem for the military. The problem was partially solved by having a RIF (Reduction in Force.) This happens after the end of hostilities when large numbers of people are not needed. People are evaluated by their individual worth towards the needs of the service. Once this is done, those of less value are forced out. Those that chose to stay on active duty and were accepted had a long, hard pull to be advanced in rank, especially officers, because Congress controls the number of those in the upper ranks.

Regardless of this college priority (and others to follow), there was always the interest in becoming a pilot. Occasionally Bob and I would check on Boeing's happenings, such as the C-97's first flight and one time we drove to Renton airport to see some surplus aircraft that were for sale, not that we had any means of buying one.

In the afternoons I had a job on the local playfield, organizing games and other recreation for kids: baseball, cricket, building balsa wood gliders, and playing with the kids.

I bought a 1946 four door black Dodge sedan. It was a nice looking car. It cost about $2,000. I saved a little more than that during the war because there was no place to spend money where I was. I kept sending my pay home by money order and Mom would bank it for me. Then, my economics got out of balance: I had a brand new car and very little money for gas. The GI Bill took care of college costs and provided a monthly stipend of $80. Bob and I gave half of ours to Mom for room and board, so I had $10 a week for pocket money.

Another source for gas money involved patrolling a Seattle beach where people would have bonfires and parties. One could find empty beer bottles lying about, pick them up and sell them. I sold my old Harley for parts; it was in pretty sad shape. I used my new car to drive other kids to the U. and they shared gas costs with me.

I took all I could on the GI Bill, going to summer school three years in a row, twice at the University of Washington and, in the 1947 summer, I went to Mills College in Oakland, California (a girl's college). Why did I do this? On a cold and wet day in one of the buildings on the UW campus, shaking the rain off my coat, I glanced at a bulletin board that said, "Come to Mills for the summer." After class, I read the rest of the bulletin and I thought, "Why not?" So,

I spent about six weeks down there and learned more about art in six weeks than I did in probably two years at the UW relative to technique. Unfortunately, there seemed to be a philosophy at the UW in the Art Department  that postulated if one were taught any technique it would stifle their creativity. I noticed this right away when I began art courses; my first thought was that the faculty had no talent. However, a faculty exhibit on the campus amazed me, showing works by those whose courses I had taken. Taking art courses was an experiment, and since I was doing well, I pressed on with a course that would prepare me to teach art at the secondary level, that is, at a high school.

I had to make up a language deficiency. The Engineering School, which I was in before military service, had no foreign language prerequisite. The Arts and Sciences College, which I was now in, did. Therefore, I had to make up this deficiency. I took French to satisfy that requirement. I was also required to take two other minors; one was in psychology, the other was in education. Some laboratory sciences were required. I took geology and physics. By coincidence, Bob and I had the same physics class, and being seated alphabetically, we were side by side, although we had different laboratory assignments.

One could easily distinguish the veterans from the other students. We had very little interest in fraternities or other campus functions, regarding these as 'Mickey Mouse,' or frivolous. Because civilian clothing was in short supply, one tended to wear portions of the uniform to school.

Les didn't come back from the war; he was a paratrooper, killed in Belgium and is buried in Luxembourg. I visited his grave once when I was stationed in France during the early sixties. Ian went back to school after the war but dropped out and went to work at Kenworth Motor Company, where his brother worked. Stan and Hugh Snow started back to school but dropped out. Stan, Hugh and I found summer jobs in a Ford Parts Depot in June of 1947. Stan and Hugh worked where the parts were stored. My job was drawing a floor plan of the entire building. Before I finished, it was time for me go to Oakland to Mills College. Stan finished the drawing, and 42 years later he retired from the Ford Motor Company. Hugh worked for and retired from the telephone company.

At the end of the summer session at Mills College in 1947, short on money, I called my Mom, asking for a loan so I could get home. Then, I found a good way to repay her. One of my high school buddies, who had gone through the Naval ROTC program during the war, was stationed on Treasure Island in San Francisco Bay. He was going to get married, but had no car. He proposed that I drive him and his bride to Providence, Rhode Island, his new station, for $100. That doesn't sound like much now but it was ample to go to the East Coast and back. So, I asked Mom if she'd like to go back to Ohio and visit her relatives at my expense. The roundtrip was to erase my debt to her. So off we went.

We had a bit of synchronicity in the middle of Iowa. We had stopped and gone into a small store to buy some ice cream cones. As we came out, two young men were coming in who turned out to be my friend's former classmates at the University of Washington. They were being transferred from Providence, Rhode Island, to Treasure Island, and my friend was being transferred from Treasure Island to Providence, Rhode Island!

Another bit of synchronicity happened on Long Island. My friend had a former schoolmate who lived at Rockville Center, Long Island, and by phoning ahead, he arranged a place for us to stay. The next morning while eating breakfast, I was mulling over the name Rockville Center, where we were. Then I remembered that one of the gunners on our B-29 bomber crew was from Rockville Center, so I asked our host if he knew anybody by the name of Frank McHugh. He replied that he'd gone to high school with him and he lived just around the corner. So, I went around the corner, knocked on the door and there was Frank McHugh!

From time to time, on my commute to the University and back, Mom would ask me to stop in town and make her house payments. I paid no attention to the paperwork until one day. I was appalled at the amount of money that went into interest and how little went toward the principal. The time for the 'birds to leave the nest' was approaching and I thought that buying a house would be encumbering, and renting, money down the tube. I mused with the idea of building a house.

In the middle of the spring quarter, 1948, I was asked if I would go on a two week active duty tour as we were required to annually by being in the Air Force Reserve. I answered in the affirmative; then, shortly I received my orders to report to McChord Air Force Base for duty. I took a copy of my orders to my professors explaining what was happening and they were all cooperative, giving me advance assignments so I could do my work while gone.

I left McChord in a C-82, arriving at Pope Air Force Base in North Carolina. There we were notified that we were to participate in a maneuver. It seems that captured plans from Germany indicated they might sometime try to invade the United States. They would come up the Mississippi Valley and split the country. Half of these plans had been put in practice by our troops. Theoretically, the Germans had advanced as far as Kentucky. Our job was to drop parachute troops to reinforce the defense of Camp Campbell, Kentucky. Before takeoff on this mission, the jumpmaster had his troops lined up with their gear on the ground for inspection. These were all black troops. The jumpmaster introduced the airplane's crew chief to the troops, saying that this man owned this airplane and they were to keep it clean. If they got airsick, they were to use their helmets and not mess up the airplane.

We flew at low level on a hot day and there was quite a bit of turbulence. Not just one, but all the troops got motion sickness and vomited into their helmets. Nearing the target, we climbed up for the jump. When a bell rang, all stood up and hooked their lanyard on an overhead cable. Then they shuffled one by one approaching the open door, each in turn, fastening his helmet on and leaping out.

As the spring of 1949 approached, my thoughts went back to building a house. This would lead to an extended hiatus relative to flying. I bought a lot in West Seattle and did preliminary work, like clearing the brush and some small trees before graduation day at the U. I did not go to commencement exercises, because it cost $15.00 to rent a cap and gown for the ceremony. Instead, I spent that money on galvanized water pipe. On graduation day I busied myself digging a trench along the road in front of the house to bury my waterline.

What did I know about building a house? Nothing. However, a contractor was putting up three houses near my lot. Each evening after the workers left, I would go over and look. This way I learned a lot.

Both Bob and Stan got married in 1948, and I believe Hugh Snow did too; I got on

The house I built 1949-50 in West Seattle.

the bandwagon in June 1949. This also contributed to a flying hiatus.

Construction proceeded slowly, and periodically I would work for a landscaper; an old football buddy and I put in lawns and rock retaining walls for him.

The winter of 1949-50 was the most severe in Seattle's history. We had no toilet or washing facilities inside. The hot water bottle in bed at night was a must. When the next evening rolled around and it was time to go to bed, the hot water bottle was retrieved for refilling; it was usually frozen. The eaves on the house were not closed and the wind would blow through. We occasionally did migrate to my mother's place some nights out in the Rainier district.

I did a lot of scrounging, watching the papers for sales of building materials.

Near the end of my project, I applied to go back into the service. I always wanted to be a pilot; however, during the war when I got into the cadet program, the Army had all the pilot trainees they could use. This is covered elsewhere herein. Why did I want to go back into the military? Besides having a chance to become a pilot, the Korean War was going on (this was 1950), and while building, I would listen to the war news on the radio, and I don't blush when I say there may have been some patriotism in me. While I was waiting to be called up, I got a job at Boeing. I sold the house.

The interviewer at Boeing asked what I had been doing. I said I had been building a house. He said, "Let's go see it." So we drove out there and he took a look. He also looked at ship models I had made when I was a teenager. He said he'd give me a job in the model shop;

so that's where I worked until I was called up.

I was working on a model of the B-52 when my orders arrived. I worked as a helper to a journeyman. We were fitting numerous tiny copper tubes inside a six-foot model of the B-52. These tubes terminated flush with the surface of the model at various places. These were to determine where the airplane's static ports should be located on the airplane. These ports fed information to the altimeters and airspeed indicators on the B-52. When ready, we would take the model upstairs to the wind tunnel. While it was being mounted in the tunnel, my job was to go through the tunnel and look for debris.

The other ends of the flush tubes we installed were connected to small rubber hoses which led to a large display board. After the tunnel was fired up and stabilized, engineers would come into the control room where the display board was and take readings from glass tubes that registered what the pressure was at each flush port. This procedure was repeated again and again with different tunnel air speeds and different aircraft attitudes. The search was to find the flush tube that showed the least variance of pressure in all these configurations. In 1985, at an air show in Canada, I walked around a B-52 on display and located its static ports. I savored the connection I had with these.

Another project in the model shop was to find the best places under a B-47's wings to hang drop tanks. Apparently jettisoning these tanks, they would sometimes strike the horizontal tail surfaces or come too close to them. It was fascinating to watch the model maker working on this problem, packing a small parachute made from a nylon stocking into a cone shaped container on the aft end of a miniature drop tank. I suppose the wind tunnel was used to test this device.

It was essential that I go on active duty before my 27th birthday because that was the cut off age for the pilot training program. I beat this by a little more than a month.

What happened to the idea of teaching? This didn't go to waste because in the Air Force I spent years in a teaching capacity both in the classroom and in the air.

Chapter Five

More Training

In March of 1951, with a few clothes and a portable sewing machine, we headed for San Angelo, in west Texas, to begin pilot training. I began flying in the North American T-6, formerly called an AT-6. Pilot training began in this airplane, whereas during WW II it was the plane in which students like my brother Bob were graduated. This phase was called Basic Training and lasted six months. I remember well my first solo flight in the T-6. There was a large hornet buzzing around inside my wind screen, so I conned myself into believing it was a welcome guest and tried to ignore it. A bifurcation took place at the end of six months. Student pilots were divided into two groups, one going to Single Engine Advanced Training and the other going to Multi Engine Advanced Training. One was allowed to state a preference; however, the needs of the service are always paramount so some didn't get their choice. Advanced Single Engine Training for me was at Bryan, Texas, about 90 miles north of Houston. We flew North American T-28s, Lockheed T-33s and Lockheed F-80s there. The T-6s and T-28s were propeller driven machines; the F-80 and the T-33 were jet powered. The T-33 was a two seat version of the F-80, our first production fighter. All of these airplanes mentioned were single engine machines.

My first solo in a jet was in an F-80. I was feeling pretty frisky and climbed up and decided to do a loop (we hadn't done them in the T-33 with the instructor yet). Well, I ran out of airspeed while going over the top and fell vertically upside down through a large puffy cloud and then recovered. I had a lot to learn.

The quiet smoothness of jet engine flight was a delight. Formation flight was a good deal different from propeller airplanes. Moving the throttle in a propeller driven airplane, the response is immediate, both in accelerating and decelerating. Hence, only small throttle adjustments make fore and aft changes easy. However, in early jet engines, throttle adjustments were not immediate. It took time for the engine to 'spool up', or accelerate, and also time to decelerate when the throttle was retarded. The response was quicker if one used more throttle than was needed, and then reduce it before it pro-duced too much thrust. This

A T-6G... The prop airplane I soloed in

was an art. If one added too much throttle too fast, a compressor stall would occur, thrust would decrease and a loud rumbling noise would come from the engine. The beginning student would hear this rumble, and if he reduced throttle too much the horn would blow (without the landing gear down, reducing the throttle, as in landing, a warn-ing horn would blow in the cockpit, warning him to extend his gear). Thus, the neophyte jet student might be called a 'rumble-beep' forma-tion flyer.

Learning to fly high-powered military aircraft required digesting a large amount of information, some of which was lengthy and complex. Mnemonic devices were used as aids to recall procedures. For example, in flying the F-80, the phrase, " I Can Fly This Thing OK" was used as a cockpit procedure reminder before taxiing for takeoff. The 'I' referred to a fuel pump called the I-16 which had to be switched on; 'Can' was a reminder to close the canopy; 'Fly' reminded one to lower some flaps; 'This' reminded one to set the trim; 'Thing' was a reminder to select the transmitting frequency and OK was to check the oxygen system. Another example, regardless of the airplane type, was used to remind the pilot of the correct sequence of information when transmitting position reports. That mnemonic tool was (and still is), "I Pee Twice A Day," standing for Identification (of your aircraft), Position, Time, Altitude and Destination.

We were graduated as pilots with shiny new wings and put into a pipeline, that is, directly headed to Korea.

On the 15th of April, while on leave at home in Seattle, I needed some money and was on my way to McChord Air Force Base to draw some pay. Passing by Boeing Field, I noticed many cars and people alongside the road. I stopped and asked what was going on. They were all Boeing employees and I was told they were waiting for the first flight of the B-52. I had two cameras with me and got some shots of the big bird on its maiden flight.

Advanced single engine school, North American T-28, Bryan, TX.

T-33... two seats; the single seat version was the F-80

Training Command F-86 at Nellis AFB Gunnery School, 1952

Lockheed F-80, the first jet I soloed in. 1951-52, Bryan TX.

After leave, the next step was to go to Nellis Air Force Base in Las Vegas, Nevada. This was a gunnery school. We knew how to fly airplanes but we didn't know how to use them as weapons yet. Six weeks here and we gained this new knowledge.

Toward the latter part of our gunnery training at Nellis, there was another bifurcation. Most of us gunnery students would go into combat in the F-80, a fighter-bomber whose mission would be attacking ground targets. Some would be fortunate enough to go into combat in the F-86, the hottest fighter in the force at that time. The swept winged jet fighter could go through mach one (speed of sound) in a dive; it was a transonic airplane. The F-100, a supersonic airplane, would be my mount later. The mission of the F-86s would be to achieve air superiority, denying the enemy the use of his aircraft to wage war. This was tantamount to going hunting every day for enemy aircraft.

It may be amusing to find out how I 'lucked-out' and became an F-86 pilot instead of an F-80 pilot. Each Friday, while in gunnery training, we would repair to the club to have a beer or two. Each instructor, with his three students, normally sat at individual tables. At the time when the bifurcation was going to occur, on this particular Friday, someone suggested a beer-drinking contest. The idea was to see who could drink the most beer without going to the toilet. Each table needed a representative. My instructor looked at me and said, "Brewer, do you want to get into F-86s?" I said, "Yes sir." Then he said that I must win the contest. I won but it hurt. This is a true story and I really don't know whether the contest made any difference or not. I hope not. Many years later in 1997 my brother Bob and I went to Nellis Air Force Base to take in an air show. There were some bleachers near the flight line with a banner that read "F-86 Pilots' Association." I was aware of this organization and had received some of its literature from time to time, but I'm not a big joiner, although I knew some of its members. I told Bob that I was going to look around the corner and see if I could recognize anybody. All I saw were old men and women, so turning away, I bumped into a man that I recognized immediately:

15th April, 1952, first flight of the B-52, Boeing Field, Seattle. I happened to be home on leave after graduating from pilot training in the Air Force upon this fortuitous photographic occasion.

he had been my instructor in gunnery school in 1952! His name was Dee Harper. I shook his hand and mentioned my name but he didn't recognize me until I brought up the subject of the beer-drinking contest that I'd won 45 years earlier!

Incidentally, the F-86 was the first airplane I checked out in where there was no instructor in the back seat for pre-solo flight because there was no back seat. You studied the pilot's handbook, got lots of 'cockpit time' sitting in the machine getting thoroughly familiar with it, taking a written test and taking a blindfolded cockpit exam given by your instructor. He'd ask you, for example, to put your finger on the radio circuit breaker so you would count down so many rows of breakers then count the right number horizontally to find it…then he would say if you are certain, pull it…and you'd better be sure. I believe only two two-seated versions of the F-86 were ever built. One of them crashed at Nellis during a demonstration I witnessed about 1954. I don't know what happened to the other one. There were no two-seat models of the F-100 either when I checked out in it later after the Korean campaign, although the later C model had two seats and came into service about 1956 or 1957.

A standing jest was used when one was about to check out in the F-86. If one had already flown it and your buddy had not, you'd ask him when he was going to. If he offered an answer, you'd acknowledge the date and add, "Good, I'll bring my colored film and marshmallows." This was one of many ways to turn danger into humor.

You could always tell when a pilot was taking off for the first time in the F-86. His wings would wobble, not being used to the sensitivity inherent in the hydraulic control system. An early model, the F-86 A, had old-fashioned cable controls attached to the ailerons which were superceded by hydraulic controls in later models. While pulling out of a high speed dive in the A model, the ailerons cables would stretch because of the 'G' force on the ailerons, thus, both ailerons would hinge upwards and act like the elevators on the tail. This would cause the nose to want to pitch up, augmenting the G force which would make things worse. Normally, back pressure on the stick is used to recover from a dive, but forward pressure had to be used to solve this A model oddity.

Annotation: Here is another adjustment observation: In gunnery school in the 'pipeline' to Korean War, a fellow pilot came to work one morning complaining about pain in his forearm. It became worse on subsequent days, so he went on sick call. Then we didn't see him for about a week. When he returned, we asked him where he'd been. He said he'd been at an Air Force hospital in Hayward, California. When asked how they'd fixed his arm, he said they'd 'talked him out of it'. Unknown to him, he had been adjusting to the idea of going to war and his body was inventing a way to avoid it. A psychologist would recognize this as adjustment by ailment. He flew his tour in combat in an F-80 unit honorably and had no more trouble as far as I know.

Home again on leave, fresh out of the gunnery school, some decisions had to be made as well as preparations. My daughter Chris was to be born in October, and I had the option of going to Korea right away or being deferred until 30 or 60 days after the birth. I don't recall which. I let my wife make this decision. I was to go. I had to make arrangements to have my family housed. We found a rental unit in Vancouver, Washington. This city was where my wife had grown up and where most of her relatives lived. I would not be present when my daughter was born.

I flew to Sacramento, California, boarded a military transport airplane and flew to Hawaii. The next leg was to Wake Island to refuel. The third leg was to Tachikawa Air Base in Japan. Yokohama looked different from when I saw it last, which was on VJ Day, the second of September 1945. At that time, there was nothing but ashes and rusting steel. Yokohama looked like it had recovered nicely. The next step was to take a train to the west coast of Japan. We had sleeper cars but found them difficult to sleep in because the beds were too short. Even sleeping on the diagonal was difficult; the best position was a fetal position, lying on your side curled up. From the west coast of Japan, we flew in a C-46 to Korea, landing at Seoul and then proceeding in a bus to my new home, K-14, also called Kimpo, where I was going to live for the next eight months.

We shared the single runway field with some other units. I was in the Fourth Fighter Interceptor Group, which had three squadrons. On the other side of the field was an Australian unit flying de Havilland Gloster Meteors, twin engine jet fighter-bombers; in addition, there was an American reconnaissance unit flying RF-51s and RF-80s. The "F" stands for fighter, "R" stands for reconnaissance. My unit flew the F-86, the newest fighter in our inventory. The 51s were propeller driven airplanes, the best fighter we had in WW II. The 80s were jets that I flew in advanced pilots' school and also in gunnery school.

On my field at K-14 in Korea, there were two other units on the field. One was a reconnaissance outfit that flew RF-80s (above) and RF-51s. The other was an Australian unit that flew Gloster Meteor fighter bombers (lower picture.)

Our primary job was to ensure air superiority; a secondary job was to escort fighter-bombers and reconnaissance aircraft to and from their targets. We accomplished our primary mission by patrolling, looking for enemy fighters that might challenge our air superiority.

Our tour of duty was one year or 100 missions, whichever came first. Most finished up their missions in about eight months; this was my case. Sometimes I'd fly a mission a day, sometimes two, then sometimes none because of foul weather. On one occasion, I flew three missions on one day; this was the day President Eisenhower came to Korea. In his campaign for the presidency he promised to come to Korea, thus, an extra effort was made for his security.

Our group had three fighter squadrons: the 334th, the 335th and the 336th. My squadron, the 335th, had an enviable record, producing 18 of the 32 fighter aces in the Korean War. An ace was a person who shot down five or more aircraft. These figures included three other squadrons of F-86s in the 51st Wing at Suwon, south of us. The Fourth Fighter Group was famous in England during WW II. It was manned with American volunteers who had come to fly with the English prior to our entry into WW II. One of my squadron commanders while in Korea had been there with the Fourth in England.

My first mission was an orientation flight, primarily used to observe landmarks and procedures. We did cross the bomb line, which is that demarcation on the surface commonly called the front. It was rare to become engaged with the enemy on orientations. However, on my second mission, which was to cover fighter-bombers, we were in and out of clouds of many layers. Because of the weather, we were flying rather close together so as not to lose sight of one another in the clouds. Normally, we would fly some distance apart, around 1,200 feet, giving pilots space to maneuver and to observe others in the flight. In your aircraft you cannot see underneath or directly behind you. This is a blind area, so you watch your buddy's tails and they watch yours. As a matter of interest, late in WW II P-51s had radar installed in the tail which would warn the pilot of aircraft in his blind spot; one of these radars was used on the Hiroshima atomic bomb, Little Boy, to measure the proximity to the ground in order to burst it at the proper altitude.

Normally, we flew in what was called the fingertip formation. If you spread your hand out and bring your fingers together side by side, the middle finger would represent the leader of the flight, the index finger, his wing man (usually the least experienced), and on the other side of the leader would be an element leader; the pinky would represent the element leader's wingman. We flew our sweeps on the same level, but not quite. If the leader were to make a sharp turn, the wingman would have some vertical clearance to avoid collision.

So, getting back to mission number two, we were rather close together because of the weather. We couldn't see the fighter-bombers because of the clouds, but we were nonetheless patrolling in case enemy aircraft were in the vicinity. Stretching my neck around, I saw two MiG-15s dropping out of the clouds about the 7 o'clock position (12:00 being straight ahead and 6:00 being directly behind); this system was used to locate objects relative to your aircraft. These were at seven o'clock high. I called my observation out to the leader and he executed the primary defensive maneuver, which was turning into your adversary. If he's not directly behind you, you make a tight turn into him, that way, he would have to turn tighter than you, and couldn't press his attack because he has to point his airplane ahead of you. If he doesn't, he can't hit you. One must aim ahead of the target aircraft, called "lead." The command for that turning maneuver, or break, involved the flight leader broadcasting, "Black, break left!" Black was the call sign of the flight. At this command, everyone made a hard turn to the left, and the MiGs couldn't stay with us in this defensive maneuver. The attackers would then tend to slide by and when they did, the next command would be to reverse the turn and try to get on their tails. So we reversed; it was quite violent. I tended to slide under my leader and I could see he was firing because the brass cartridge cases were pouring out of the chutes on the underside of his fuselage. About that time, we popped into some clouds; I kept my heading in a dive. Then I popped out of the clouds and looked around -- I saw nobody. My leader asked if I had him in sight; I said, "negative," which means no, and he said he had me in sight. At that moment I spotted an airplane below and going away to our right. I called the leader and told him I had a bogie in sight. He replied, "Go get him." At that moment I became the leader. This change from being a wingman to being the leader is because, if you take your eyes off the target, chances are you'll never see it again. This is because of the speeds involved, each going about 600 miles an hour, and looking away, it's difficult to reacquire a target. Once acquired, the expression used was, "I'm padlocked," meaning that you could not look away, thus, your blind spot is exposed. So the original leader assumes the wingman role and 'checks your six,' that is, he keeps your tail clear. I was overtaking my target at a high rate of speed and the adrenaline was pumping, then I recognized the aircraft as an F-86. F-86s trailed a bit of black smoke from the engine and the MiG fifteen did not. I called and said that I identified my target as an F-86. Black Flight was called and told to rock their wings. Rocking wings was proof positive that my 'target' was friendly. So, I had some action on my second mission. One might fly 50, 75, or maybe even an entire tour and never see an enemy aircraft, but when you did you had your hands full.

That was an escort mission. Most missions were not escorting missions but sweeps or patrols. We would take off, fly the 200 nautical miles to the Yalu River, which was the boundary between Korea and Manchuria, then cruise along the river in a shallow figure eight, closely paralleling the river. At the mouth of the river, where it poured into the Yellow Sea, one could look down and see two air bases: one was called Antung, and the other Fengcheng. The leader of the first flight up into the area we called 'MiG Alley' would take a pair of binoculars and look down on these Manchurian airdromes to see if any aircraft were taking off. If so, this could be an indication of possible engagement. Normally, this border was not to be violated, depending upon the political situation. Thus, the enemy had a sanctuary; this was frustrating for us. Sometimes this prohibition would be altered to allow border crossing if one were in hot pursuit. On one occasion we were authorized across the river when the fighter-bombers were going to hit the power plants on the Suiho dam. We also had cheaters that would go across the fence to hunt. Sometimes tacit permission was given to cross the fence. The "Old Man" (our boss) would say he believed a strong south wind was blowing that bends the boundary a bit, which meant it was OK to cross the fence.

Now our enemies were not just Koreans; some were Chinese and some were Soviets. How do we know this? Well, it's impossible to fly this kind of combat without radio communications between aircraft. Our intelligence people monitored the enemy communications. Sometimes they would find the Chinese language with a Russian accent, and in stressful moments, sometimes the Soviet pilots would use their own language, replete with epithets. One time a transmission had a pilot speaking Russian with a German accent. Because Soviets flying in Korea was supposed to be a secret, Stalin would not let his pilots fly over the Yellow Sea. The reason was that we controlled the Yellow Sea and if one of their aircraft went down in the water, we might be able to retrieve the pilot and show that the Soviets were involved. On the other hand, Stalin really wanted to get his hands on an F-86 because we were waxing them, and they wanted to know why.

Because the MiGs would not fly over the Yellow Sea, it was a place for us to head if we were in trouble. If one became separated from his flight, he was required to head for the Yellow Sea and fly over the water back to base. In case of emergency, we had helicopters, flying boats and ships that could perform rescue services in the Yellow Sea. The procedure for being alone, not being able to see underneath nor directly in back of you, was to make shallow turns which allowed you to look over your shoulder down and back and complete your field of vision and head for the water. The Yellow Sea would freeze in the winter out to a mile or so from the shore, and there were sharks there in the summer.

Living conditions on our base were quite good. We lived in stucco buildings that had tile roofs, former quarters for the Japanese who occupied Korea for 40 years. In each room, which housed six or seven pilots, there was an oil stove, which seemed to blow up about once a week and spread soot all over. We had a Korean house boy who swept the floor, cleaned the oil stove and kept an eye on things. The food was good, much better than the food I ate during WW II overseas. Perhaps once a week we might have steak or perhaps ice cream. Occasionally, if one wanted a better meal, one could go into Seoul to the 5th Air Force Headquarters Officers' Club and splurge. This was rare for me. We had an Officers' Club which, when I arrived, was just another room in a stucco building with some wood picnic tables. A new club was built during my tour. It was interesting watching the Korean building methods. I watched one man making gutters and downspouts by hand using only a mallet made of pieces of two by four with a stick for a handle.

The enemy had some old biplanes called PO-2s (Polikarpov-2s) and occasionally they would show up about 10:00 at night about the time we went to bed, tossing mortar shells on us. These aircraft were dubbed 'Bed Check Charlies.' They were mostly harassing, and as far as I know did very little damage, although I believe they hit petroleum storage sites at Inchon once. We had anti-aircraft guns nearby, consisting of .50 caliber machine guns and 40mm antiaircraft guns, both of which I trained on when I was in the Coast Artillery. I don't know if these defenses ever hit the PO-2s. One morning I went down to fly and walking around my aircraft making my preflight inspection I noticed one of the external fuel tanks seemed empty because the airplane was sitting cockeyed. Quizzing the crew chief, he said that he had filled the tanks the night before. Kicking the tank proved it to

Polikarpov PO-2, aka 'Bedcheck Charlie.' (photo courtesy of Aviation History, Nov., 2008)

be empty. An inspection showed a gash on the underside of the tank. This apparently was caused by a 'short round' (which is a term for a faulty cartridge) whose projectile had ricocheted off the pierced steel planking on which our aircraft were parked, and had come up and cut a gash in the tank, allowing the fuel to escape. The source of the projectile was probably from one of anti-aircraft machine guns.

Bed Check Charlie was a nuisance. On another field we had some all-weather interceptors called F-94s. They had radar in their noses to seek out other aircraft in weather or at night. One was dispatched to shoot down a PO-2. The interceptor found the PO-2 all right, however, the speed difference was a problem. The PO-2 was probably going all of 70 or 80 miles an hour, a speed at which an F-94, a jet plane, would probably fall out of the sky. The interception was made and they collided; all were killed. Next, the Marine Corps was called. They were flying some WW II propeller driven airplanes called F4U Corsairs, able to maneuver at low speed, hanging on a 9-foot propeller. I believe the only ace the Navy had (the Marines are part of the Navy) in the Korean War was from shooting down PO-2s. Officially we were in a United Nations Police Action, not a war; however, it was war, so I give it this label.

When Bed Check Charlie visited us, sirens would sound and we'd go outside and get in a trench that was there for shelter, grabbing a coat and some blankets for warmth. (Korea is very cold in the winter, it being very close to Siberia.) One odd thing was that, walking to and from my squadron operations on the flight line, I saw a yard that contained several large searchlights. Why these were never employed

Maintenance: vital and essential aspect of aviation. Above: F-86 in Korea. Below: an F-80.

against the PO-2s I don't know. Incidentally, these PO-2s were flown extensively by female pilots in the Soviet Union during WW II, mostly at night attacking small targets such as unit headquarters. They were called the 'Night Witches'.

Annotation: Microsoft billionaire Paul Allen has a PO-2 in his Heritage Collection at Paine Field, Everett, Washington.

In our living area, the shower and latrines were primitive. The equivalent of an outhouse was a seat superimposed above a 50-gallon barrel. Periodically, the Korean farmers would come and take them away, using the contents as fertilizer on their fields; these were called 'honey buckets.' It was common to see Korean farmers on the field cutting grass for fodder. They had a device called an 'A frame', which stood like an artist's easel, propped up with a staff. After loading a prodigious amount of grass on it, the prop would be removed and the farmer would carry the frame on his back, using the prop as a walking stick.

There was a barbed wire fence around the base, and at night sentries would patrol it. One portion of the fence was not far from our door. One cold night, walking back from the flight line to my quarters, I saw a sentry walking there. I spoke to him and told him, if he wanted, I would bring him some toddy (a chocolate drink in a small can.) I told him I would heat it on our oil stove and bring it out. When I took it out and approached him, I was told to halt. I remarked that it was just me and I had the toddy for him. He repeated his order and I heard the bolt go home on his carbine. Needless to say, I froze

Squadron patch that I redesigned for the unit.

in my tracks and went through the procedure of laying down my identification, backing away and then waiting for him to come and inspect my ID. What had happened was, while I was heating up the toddy, the guard had changed. All ended well.

Chapter Six

Combat in the Korean War

Unlike my overseas base in WW II, we had a laundry on our base in Korea. On Tinian, in WW II, we had to do our own laundry. Many built small windmills to do this; I built a gasoline-powered machine to do my laundry. Many others used it. Koreans operated our laundry on K-14; it was efficient and inexpensive.

In leisure time, we could go to movies. These were shown outdoors, sitting on planks embedded in a slope so one could see over others' heads. This was weather-dependent, however. We had no USO shows. On the flight line, a good deal of time was spent playing ping pong, and it was seldom that the ping pong table was idle. I found out that I wasn't the best ping pong player in the world. My backhand was OK, but my forehand was wanting. I spent some time painting, using watercolors that I had bought in Tokyo. I also painted a sign that hung over the doorway of our group briefing room. It said, "Fourth Fighter Interceptor Group, Home of the MiG Killers." It turned out to be a favorite place to have one's picture taken. In books and magazines, over the years, I have seen it reproduced several times, often with former fellow pilots. I also made some diagrams showing what a MiG-15 looked like from dif-

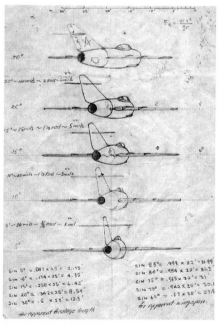

Drawings I made showing the enemy Mig-15 from different angles. I enlarged this and made a poster for our squadron bulletin board.

ferent angles from its tail and posted these on the unit bulletin board. Some made model aircraft in their spare time. I also did this; however, I never finished mine, leaving its balsa wood frame behind when I left to go home. Some recreated by drinking; some to excess. On one of my early missions, the flight leader and one other in the flight were noticeably drunk, and had been up all night. Perhaps some flew better drunk than sober, but I doubt it.

We had a single runway at K-14. At the east end was a Quonset hut that served as a shelter for pilots who had alert duty. Each day, prior to dawn, four aircraft would be taxied to this area, their tanks topped off, and the pilots would go inside. Some would read, some would sleep and some would play cards. I spent some time outdoors whittling on a stick or making sketches. When our radar station would show unidentified aircraft approaching, a telephone would ring in the alert hut, answered by a clerk who would relay the order to 'scramble.' This would trigger a response, depending on the magnitude of the threat. Either two or four aircraft would be scrambled. The clerk that received the call would shout, "Scramble two,

Kimpo, standing alert, whittling on a stick.

or "Scramble four." This was the signal for the designated pilots to run to their airplanes, don their parachutes, climb in the cockpit, and while strapping in, the crew chief would lean over your shoulder and start the engine. From the scramble signal to rolling down the runway would only take about two minutes. Jet engines don't require a warm up, as do piston engines.

We would take turns for this duty. There would be a

F-86s on alert pad, Kimpo, Korea, 1952-53

roster scheduling individual pilots for this. One would be either on the morning shift or the afternoon shift. Alert was from dawn to dusk. One time when I was on the afternoon shift, while doing my walk around inspection, I discovered a dust cover inside the engine air intake, lying against the screens. These covers were designed to keep out foreign objects when the aircraft was shut down. They were made of plywood, painted red with a red lanyard attached to attract attention, and inserted in the nose. Prior to starting the engine, these had to be removed. Evidently, the pilot who had been on the morning shift either had not done his inspection or had not seen the cover lying on its side deep inside the intake. Had he been scrambled, chances are that on the takeoff run, the cover would have stood up by the incoming air pressure and would have caused the engine to stop. This was an accident waiting to happen.

To alleviate boredom while waiting to be scrambled, sometimes we would play pranks. If we knew there was a newcomer using our corrugated sheet metal outhouse, we would wait until he was well positioned, then throw rocks at the building, which would make a terrific racket. One time we took a length of rope, put it around the outhouse so the door would not open (after the victim was well positioned) then call, "Scramble two," knowing that he was one of the two. We got a good laugh watching him trying to get out.

Incidentally, the pilot that had overlooked dust cover removal was sent home early. He was involved in the death of an airman. To harmonize our machine guns so that the bullets went where the sight was set, the guns were fired at short range at targets that were backed by bags of earth. Although pilots were not required to assist in this task, one pilot chose to help. He was in the cockpit. The guns had been fired and the hot gun barrel had heated a cartridge until it cooked-off. Unfortunately, an airman that was in front of the airplane was killed. I don't know if this had anything to do with pilot carelessness in these two incidents, the dust cover and the death, or the fact that he had contacted hepatitis, but he was sent home early.

My flight leader and I were scrambled once. We followed the radar station's vector, but saw nothing. On the way back to the base, I noticed my leader flying a bit erratically, not holding a steady heading. I called him and asked if he was OK. He said he was. His wanderings continued, so I asked him specific questions. I'd ask how much fuel he had left. His head would go down in the cockpit and slowly he'd give me an answer. Other questions about oil pressure and oxygen were asked. Slow responses were made. I suspected oxygen or carbon monoxide problems. I advised him to go on 100% oxygen and look at his fingernails (they turn bluish with carbon monoxide poisoning).

He took his gloves off and looked, but didn't answer. Then I called the base and alerted them of a possible problem. I asked my leader if he wanted to fly my wing in the traffic pattern; he laughed at this. He landed OK and was taken to the hospital. He was saturated with carbon monoxide.

I was assigned to lead three new pilots on a local training flight one time. We were all lined up to take the runway when an emergency occurred. An F-84 pilot had been hit and blood was interfering with his vision. His wingman was flying alongside him, trying to help him land. The wounded pilot was coming down the runway too fast so the wingman was yelling for him to retract his gear and belly in. The airplane touched down in front of us, leaving a trail of sparks. It then rotated sideways about 90 degrees and skidded off the end of the runway in a cloud of dust and came to a stop. The pilot stood up in the cockpit and began to climb out. Apparently he triggered the ejection seat and was projected up into the air about 30 or 40 feet. He looked like a rag doll going end over end. When he came down. I couldn't see where he landed. Thinking I'd witnessed a fatality, I was surprised to see the pilot in our club later with only minor injuries. He had landed on the horizontal stabilizer of his plane and that absorbed most of the energy of his fall.

There was a pilot in another squadron who thought he was the quintessential hot fighter pilot. To achieve notoriety, he liked to do an aileron roll immediately after take off. He tried to do this one too many times, dishing out of the roll and taking the head off a worker who was driving a grader near the end of the runway. He also killed himself.

Here is a bit of history that unfurled at our alert pad: after I had left to come home, the pilots on alert were surprised to see an enemy aircraft land on our runway, taxi off the runway to our alert building, shut the engine off, and stand up in the cockpit with his hands raised. A North Korean had defected in a MiG-15! Our radar had not detected him approaching because it was shut down for maintenance that day There was a reward offered for such action, however, this pilot was not

Kimpo (K-14), Korea, July, 1952. This F-86 of my unit has downed 14 Migs, one for each red star you see on the fuselage.

aware of it. He had defected for personal reasons. Because truce talks were going on in Panmunjon, we thought we might have to give this airplane back. It was a valuable prize and we wanted to test it to assess its capabilities. Chuck Yeager, the test pilot who had first broken the sound barrier, and one other pilot were summoned from the States. The airplane was dismantled and shipped to Okinawa. Reassembled there, it was never returned. Incidentally, the North Korean pilot landed downwind and passed one of our aircraft taking off in the opposite direction, the two barely missing each other.

Man and his machine

During questioning, the Korean pilot was asked why there was an inch wide white stripe painted vertically down the center of the instrument panel. He said it was for spin recovery. Puzzled, he was asked how? He replied that was where you put the stick. In a normal spin, the stick does go forward to lower the nose in order to gain air speed for spin recovery. This was an indication of a difference in pilot training. We would never teach such a mechanical approach to flying. Besides studying the manual and taking a written examination on the aircraft systems, we were required to take a blindfolded cockpit check. An instructor would ask you to put your hand on various controls, for example, he might ask you to pull a certain circuit breaker.

While preparing to fly the MiG-15 on Okinawa, the Russian markings on cockpit controls had been translated into English to simplify our test pilots' task. The Russian markings had been taped over with English. While asking the Korean pilot what the various knobs, switches and controls were for, there were some whose use he didn't recall until he lifted the tape and read the Russian. Apparently this pilot had never had a blindfold cockpit check.

In some respects, the MiG-15 was a better airplane than the F-86. The MiG was lighter and had a higher rate of climb (thanks to its

British designed engine). Its armament was greater; it had two 23mm cannons and one 37mm cannon. Our airplanes had six 50-caliber machine guns. The difference between a machine gun and a cannon is its projectiles. The cannon has shells, which on contact explode, making many pieces of shrapnel. Our machine guns, on the other hand, had solid projectiles of three types: ball cartridges with solid steel-jacketed bullets; interspersed with these on the belts that fed the machine guns were API (Armor Piercing Incendiary) cartridges; and tracers which, when fired, left white paths

A painting I made of an old Korean farmer.

My cousin Dale McMullen and me with my F-86, 'Trouble Brewer.'

through the air so you could see where the bullets had gone.

When diving, the F-86 was superior. It could go through mach one, the speed of sound, with very little trouble. Approaching mach one, one wing tended to be heavier than the other; then the other wing would feel this way, finally, all would feel normal and stable. In a high-speed dive, the MiG-15 tended to yaw, weaving from side to side. The F-86 had a superior gun sight that used radar ranging; MiG sights had no radar. All told, perhaps the aircraft were nearly equal in capability; however, it seemed that what was in the cockpit made the difference. Attitude also was a factor. I don't know any fighter pilot that was in Korea who doubted what he was doing or why he was there. The aggressive nature of our fighter pilots was personified by the motto, "Every man a tiger." I don't know what the attitude among the enemy pilots was. At least there was one who didn't relish communism or he would not have defected. Fighting performance varied widely among the enemy. We observed that some when hit would bail out right away. Some would bail out if they'd get into a spin. Some would hit and run; however, there were some aggressive enemy fighter pilots that would challenge you and hang on like a junkyard dog. These we called 'honchos', a Japanese word meaning boss or leader. Just as the Germans and the Soviets did in the Spanish civil war testing out their equipment and tactics, so did the Soviets in Korea in order to find out how they would stand in a larger conflict. One learns by doing. Whatever, the overall score was about ten to one in our favor when the armistice was signed.

Just about everyone was eager to achieve the 100-mission goal and sometimes it led to problems. One such problem concerning myself occurred when, after eight days of being grounded because of weather in the form of thick fog, we were finally going to fly a mission. I checked the scheduling board and saw I was slated to fly as a 'spare.' A spare was an aircraft that the took off first, proceeded to a specific point and waited, so if another pilot aborted for any reason and needed to be replaced, the spare would fill in to maintain the flight integrity, which is essential for defense. So I was a spare. I took off and went to my point, which was over an island that we controlled in the Yellow Sea called Cho-do. It had our major radar station as well as a point to launch air sea rescue services.

Well, that day no one needed a spare. One got credit for the mission, however, because Cho-do was north of the bomb line. So there I was with an airplane with lots of fuel and nothing to do. What

I should have done was go back to base and land; however, a couple of weeks before we had an airplane that had tried to land on a beach on another island called Pen-yang-do. According to the pilot, the beach was replete with boulders, so he put the airplane in shallow water, the first ever ditching of an F-86. Because of this, I thought it would be valuable to know whether any beaches on Cho-do were suitable for forced landings. So I let down, meaning to find out if a beach in particular on Cho-Do's west side was suitable. Most of Cho-do's perimeter consisted of cliffs. As I got down to the surface I saw, to the west a mile or so away, an SA-16 amphibious flying boat, part of the rescue service. Although I was not close to it, apparently they were alarmed because the pilot made a steep turn toward me, a primary defensive maneuver. I turned away from there and went to the beach and slowed down by putting my gear down, dive brakes out and flaps down to take a look. It didn't look suitable. I headed home. Off the northwest corner of the island, there was a large stack (a large rock mass) and I went between it and the island, cleaning up the airplane by retracting the gear, dive brakes and flaps, and adding full power to climb out. Making a turn to the right, I paralleled the north shore of Cho-Do, which was very steep, almost a cliff, although it had vegetation on it. I looked to my left, saw some vessels there at some distance, glanced at the greenery, looked back at the boats, then over my right shoulder I noticed something happening behind me. There were shells going into the rock face of the island! These were coming from the ships. They were tracking me nicely; however, I was accelerating, and apparently the gunners didn't compensate for that. This scared me. Another close one! That would have been an ignominious end, being shot down by my own Navy.

After each mission, a pilot would go through debriefing. The intelligence people would want to know what you saw, how many, what color, what maneuvers and anything else they could glean from your experience. This time the interrogator remarked that I had been a spare and not used, and so waved me on. I breathed a little easier. However, that night about 8:00, I had a telephone call. It was a Major Eagle from Fifth Air Force Headquarters in Seoul. He said, "Brewer, you were a spare today." I said, "Yes." He said, "You weren't used." I said, "Yes." He asked if I'd made a pass at a SA-16 up there. I said no, and I told him what I was doing, that is, taking a look at the beach. I didn't mention that I had seen the amphibian turn into me in defense. Then he told me that I'd scared the hell out of those people; he said they didn't know a MiG-15 from an F-86. Then he said nothing for a while. Then he asked if I had seen any gunfire up there. I didn't want to say yes and I didn't want to say no, so I said, "Gunfire?" Then he said that those people on the boats up there were very vulnerable and didn't know the difference between a MiG-15 and an F-86 and I'd scared the hell out of them too. He made me wait some more, perhaps deciding what, if anything, to do about me. He finally said not to 'sweat' this and hung up. I

Celebrating the birth of my daughter Christine

was greatly relieved; my intentions were good; my judgment was less than it could have been.

We had instances where we shot at our own people. On my second mission I was ready to do this until the last second when I realized my target was one of our own. My cousin, Dale McMullen, who was in my unit and who had followed me through pilot training, was flying wing with the group commander Colonel Baker, an ace. They got into some MiGs, and my cousin called that he had a bogey and was padlocked. Immediately, the Colonel who was leading became the wingman. My cousin fired once, missed, and then realized his target was an F-86. Upon landing, my cousin expected to catch hell from the Colonel for his mistake. However, the Colonel said, "Mac, you had that guy wired. Why didn't you press in?" Then Mac replied that it was an F-86. The Colonel said, "The hell it was." They removed his gun camera film and had it developed. Indeed it was an F-86. As one pulls the trigger, the first travel of the trigger starts a recording device, in our case, a motion picture camera; nowadays, probably a video camera.

On another occasion, one of our pilots did shoot down one of our own. The first ace of the Korean War was a fellow named Jabara. Because of his accomplishment he was rotated to the States as a celebrity, encouraging people to buy war bonds and attending gala events. However, he, like everyone else, was required to fly his 100 missions. So, when he returned, I was there. We called him 'Cousin Weak Eyes,' because of his propensity to shoot at anything. On one occasion, he attacked one of

Above: My sympathy was with the antiaircraft gunners protecting our base in Korea, just where I would have been if I'd not transferred to the Air Corps in WW-II.

our own aircraft, fired at it nine times, hit it three times, and caused the pilot to bail out. He realized his error and told the pilot to bail out. The victim was reluctant to bail out because he'd lose his new camera that he had with him. Jabara told him he'd buy him a new one. He did bail out, landing in the Yellow Sea, not too far from shore. An SA-16 air sea rescue amphibian picked him up, dodging ground fire in the process.

Now each unit had many administrative jobs for which no one was staffed. These were additional duty assignments. I was Awards and Decorations Officer in my Squadron. Another job was being Unit Historian. That person would log the daily activities of the unit for the official record. There was such a historian in the squadron that Jabara and his victim Dick Fraley belonged to. This historian was ordered by his superiors not to record this incident in the records and he complied. However, some 48 or so years later, this historian wrote an article in the Smithsonian's Air and Space magazine in which he told the truth. Jabara had died many years before in an automobile accident in Florida. The historian, John Lowery, was criticized by a retired Air Force general over the phone for telling it as it was. I recognized the story and I wrote a letter to the editor of Air and Space about my cousin's mistake and a couple of other ones. A copy of my letter was sent to Dick Fraley by the editor before the magazine was printed and, after 48 years or so, out of a clear blue sky, I had a telephone call from Dick Fraley from Arizona. We talked a while and recounted the incident and the 48-year-old cover-up.

This same retired general wrote a letter to the editor repeating his criticism of John Lowery, saying that friendly fire is known to happen but there is an unwritten code amongst fighter pilots, and we don't talk about it. This is baloney. Lowery's response to the general was that he wondered what the repercussion would be for having destroyed government property (the F-86) and being ordered to falsify official records (being ordered not to include the incident in the unit's history) just to protect a celebrity.

A photo of Jabara, a fellow pilot named Mailloux (we called him 'Mailbox'), and Dick Fraley is shown herein; the sign above them was made by me and was a favorite spot to have pictures taken.

Another piece of my artwork shown has the name "Trouble Brewer" painted on my airplane. Brother Bob originated this name and had it on his P-51 during WW II.

This sign I painted became a favorite place to have photos taken.

My brother Bob in his P-51, in WW II. This was the original Trouble Brewer.

Here are more tall (but true) tales from frozen Chosen. Chosen was the Japanese name for Korea. This is common. Japan isn't called Japan in Japan, it's Nippon. Germany isn't Germany in Germany, it's Deutschland. Spain in Spain is called España.

On one sweep, we were attacked by some MiGS, and violent maneuvers ensued. Rolling out of a turn, I looked around and there was nobody in sight. Making some calls to see where everyone had gone resulted in nothing, so I headed for the Yellow Sea. As explained earlier, the MiGS would not fly over the Yellow Sea, which we controlled; they didn't want us to recover any of their pilots, showing that some of them were Soviets. We had air-sea rescue services that would pick us out of the water if need be, so the procedure was to head for the sea, making shallow turns to see what was in one's blind spot, the area behind and under the airplane. After three or four shallow turns, I spotted an aircraft at my level to my left; it was a MiG. I immediately turned into him and he'd turned into me. This results in what we called a scissors maneuver, each trying to out turn the other and get on his tail. When we crossed, we were quite close. On the third turn, which was to my left, I decided to take a snapshot. A snapshot is firing when the gun sight isn't necessarily on the target. In this case, when we crossed, I was slightly above and fired. I saw hits on the MiG's uplifted left wing. On the next turn, I noticed that he did not choose this maneuver any longer but he climbed up and away and headed to the north. Because they could out climb us, there was no reason to pursue, so I continued my shallow turns heading for the Yellow Sea. About five minutes later, I saw an airplane below and well ahead of me trailing white smoke. As I approached, I could see that it was an F-86, obviously in trouble. I slowed down to see what was happening. About that time, I looked over my right shoulder and there was a MiG, perhaps the same one I maneuvered with. I had to turn into him and increase my speed because I was only going about 140 knots to match the speed of the crippled airplane. The MiG slid on by and I reversed my turn. It climbed up and away. I kept my eye on him for several seconds and then looked back at the smoking airplane and identified it as one from the 51st Wing (they had a checkerboard on their tails). Then I saw a parachute. I radioed our base and described what I saw and they asked me for my position. We did not use latitude and longitude because the enemy could use those as well. We had a grid system, which was overlaid on our charts and in the cramped cockpit it was quite difficult to determine the numbers and letters needed to transmit, keeping an eye out for the enemy. A rescap was launched from homeplate (our base). This was an effort to rescue or track pilots who had bailed out. I did not stay in the area but headed for homeplate because of low fuel. The search effort yielded nothing.

I was stationed at Nellis Air Force Base at Las Vegas, Nevada after the campaign in Korea. One evening I heard a knock on my door and when I answered, it was the pilot of the airplane that I saw bail out in the story above. He said he had hit the ground and had run west toward the Yellow Sea for two days without stopping, going through fields, villages and woods. Finally, he had to rest. A farmer found him in a ditch covered with vegetation and had notified soldiers. He was a POW and had a rough time until released. He told me that he hadn't seen the MiG or me. He said he was having a bad time. His engine was dead and the cockpit was filled with smoke. He could not fire his canopy off the airplane nor open it manually, nor could he fire his seat through the canopy. The way he got out of the smoking cockpit was unique: he took his .45 caliber pistol and shot a large hole in the canopy, crawled out and jumped. He had jumped before as a 'smoke-jumper' (forest fire fighter).

As an effort to understand our counterparts in other branches of the service and among our Allies, we would exchange pilots. Once in our squadron we had a Canadian Wing Commander, an English Flight Lieutenant and a Marine Corps Major. One day the major's airplane was disabled in a dogfight. His engine was out and some of the damage was in the cockpit. He was heading toward the mouth of the Yalu River (which empties into the Yellow Sea) with a gaping hole where the throttle had been. The radio transmission button was located on the throttle lever, so he reached down inside the hole and tried crossing different wires and managed to make the right connection for the radio and told of his plight. He bailed out and was picked up from the water all right except he hurt his shoulder somehow.

On another mission I was flying as a wingman with our Canadian exchange officer. We came across some MiGs, which were climbing away from us. My leader was trying to catch up to them and I was keeping us clear. Then I saw two MiGs coming in at 5 o'clock. I called my leader and informed him of this; I had no response and the MiGs were getting closer. I made multiple calls, but no response. It came to the point where I would have to break into the attackers. I made another call. No response. Then I turned into the enemy in defense and no longer saw my leader. When I got back to base I thought maybe he had been lost; however, he wasn't. I expected some flak because I had left him. Instead, he apologized, saying that he heard the calls but didn't realize they were for him; he had 'target fixation,' a deadly disease.

On another mission, I was flying wing on the English Flight Lieutenant. We got into a battle and my leader was trying to climb after some MiGs, which were pulling away and we were running out of speed. Keeping us clear, I spotted two MiGs coming at 5 o'clock. I called for a break to the right and I didn't wait for my leader to break because there were things that looked like orange golf balls streaming past my tail from right to left. These were cannon shells fired at me. My turn was violent and I had a high-speed stall shudder. The MiGs climbed away; we reversed to no avail. After this, I could not keep up with my leader. I called him and asked him to reduce power so I could stay with him. He did this and we flew at this rate back to base. As I came over the fence to land, the people in a small-wheeled observation unit called mobile control (beside the end of the runway) asked me if I'd been hit. I answered that it was possible. I really didn't know it, but I was hit twice. I didn't notice it because of the stall shudder I mentioned. Cannon shells had hit the tail of my fuselage. The shrapnel made many holes in the airplane's skin and tailpipe, some of it barely missing the hydraulic actuator for the elevators by about 5 inches. Two pieces of the shrapnel made spiral scratches up inside my tailpipe knocking pieces off two turbine blades. This damage and the drag caused by the holes were why I couldn't keep up with my leader. This was a real close one!

Four trouble-makers

About 50 years later in the December 2002 issue of the magazine, *Flight Journal*, there was an article called "Master of MiG Alley" written by double ace "Boots" Frederick Blesse, whom I knew in Korea and later at Nellis. It was a good article accompanied by a two- page photo of some F-86s with my Group markings. I noticed the photo credit was given to Karl Dittmer, a pilot in my squadron. I also noticed the number on the lead airplane in the photo, '963'. Later in the day after I had read this article, I found the number '963' stuck in my head. I thought perhaps that was the number I had put on a watercolor of an F-86 I had made, however, it was not. Then I looked through some photos I'd taken in Korea; '963' was the airplane I'd been shot up in! I wrote a letter to the editor of *Flight Journal* about this coincidence and he printed my letter and photos I'd sent showing myself and

Two canon balls in my tailpipe

the damage to '963' in his February 2003 issue. That was probably me in the two-page photo of the flight of F-86s, flying '963'!

On some missions, we would stay in MiG alley longer than I thought we should have. There was a code word broadcast when an airplane reached what was the minimum amount of fuel to get home. Wingmen would burn more fuel than the leader because of throttle changes. The first aircraft to reach minimum fuel would make a radio call identifying himself and saying, "Bingo." In some of my early missions, the leader would not head home at bingo but would stay

The day I got the worse of a dogfight. The holes were made by canon balls. One hole came within 5" of the elevator actuator... a close one!

Shrapnel Holes on the right side of 963. Marked by paper strips.

in the area to find some action. So there were times on the way back to base that we would have to shut the engine down in order to make it home. We flew 'heavy gliders'. Once near the base one would make an air start and land. The jet fighter is very clean aerodynamically and has a glide ratio similar to that of a Piper Cub, about thirteen to one. So if we were at 45,000 feet (about nine miles), multiplying nine times thirteen, an altitude of 45,000 feet would provide over 100 miles of range. It would be quiet and cold and sometimes the windscreen would freeze and make visibility difficult. I swore that when I got to be the leader I would never do this. Staying in the combat area so long would compromise your ability to get home if engaged. I know of one case, not deliberately done, which resulted from a lengthy battle where fuel was exhausted on the way home so the pilot had to bail out. He was picked out of the water, but the airplane was lost.

On one escort mission, we were flying cover for two RF-80s. We were way up in North Korea and these two aircraft were flying up and down a valley taking pictures of enemy installations. In the process, one of them was hit by ground fire. Although damaged, the airplane was flyable at least until we got out over the water where the pilot could eject. One of the pilots was the commander of the reconnaissance unit; the other was a lieutenant. Once over the Yellow Sea, the commander told the lieutenant to go ahead and punch out. There was no response. He called again and the lieutenant replied that he elected to stay with the airplane. Then the commander got on his case and shouted at him, ordering him to bail out. Knowing he was going to ditch, he had the canopy open. When he hit the water he was thrown forward out of the cockpit, probably leaving his legs inside. He made a splash and the plane made a splash and that was all.

There was an Australian unit on the other side of our airfield flying de Havilland Gloster Meteors, twin-engine jet fighter-bombers. One time, monitoring their channel, I listened to four of them working over a ground target. In succession, they were calling in on the target and then calling off the target, one after the other. The sequence was interrupted by one of the pilots saying, " I believe I've been hit." The response from the leader was, "I believe you have." The next transmission was, "I believe I'm going in." The leader's response was, "Yes, I believe you are." And that was the end of that.

Coming back to base from a mission one day, when I went to put my flaps down on downwind leg, my airplane made a violent roll. I was able to stop it by retracting the flaps. Apparently, only one flap came down. I went ahead and landed with no flaps. As I turned off the runway, the flying safety officer was there and flagged me down and gestured to shut the engine off. I complied and opened the canopy. He asked me what the big idea was landing with no flaps. I told him I only had one flap. He said that was not possible. I told him I knew that. Then he told me to put the battery switch on and put the flaps down. One came down and other didn't. He said I'd made a nice landing and walked away. The flaps on the F-86 are interconnected with a large shaft; if one comes down, the other comes down. This airplane had suffered some battle damage some weeks before and the damage had been traced as far as possible and repairs

Let's go hunting

made. What they didn't see was an apparent crack in the shaft, and the subsequent stress caused it to break completely when I put the flaps down. We took off with partial flaps. Had this happened on takeoff, there would have been no time to recover. Another close one.

These things that I am relating are not typical; these are exceptions, although I have some other incidents to relate that were not related to combat. The majority of our missions were almost routine except the elements of danger were there not only from the enemy but also due to the fact we were flying in one of the hottest airplanes in the world. One might fly an entire tour and not have any problems at all.

Wingmen were usually young lieutenants right out of gunnery school. It took a long time to work your way up to lead a flight. This was true especially in our unit. One reason was there were pilots in our headquarters in Seoul who would come and fly with us. These were usually people of rank and would be put in lead positions. Since most of our pilots were lieutenants, we were at the bottom of the totem pole. RHIP. (Rank Has Its Privileges.) Consequently, if you peruse the list of aces from the Korean War, you will find it top heavy with rank. You will see very few lieutenants in the list. It's the leader who gets first crack at the enemy; the wingman is there to protect the leader.

Korea gets bitterly cold in the winter. It's right next door to Siberia. To combat the cold, we were issued immersion suits. These resembled old-time diver's gear. They were made of rubberized fabric that had tapered sections through which your hands and wrists would protrude; your head would protrude in like fashion. Personal equipment people would cut the tapered portions so they fit snugly and made a waterproof seal. The rubber seal around the neck chafed it badly when turning your head, and it was imperative to turn your head if you wanted to stay alive. So, parachute nylon was wrapped around the neck inside the rubber seal. Insulated rubber boots were sealed to the legs of the suit. One donned the suit by climbing into it, rolling up the material and closing it. With this suit on, you could not climb into your airplane by yourself with all the other gear you carried. This reminded me of having a hoist to lift an armored knight onto his horse. The crew chief would assist you up with a shove on your butt. We called these "Poopy-Suits."

The first time I wore one of these suits, I neglected to open the valves on the boots before takeoff. So, as I ascended, the air pressure inside the boots squeezed my feet. It became painful and problematic because we were climbing through clouds in close formation. I could not take my eyes off my leader in order to reach down and open the valves.

I drew a cartoon showing some of these suits hanging on a wall, one of which had the conformation of a woman. At that time (1952) I meant this to be humorous because we had no female pilots in the Air Force. Things change.

We were doing a sweep at high altitude as usual. All of a sudden I had no oxygen, so I notified my flight, did a split-S (rolling over on your back and pulling through to descend rapidly) down to about 12,000 feet, engaging the emergency system on the way down. Attached to our parachute was a high-pressure oxygen bottle with a gauge that one would check while inspecting the parachute before flight. After strapping in the cockpit, one would take the hose that came out of the bottle and attach it to the side of your oxygen mask. On one end of the bottle there was a short cable whose end had a small wooden ball painted green. Pulling the 'green apple' supplied a continuous flow of oxygen for about twenty minutes. This was plenty of time to get down to lower altitude where supplemental oxygen was not needed. I never did find out why my system failed. Such an emergency was anticipated; equipment was in place and operated nicely.

I was flying wing in a flight of two when apparently my leader got bored, and I followed him down through the mach as he made a firing pass at a fishing boat. I didn't fire and wondered why he was doing such a thing. In order to not overrun him in the dive, I had extended my dive brakes, and leveling out, retracted them. They would not retract all the way. I recycled the brakes a few times, but they just wouldn't come in flush. We were at sea level and 200 miles from base. This was serious because if I needed speed it wasn't available and more fuel would be burned to overcome the drag. However, I got back OK even if it was slow.

Toward the end of a routine sweep one time, we were a flight of two and saw a MiG overhead and turning to the left. My leader immediately pulled up trying to get on his tail. By lowering my nose in a shallow turn, I stayed underneath the MiG while my leader had killed off his airspeed by pulling up sharply. So I ended up ahead of him. I eased my aircraft up, and even though the distance between the MiG and me was lengthening, I decided to make a snapshot out of range. I saw some flashes in his left wing root, which were verified by the leader. In order to make a claim of aircraft damaged, probably destroyed, or destroyed, one must have proof. This came in two forms: an eyewitness or evidence on your gun camera film, otherwise every pilot would be an ace.

The MiG was better armed than the F-86. In an effort to equalize things, some of our airplanes were modified to carry four 20mm cannons (The Gun Val Project) in lieu of the six .50s. These were called F-86 F-2s. An effort was made to deceive the enemy by painting two more black spaces on each side of the noses of these airplanes so that it appeared to have six guns as usual. We had some trouble with these guns because sometimes the muzzle flashes would rob air from the engine intake and cause the engine to flame out (stop). So, if you flew one of these models, you were required to test fire the guns on the way home. Such was the case with my flight leader once. He took the precaution to be over the Yellow Sea where we had rescue facilities before firing. He notified the flight that he was going to fire. His engine quit. We circled above him to keep our speed up while he descended to 25,000 feet. (It was difficult to air start the engine above that altitude, there not being enough oxygen.) Once at the lower altitude, he tried to start the engine. It wouldn't start. There was fuel coming out of the tailpipe, looking like white smoke, but no fire. He tried several times in vain and finally got down to where he had to punch out. A helicopter picked him up. Talking to him later, he said he heard an explosion in the airplane when he test fired the guns. It was assumed that one round did not get fully seated in the gun's chamber and blew some sheet metal into the air intake. That would account for the engine's reluctance to start. So this pilot essentially shot himself down, and having 4 MiGs to his credit already, one could say that he was the only unheralded ace of the Korean War.

The aggressive attitude of our pilots was great, but like any endeavor, it could be carried to extremes, and we had some people who fell into this category. It seemed that to further self-aggrandizement, some would cheat. If it looked like there was going to be an engagement, we would drop our external fuel tanks to get rid of the extra weight and drag. At times a tank would not release and this could be faked by pulling a circuit breaker on the release mechanism. Therefore, being unable to stay with the flight, one would have an excuse to leave the flight and be on one's own. Of course, the wingman would go with him. Being essentially alone, the cheater could do as he pleased, crossing the 'fence' flying into the interior of Manchuria (where there were other airfields), drop down to a lower altitude, circle and wait for aircraft either to take off or land where they would be very vulnerable to attack. One might even use his wingman as a pawn and have him maneuver as bait while he gained an advantageous position.

Being overzealous (we called this 'MiG fever') led to some pilots firing on our own aircraft. Such was the Jabara case already mentioned. Another time a pilot was seen firing on one of our own aircraft that was already going down. To hide the fact, it is believed that he destroyed his own aircraft to hide the evidence, the evidence being gun camera film in the nose of the aircraft. He ditched the aircraft in shallow water and of course, it sank with the film. However, the pilot said he had been in a fight, shot down a MiG, was damaged himself and decided to put the airplane on a beach. However, the beach was unsuitable so he put the airplane in the shallow water, then stood on the canopy rail to get into the water. The airplane sank, denying him of the chance to retrieve his film from the nose of the airplane to prove he had a victory, or to destroy the film, which could be incriminating evidence that he had polished off one of our own. So, here are two versions to account for the loss of an F-86. He flew no more missions and was sent back to the States. Which do you believe?

When I was in combat in Korea, we had a disadvantage in our

combat against the enemy fighter aircraft because they could out climb our F-86s. The MiG-15 could initiate an attack and then climb away before we could achieve a good firing position. An attempt to even the odds involved installing a couple of JATO (Jet Assisted Take Off) units on some of our F-86s. These were essentially small rocket devices that had been used for additional thrust on takeoff of heavily laden cargo and bomber aircraft. They were installed near the trailing edge of the F-86's wing, aft of the center of gravity of the airplane. Their position and weight caused an odd flight characteristic. At cruising level with the airplane trimmed properly, the airplane would pitch nose down without warning. Then, trimming again for level flight, the airplane would pitch up without warning. This oscillation would continue until sufficient fuel weight was diminished, allowing the touchy center of gravity to fall within normal limits.

These JATO units could also help us climb to the higher altitudes that the enemy could achieve. I have no knowledge of their use in action.

In an effort to recover downed airmen behind enemy lines in the Korean war, an unusual device was assembled. To show pilots in my Group how it worked, a demonstration was made. The device consisted of poles set apart with guy ropes to keep the poles vertical, looking much like the

Patch I designed for those that survived beiong shot at and/or hit by MIG cannon fire.

goal posts on a football field. A rope was put across the tops of the poles, and the two ends of it led down to a parachute harness on the ground between the poles. The downed airman would strap himself in this, facing in the direction of an oncoming rescue aircraft, a twin engine C-47. A hook on a rope dangling from the C-47 would engage the line stretched across the tops of the poles and the airman would be snatched from the ground and reeled into the airplane by a powered winch. The poles, ropes, harness and directions were dropped from the aircraft to the airman. I don't know if this system was ever used, but I did see it work.

When our F-86s needed major maintenance, we would take them to another base. This base was called Tsuiki, located on the north shore of Kyushu Island, Japan. A pilot could take an aircraft down there but he would have no means of returning unless there were repaired

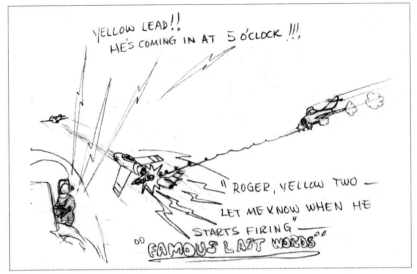

Yellow three asked his leader if his gear was up; he sensed that something was wrong!

The' motor-mouthed' flight leader was sometimes the worst offender of radio discipline.

aircraft ready to come back. The usual procedure was to fly two aircraft down, one of them being a T-33, which had two seats. The two would fly down in formation, sign over the F-86, and come back in the T-33. This procedure didn't always go smoothly. One time I went down in a T-33 alone to pick up a pilot. En route, my radio compass failed, and there was an undercast. I had no means of making an instrument letdown, and I didn't have enough fuel to return to Kimpo. I used my dead reckoning position and let down through the clouds. When I broke out, I was near the shoreline. Believing I was east of the base, I turned to the left and cruised along under the clouds. I noticed some water splashing off to my right. I didn't know what it could be unless it was whales. Then I discovered it was not whales but artillery fire. I was flying through an artillery firing range. I could actually see the shells in flight. I located the base OK and landed.

On another occasion, I found myself at Tsuiki in a T-33, getting ready to return to K-14 alone. The T-33 had no baggage compartment and anything to be carried had to be strapped in the rear seat. As I was getting ready to go, an enlisted man from my unit asked if he could go with me. I agreed to take him, so I checked him out on the use of a parachute and the use of the ejection seat and told him that he'd have to hold a box containing cartons of milk on his lap. We would bring milk from Tsuiki because it was much more palatable than the milk we had at Kimpo. So off we went. Arriving near Kimpo, I still had fuel in my tip tanks. We didn't land this airplane with fuel in the tip tanks because, if one made a hard landing, the weight on the wingtips might over stress the wings. I notified the base that I was in the local area and was going to burn out the tip tanks before I landed. The base was not far from Inchon, a large port on the Yellow Sea, so I flew over there and decided to amuse some troops on some hospital ships. (Hospital ships were well-marked with large white crosses.) I flew down between two of them, climbed up, made a lazy turn and came back between the ships again. I saw troops so I rocked my wings to acknowledge their waving -- then a red light came on, meaning the tip tanks were empty. This airplane has other tanks: wing tanks and leading edge tanks, all of which feed into a fuselage tank and then the fuel goes to the engine. The fuselage tank holds 90 gallons. The tip tanks being empty, I switched to the wing tanks. At that moment I suffered complete electrical failure. There was no radio, no interphone, no indicator lights and the fuel pumps in the wing tanks were inoperative. The total usable fuel at that moment was 90 gallons in the fuselage tank, so I headed for Kimpo. Arriving there, I flew a pattern, rocking my wings on approach to indicate that I had no radio, put the gear down and came in to land. There was no way to check to see if the gear was down because the indicator lights were inoperative. I had no flaps or dive brakes because they were controlled electrically. The runway people on the ground fired red flares, so I went around (going around means to apply power and fly another pattern). Had it been a sun shiny day, I could have put the shadow of my landing gear on the tip tanks to see whether it was extended or not; however, it was overcast. I attempted the emergency gear down system, which involved rotating a handle that was safety wired in place, but I could not move it. So, in the pattern, I loosened my straps, pushed myself up and back in the seat and put my boot on the handle; this moved it. However, it did nothing. Approaching for the second time, I received more red flares. Now this airplane consumes 30 gallons of fuel for a go around. I had made one, and now I was making a second, and of course, I had burned fuel coming from Inchon to Kimpo. I realized that the tank was just about empty, so on the third attempt I was going to put the airplane down, regardless.

If the main gear was not down, the procedure was to pull all wheels up and slide in on the belly. I touched down on the left wheel first; it was locked down, then I touched down on the right wheel and it was locked down, so I figured it was the nose wheel that was causing the red flares. The procedure then was to hold the aircraft's nose off the runway as long as it was controlled, and, when it began to descend on its own, allow it to come down and land on the main gear and skid on the airplane's nose. When I lowered the nose, it was locked down. Normally, one would stop straight ahead to allow ground crewmen to put pins in the strut to prevent it from collapsing. However, there was a war going on and we only had one runway and it could not be blocked by stopping straight ahead, so I made a shallow turn off the runway; as I did, the engine quit. I was out of fuel! It was a close one. The young man in the rear seat asked why I was parking way out by the runway. I asked him if he didn't notice anything wrong. He said he saw the red flares but didn't know their meaning. Had the engine quit in the pattern, I could have bailed out but I don't think the passenger would have reacted to the emergency and I am afraid he would have been lost. Actually, the person in the rear seat of that airplane is supposed to eject first. This was a close one not involving combat.

Why all the red flares? I was told my right gear was not completely down on all three approaches. When I touched down on the third approach, and tried the left gear first, observers told me that the right gear was almost down, still moving, and as I touched down on the right gear, it locked into place.

Let me draw a contrast here for a moment. Flying an airplane is not just flying an airplane. One may go out to the local airport, and with a private pilot's license, climb into his puddle jumper and become airborne. This type of flying is much like driving a car. These simple machines are forgiving and there's very little danger involved. Contrast this with climbing into the hottest airplane in the world under combat conditions where your life is on the line each day. You can see that there are differences in flying. Nowadays, there are commercial enterprises that advertise that you can come and join them and fly 'actual combat.' There are no guns and they 'shoot' at each other with video cameras. An instructor is with the customer, and in no way can this simulate reality. There's nobody in your adversary's plane who is bent on killing you.

The real thing involves some inevitable stress. Some can absorb stress better than others. I once knew a pilot who had flown a combat tour in the F-86 in Korea and returned to the States, becoming an instructor in one of the most prestigious units in the Air Force, always flying front line jet fighters. However, when he was transferred to Europe, he walked into his commander's office one day, took his wings off, put them on the desk and said, "I quit." (One has that option once the obligation to the service is met by a certain number of years after pilot training.) This pilot was asked why he was quitting. He replied that he'd always been afraid of flying. He must have suffered greatly for years. He could have quit earlier; perhaps he didn't for fear of losing face with his peers, but the stress finally got to him and he did something about it.

As I mentioned earlier, most of the missions I flew in Korea might be called almost routine. One took off, flew up to make a patrol, saw nothing, came back

June 25, 2000

Dear Veteran

On the occasion of the 50th anniversary of the outbreak of the Korean War, I would like to offer you my deepest gratitude for your noble contribution to the efforts to safeguard the Republic of Korea and uphold liberal democracy around the world. At the same time, I remember with endless respect and affection those who sacrificed their lives for that cause.

We Koreans hold dear in our hearts the conviction, courage and spirit of sacrifice shown to us by such selfless friends as you, who enabled us to remain a free democratic nation.

The ideals of democracy, for which you were willing to sacrifice your all 50 years ago, have become universal values in this new century and millennium.

Half a century after the Korean War, we honor you and reaffirm our friendship, which helped to forge the blood alliance between our two countries. And we resolve once again to work with all friendly nations for the good of humankind and peace in the world.

I thank you once again for your noble sacrifice, and pray for your health and happiness.

Sincerely yours,

signed
Kim Dae-jung
President of the Republic of Korea

존경하는 참전용사 귀하

6·25전쟁이 발발한지 반세기를 맞아 세계의 자유 민주주의와 대한민국을 수호하는데 기여한 귀하에게 진심으로 감사드립니다. 아울러 고귀한 생명을 바치신 영령앞에 무한한 경의와 추모의 뜻을 표합니다.

대한민국이 오늘날의 자유 민주주의 국가를 유지할 수 있도록 귀하께서 보여주셨던 불굴의 신념과 진정한 용기, 그리고 거룩한 희생정신을 우리는 가슴속 깊이 간직하고 있습니다.

특히 귀하께서 50년전에 몸으로 실천했던 자유민주주의 이념은 이제 새로운 세기, 새 천년을 맞아 세계 인류의 보편적 가치가 되었습니다.

이에 6·25전쟁 50주년을 맞이하여 귀하의 명예를 드높임과 동시에 과거 혈맹으로 맺어졌던 귀하와의 우의를 재다짐하고자 합니다. 아울러 인류의 발전과 평화를 위해 세계 우방들과 함께 노력해 나갈 것입니다.

다시 한번 귀하의 숭고한 헌신에 깊이 감사드리며 행운과 건승을 기원합니다.

감사합니다.

2000년 5월 25일

대한민국 대통령 김 대 중

Letters of Appreciation from the President of Korea

to Kimpo, landed and chalked up one more toward the 100. However, you look death in the face periodically. On these occasions I have asked myself out loud, "Brewer, how the hell did you get here?" The answer to that question is that I got there step by step in small

The road from Kimpo going home, March, 1953

increments of excellent training. The process is lengthy and gradual. Why did I start in this direction in the first place? I was always interested in aviation when I was young, digesting the news of aviators like Lindbergh, Wiley Post, Howard Hughes, Roscoe Turner, Clyde Pangborn, Eddie Rickenbacker, Billy Mitchell, Amelia Earhart, Jimmy Doolittle, Kingsford-Smith and many others. In addition, I seem to have an appetite for adventure. Adventure has an element of danger which can be exciting and at times, romantic. I may add that I'm not shy to admit that I'm a patriot and fought in combat in two of my country's wars…so that's how the hell I got there.

When I was a navigator in B-29s in WW II, I was a little disappointed in aviation. I was a cog in a machine, and at times I was ignorant of what was going on. I always wanted to be a pilot, but when I got into the cadet program in WW II, the army and had all the pilot trainees they needed; in fact, they had too many. I had qualified to become a pilot, but was told I would probably never see an airplane because there were thousands waiting to get into pilot school. I could have been one of the 38,000 that were put in the ground forces and

My sanctuary, the beach shack on Hood Canal

sent to Europe. (This missed me by two weeks.) Being a fighter pilot is better than being a navigator. In most cases, you are alone in the driver's seat. You make the decisions. I am now 85 and I still enjoy 'kicking the tire and lighting the fire' as a pilot.

Some of the pilots I went through flying school with were on the same airplane flying back to the States with me when our tours in Korea were finished. The leg from Japan to Wake Island was at night. The seats were of canvas with straps for the back; these were close together and uncomfortable. While at the 'head' (it was a Navy airplane), I noticed a stretcher hanging on the bulkhead. I asked the attendant if anyone was going to use it. The answer was no, so I took it off the bulkhead and stretched out for the night. The next leg was to Hawaii. The following leg was from Hawaii to Sacramento. It was night again and I waited to see if someone else might claim the stretcher, but no one did. So I had a semi-comfortable bed one more time while my buddies suffered, trying to sleep sitting up, crowded together. I flew from Sacramento to Portland, Oregon, and where I met my five month old daughter for the first time and had a reunion with family and in-laws.

Prior to going to Korea, I bought some waterfront property on the saltwater in Washington, at a place called Hood Canal. The objective was to have a place to spend my leave. As it had been, when home on leave, I would spend the daylight hours awaiting the man of the house to arrive after work, have dinner and then visit. This would be repeated day after day. My memories of leave were largely those of waiting for somebody to come home. To interrupt this sequence, I decided to buy some property, put up a small building, then, when I came home on leave, that's where I'd be. If people wanted to see me, they knew where I was. It worked out this way; in addition, friends and relatives used this facility in my absence.

So, when I got back from Korea, my brother Bob and Stan helped me put in some concrete work on the property to get a building started. I built a small shack, twelve feet square, big enough to get in out of the rain or for changing clothes. The architecture came to be known as an ' A frame'. I had electricity but no water. I noticed when the tide was low (this was salt water beachfront), there was a section of the beach that never dried out, so I assumed that, in essence, it was a spring and that marked the level of the water table. I bought some materials from Sears and Roebucks and drove a well point into the beach near the bank, next to the shack. I put a pitcher pump on this and I could draw fresh water, even with the tide at flood stage. I had gone down about 22 feet. It was necessary to prime the pump, but water was available from a small stream nearby on a neighbor's property.

In the fall of 1955, a photographer from Sunset Magazine came by and told me they were going to run a series on beach cabins and he wanted to know if he could take some photographs of my shack. I also gave him some drawings of the building. These were published in Sunset Magazine in October 1955. One of the pictures shows my daughter, Chris, in a swing that was hung from a picturesque Madrona tree next to the cabin.

Hood Canal is popular at the lower end because it is quite shallow, and during the summertime the water warms up from the sun and makes it tolerable for swimming. Oysters abound on the canal, and one time an elderly neighbor asked if it was okay to kill the starfish (which prey on the oysters) on my beach when the tide was low. I was agreeable. He would walk along with a bucket of quicklime, a small shovel and a gaff hook. He would turn the starfish over with the hook, put a dab of lime on it and then do this to others. Soon the oysters were so thick that they stood on edge.

Why choose Hood Canal for my sanctuary? Well, as teenagers, immediately after school was out in June, we'd go up to Hood Canal for a vacation. Before this, we tried camping near home in vacant lots, taking potatoes from home and other tidbits for sustenance. We used toilets and other facilities at home when needed. Later, we'd go to the Canal and camp. One year we hitchhiked, having made some packs for our backs, loaded them up with canned goods and added some blankets. We took the ferry from Alki to Manchester and hit the road. The first day we made it as far as the Union River near Belfair, at the end of the Canal. We had a tent and that night it rained so much the sluggish river rose and came into the tent. We were soaked and had to carry the sodden tent on a pole between the two of us. Stan and I each had a wool watch cap; they both faded. I don't remember whether he had the red one and I had the blue one or vice versa; anyhow, we had colored faces. We went into an empty barn to dry out a bit and then hit the road again. A fire warden picked us up in his truck. We got out where there was a stream of water. At this site, there were the remnants of some old loggers' shacks. We stayed there. At this time, there were neither houses on the north shore of Hood Canal nor any road traffic. We would run around naked on the beach. The fire warden would drive by on his daily patrol in the mornings and return in the afternoons. He was the only person we saw. We would stay until our groceries were consumed and then head home.

Another time we went to Hood Canal on bicycles and camped at a different place. The third time, we went in Ian's father's '29 Buick. Towards the end of this stay, some other friends came up and joined us. We attempted to eat the remainder of our groceries on the last day so we wouldn't have to carry them home. I recall that I ate nineteen small pancakes for breakfast; 119 were cooked. Several pounds of potatoes and cans of vegetables were all cooked together, and we stuffed ourselves with this for lunch and supper.

Chapter Seven

Gunnery School Instructor

When my leave was over, after returning from Korea, my new station was Nellis Air Force Base at Las Vegas, Nevada. I had been there before, going through gunnery school on my way to Korea. I found a place to live in town, went to the base and checked in for my assignment. The group commander looked at my papers and made a comment to his secretary, saying I was a man who had made a great recovery from being a navigator on a B-29 to being a fighter pilot! He told me he was going to send me to a place called Sandia Base in New Mexico. I was to attend a course dealing with special weapons; this had to do principally with nuclear weapons. Up to this time, there were no nuclear weapons that could be carried on fighter aircraft, primarily because of their size, one being about 5 feet in diameter. However, there were weapons under development to be carried by fighters. So, off we went to Albuquerque. We encountered a dust storm en route and had to stop because of poor visibility. My infant daughter had diarrhea and the convertible top of my Oldsmobile allowed the dust in. The poor thing looked like a red clay doll. We found an apartment to stay in at Albuquerque during my course there. I bought a second car there, a 1948 Lincoln Continental Coupe. I had always admired these cars and almost bought one in place of the 1950 Oldsmobile three years earlier. While at Sandia, we visited Santa Fe and the Acoma Indian Reservation.

Returning to Nellis, my new boss was going to Alabama to a school temporarily, so I sub-rented his house in the base housing area. My name came up on the list for housing in the same area before he returned, and this became our home for five-and-a-half years. My immediate job was, for myself and a non-flying lieutenant, to establish a course to teach what we had learned at Sandia Base. Some of this information was Top Secret; however, we didn't have to teach that. Most of the course was classified, so security was a concern. Our special weapons course was part of the academic section, which taught aircraft systems, armament, tactics, engines, and other subjects. The primary mission of the base, as part of Air Training Command, was to produce fighter pilots. The instructors based at Nellis were mostly combat experienced. The students were either pilots fresh out of flying school (who had not yet learned how to use the airplane as a weapon) or older pilots we called 'retreads,' who were to be upgraded in gunnery proficiency. Gunnery included bombing, air to ground strafing, air-to-air firing on towed targets, formation flying and tactics. At one time, Nellis was the busiest airfield in the world, averaging a takeoff or landing every 28 seconds. Attrition was bad. Sometimes we would lose a student a week. And during the first 32 months that I was at Nellis, we lost eighteen instructor pilots from multiple causes. If there was a pall of black smoke visible from the housing area and you were driving through the area, you might see knots of housewives standing outside with concern on their faces, probably wondering if that pall involved their husband. The student loss was so alarming that our headquarters in San Antonio, Texas, decreed that the next instructor who lost a student would be court-martialed. Of course, it happened. Among the questions the instructor was asked was, "Did you brief your student not to fly into the ground?" He was acquitted. Why such an attrition rate? You have to consider not only the airplane, it being the hottest thing going, but the complexity and volume of training going on. It is a well-known fact, for example, in WW II, B-29s in training had a greater attrition rate than those in combat.

Having lost almost two instructor pilots that I knew per month, it had an effect on me. The effect was that I tended not to become close friends with any of my fellow pilots.

In early 1954, a close friend of mine that I had gone through pilot school with and with whom I had gone on R&R in Tokyo, bit the dust at Nellis. His brother, an airline pilot, came to assist his brother's family. He asked me if I would go downtown to the funeral home and help him make a decision. That decision was whether to have an open casket funeral or not. People sometimes get torn up in an aircraft accident. The funeral home had a photograph of the pilot and they did wonderful things with wax, but it didn't look like my friend. His brother asked me what I thought. I said no, and he agreed. We attended the funeral in Salt Lake City and when his mother arrived and learned that it was to be a closed casket funeral, she became hysterical; she'd never see her son again. Then at the last minute the pilot's wife asked me if I would stand up before the gathering and account for the pilot's time in the service. This was one of the toughest things I ever had to do in my life, and I decided not to go to any other funerals.

Losing close friends in a dangerous business causes one to reflect on the probability of one's surviving. This is quite sobering and you have to make up your mind to press on or give it up. I have never considered quitting, as I know that some have done. Some figure it will never happen to them. I consider this a bad philosophy. You need to realize that there is a probability that it will happen to you and do everything you can to avoid it. Later on, I'll relate a time when my engine blew up and I had eight seconds to get the airplane on the ground.

No matter which kind of flying it is, it's valuable to practice. For example, do simulated forced landings; practice them and note them in your logbook. Instead of being fat, dumb and happy while boring holes in the sky, you should discipline yourself each flight to assume that something's going to go wrong and decide what you would do about it. Emergencies are always surprises. If you have practiced for them and give them some thought ahead of time, you are not likely to panic, but rather keep a cool head and do what you have to do.

My job at Nellis involved going on temporary duty to Sandia base several times: once to the Rocky Mountain Arsenal in Colorado,

1948 Lincoln Continental Coupe

once to North Carolina, and twice to Montgomery, Alabama, mostly traveling by car. we saw a good deal of the country.

Because we were dealing with classified information, security was paramount. Much of this time at Nellis I had an additional duty job of being security officer for my unit. One time there was an attempt to penetrate our security. A lieutenant came to our door and was stopped by the air policemen on duty who checked his ID. The lieutenant produced some orders saying he was to be allowed to check some bearings on our dummy A-bomb. This was suspicious, so I had the air policeman escort him to the Wing Adjutant. The adjutant was not satisfied, so he turned him over to the Office of Special Investigations. There, he was strip-searched and a copy of his valid orders was found inside one of his shoes. His job was to test our security. It was well that we passed this test.

On one occasion, one of our documents was missing. The last known person to have it was our boss, and he was gone on temporary duty. I went to his house and asked his wife if there were any papers lying around that her husband had brought home. I found the document on top of the chest of drawers in the bedroom. Another time, another document was missing, and again, the last man known to have it was our boss. When I asked about it, he grinned and led me to his car. It was in the trunk of his car. After this officer was transferred, the person that took his place was later being transferred himself and there was another document missing. He was the last one known to have it. He came to me on a Saturday morning after having said goodbye, and wanted me to come back to our building and make out a false destruction certificate for the document. I told him that I couldn't do it. He was upset because he couldn't leave the base until the document was accounted for. He came by the house later and apologized; he probably found somebody else to falsify the record.

After this officer left, we had another boss. One day he didn't show up for work. When I called the Wing Adjutant and told him our boss hadn't come to work, he told me that he wasn't coming to work any more. Later, we found that he was dismissed from the service for being a homosexual; he had been paying young airmen $50 each for their favors. Was this discriminatory? Probably, but this man's head was full of military secrets, and being associated with special weapons, that apparently was judged to be a security risk. In order to keep his sexual leanings secret, he was vulnerable. I would guess that he was watched for several years to ensure that his vulnerability wasn't exploited.

The housing we had at Nellis for five and a half years was a two-bedroom unit with a swamp cooler on the roof, a carport, a small storage room and one tree in the front yard. I spaded up the back yard and planted it with clover and built a chicken wire fence around it to have a bit of greenery. The building was made of cinder blocks and when we had dust or sandstorms, the wind would drive some of the dust and sand through the cinder blocks, which apparently had very small holes in them. These houses were unfurnished. They had washers, dryers, refrigerators and stoves only. We went down to Los Angeles and bought carpet, chairs, a sofa and all it takes to furnish a house. I made some furniture out of mahogany: a couple of bookcases, and later, a cabinet to house high fidelity music equipment. I made a dining room table and four chairs.

There were swimming pools on the base and we spent some time there. I taught my daughter how to swim before she was three years old. I did this by having her hold onto my thumbs in the water, then squeezing her little hands off my thumbs; down she'd go and she automatically paddled and came to the surface. Then I would grab her and laugh, and she'd laugh. At the end of the summer, before her birthday in October, she could swim almost halfway across the pool.

If a base has housing available, you must occupy it and forfeit an allowance, which is provided in case the base cannot accommodate you. This allowance varies depending upon rank; the same applies to the rations for meals: if they've got them, you eat them; if they don't have them, they pay you an allowance.

Much of the above doesn't involve flying. However, I lean on your ear (eyes, in this case) with a few mundane facts to show that all isn't just about being airborne if you are a military pilot. There are many things that bear on you that determine your will and attitude when you are airborne. 'Flying a desk' is one of these. We all get a turn at this.

As you probably know, if an airplane goes faster than the speed of sound it makes a sound, heard as a loud ka-boom. Under standard conditions at sea level, this is 759 miles an hour. An F-86 could exceed this speed, but only by lowering its nose and getting a boost from gravity. The next generation fighter, the F-100, could exceed this speed in level flight. At first, achieving mach one was a novelty. A prank we played was to see if we could hear our own boom. You don't hear it in the cockpit. What we would do was climb to about 25,000 feet, find a local AM broadcasting station, tune in their frequency on the aircraft's radio compass, roll over and dive (a split S), put the gun sight on the broadcasting building, go through mach one and then pull out. If there were a live broadcast, your boom would be broadcast and you could hear it in your headset.

F-100, Nellis, 1957

Booms became a nuisance. Sometimes they broke windows; sometimes they broke plaster and almost always they broke the peace. It was fairly easy to refrain from booming with the F-86, however, the F-100 would slip through mach one with ease and one had to be careful not to be a nuisance. We had a student at Nellis who, when he first checked out in the F-100, flew to Cedar City, Utah and repeatedly crossed the town through mach one. He broke windows, cracked plaster and did other damage. The general was waiting for him when he returned; he was going to be court-martialed. An investigating team was sent to Cedar City to gather evidence. However, they came back with none. Why? The townspeople learned who it was that beat up their town: he was a local boy; he had gone to school there and he had done well, becoming a pilot. There were no complaints, therefore, no evidence. There was no court-martial; however, you can rest assured that he was reprimanded severely.

In a training program, the student has to fly his aircraft on the edges of its envelope; that is, in order to fight efficiently, you must know what the airplane can do. Going through mach one was one of those things. So, an unpopulated area was found north of the Grand Canyon where it appeared there were no towns, no residences nor highways; very little but sagebrush. This was designated as the booming area. Students would go there to practice supersonic flight. However, once the area was designated, it didn't take long for a letter of complaint to arrive at the base. There was a shepherd, an elderly woman, who, over a period of several months, would graze her sheep in a large circle, ending up at home where she had started. It so happened that she was in the boom area when it was designated. Some of our people went out in a helicopter and talked to her. They copied her schedule and altered the boom area to avoid her. Her complaint was that the booming caused her sheep to panic and hurt themselves.

Formation flying was part of our program. As a treat, if my students were doing well, I would take them into the Grand Canyon, let down, spread them out a little and have them look around. We had to curtail this because we got a letter from a mining company which was stringing a cable across the canyon to a cave on the opposite wall in order to extract bat guano. Another treat was to take my students to Death Valley where they could fly below sea level. This could be done at the Salton Sea also, but Death Valley was closer.

At Nellis, which was an Air Training Command Base, there were two tenant units. One was the Air Force demonstration team, The Thunderbirds. The other was the Fighter Weapons School. This latter unit belonged to the Tactical Air Command. When the Navy wanted to establish their Top Gun School, they came to the Fighter Weapons School for guidance. This was a prestigious unit. Many of the top

USAF Fighter Weapons School Staff, 1958, Nellis AFB, Nevada. I am third from the left, bottom row.

Old Harry with the USAF Thunderbirds

fighter pilots in the Air Force were instructors there. I was asked to join them in 1957 because of my special weapons expertise, but I'm getting ahead of myself; more about this later.

It was about this time that we had an incident of note at Oxnard, California. Each year a pilot was required to log a certain amount of instrument time in weather or under a hood. An additional requirement was so many GCAs (Ground Controlled Approaches). This is an instrument approach to land, guided by radar on the ground. One contacts the radar station and they give the pilot headings and altitudes to align him with the runway and bring him down to his final approach. This is the surveillance radar. As the pilot turns on final approach,

USAF Fighter Waepons School Patch. It was here that the Navy came to see how we operated and then organized their 'Top Gun' school.

a second controller takes over; the pilot remains mute and follows headings and altitude changes given by this precision controller who brings the pilot down to the runway. We had no GCA at Nellis because the weather was so good it didn't warrant a station. So, in order to practice GCA approaches, we had to go somewhere else; one place was Oxnard, California. Two of our pilots in a T-33 were shooting GCAs at Oxnard, and after two or three approaches they were given a different climb out heading than before. The pilot in the rear seat was flying on instruments The pilot in the front seat would take off and land, and while the patterns were flown, he would act as an observer to keep the aircraft clear. Climbing out in the clouds with this different heading, the observer looked to his left through a rift in the cloud -- he was looking into someone's living room. Needless to say, he took over the airplane, added power and climbed out. It so happened that there was a second aircraft shooting GCAs at Oxnard at the same time. It was a two engine transport aircraft, a C-47. The controller was working both of these airplanes at the same time, and he made a mistake: he did not change channels and gave the C-47s heading to the T-33. At that time, an aircraft's call sign was 'Air Force' and then the last four digits of the airplane's serial number, (for example, "This is Air Force 1234"). It so happened that the C-47 and the T-33 had identical call signs. This incident prompted a change in call signs for aircraft in the Air Force. Thereafter, five digits were used instead of four.

We had an Army liaison officer at Nellis. He was leaving and had a TV set for sale. I agreed to buy it and when he came by to deliver it, he notified me that I'd been promoted to captain.

I made a couple of trips on temporary duty in 1954. One was to The Rocky Mountain Arsenal in Colorado. Nerve gas (it's really a liquid) was manufactured there. Since special weapons not only meant nuclear weapons but also biological and chemical weapons (ABC: Atomic, Biological, Chemical), I got to see the assembly line where the liquid was put into containers. It involved hermetically sealed cases into which workers with long rubber gloves would work. Sitting on the floor here and there were some albino rabbits in cages. They have large pink eyes. These were alarms. One of the first symptoms of nerve gas poisoning is the contraction of the pupil. It was easy to see this in the rabbit's eyes. This system is reminiscent of the canaries used in mines to warn of noxious gases.

Another trip I made was to North Carolina to the Air-Ground Operations School. The purpose of the school was to orient both Army and Air Force officers to the system in place that coordinates the two services in battleground operations.

In 1955, I went on TDY (Temporary Duty) to Maxwell Air Force Base in Montgomery, Alabama. There I attended a school. The mission of the school was to produce staff officers to advise a commander of the probability of success in attacking special weapons targets. The course was based on the mathematics of probability.

At times, people question why some of our exacting space efforts fail. This can be explained by mathematics of probability. Probability works like this: If a component in a space launching has a reliability of 99%, that is, it will do its job 99 times out of 100, and a second component has a 99% reliability, one multiplies 99 times 99, getting about 98. This number represents the probability of success of the two components working properly together. Introducing a third component of like reliability, the probability of success drops to 97%. Even if the reliability of each component is 99.999%, there might be 10,000 components. Now you see why failure can occur.

A special weapons staff officer takes many things into account to calculate the overall probability of success of a given mission. Some factors considered are the accuracy of bombing, the dud rate of the weapon, weather, the attrition rate by enemy action, the abort rate, and the bomb's effect that is desired. Putting the figures together for all these factors yields a probability of success that can be given to the commander, who then decides whether the mission is worth launching or not.

During the last week of this course I had a sleepless night. I had a vague pain in my abdomen and about 10 o'clock the next morning the pain got worse. I left class and went on sick call. Two doctors made two diagnoses; one thought it was the appendix, the other, the pancreas. A $5.00 wager was made between them. They sent me home to spread the news and had me return at one o'clock in the afternoon. They operated using a spinal; I was a bit nauseated for a while but I felt nothing. The doctor asked if I would like to see what was bothering me and I agreed to look. He pointed out the greenish tip on the appendix. The doctors then settled their bet. This was on a Tuesday. I was kept overnight in the hospital and the next day the family came to visit. The first thing my nearly three year old daughter, Chris, said was, "Where have you been my big friend?" That made me laugh and it hurt. The following weekend, we went to Fort Walton Beach in Florida. I looked a little odd on the beach because the medics had shaved me from my chest down.

Flying in school situations like this is sparse. One must fly a minimum number of hours by regulation, so 'sand-bagging' is common. This is flying as a co-pilot with an instructor pilot and another pilot actually in the left and right seats at the controls.

One morning when I was driving to this school on a back road, I noticed some vehicles parked along the road, and looking out into a cornfield, I saw the tail of an F-100. I stopped, walked out into the field and there was a pilot from Nellis. He was a member of the Air

Force Demonstration Team, The Thunderbirds. His name was Lucky Palmgren. When he saw me, he said, "What the hell are you doing here?" I looked at him and asked, "What the hell are you doing here?" I told him I was going to school at Maxwell, and he told me that they had been practicing for an air show to be flown at Maxwell Air Force Base. They had been practicing over the civilian airport, Danelly Field, and he lost power. He thought he could make it back to Maxwell where maintenance facilities were available, but he didn't make it. Consequently, he put his aircraft down in a cornfield. Meeting in a cornfield in Alabama with a friend from home was another bit of synchronicity.

In landing a fighter on a surface other than a runway, the procedure was to land with the landing gear retracted to avoid cart-wheeling. As fighters became heavier (the F-100 weighed 28,000 pounds), the procedure had been changed. The heavier machines weren't likely to cart-wheel, and with the gear down it would probably act like a shock absorber. This Alabama cornfield incident was the first time the new procedure had been employed in the Air Force. Had he not used it, he would not have survived, because he touched down in one cornfield, sheared all three landing gears off on an abandoned railroad embankment, crossed a road, sheared off a utility pole and slid to a stop in a second cornfield. With the gear retracted he would have piled the airplane up on the railroad embankment.

In 1956, I was again on TDY at Maxwell Air Force Base. This time I attended Squadron Officers' School. This was basically a leadership course, taken as one advanced through an Air Force career. The only physical problem I had at this school was dislocating the same finger joint twice playing baseball. A member of the staff of this school and I would cross paths again when we were both stationed in France in 1960-3.

My son Mark was born December 9, 1956 on the base at Nellis. This time I was on hand to greet the newborn, whereas I didn't see my daughter until she was five months old, being in Korea at her birth.

At Nellis, we had some other aircraft besides our fighters. A neighboring pilot was checked out in some of these. He asked me why I didn't check out in some and get to fly low and slow periodically and enjoy the scenery. Flying jets necessitated high altitude flying because of fuel consumption. For example, in the T-33, the rate of fuel consumption was the same taxiing on the ground with the throttle at idle as it was cruising 360 knots at 35,000 feet. Each base had a couple of L-20s, a propeller driven airplane with a 450 horsepower engine. These were Canadian-designed, called de Havilland Beavers. They were used for liaison and transport of cargo and a limited number of passengers, sort of a utility airplane.

A tragic accident occurred on the day I got checked out in the L-20. Another aircraft we had on the base was a B-25, a twin-engine medium bomber left over from WW II. There were at least two pilots on the base that flew this aircraft. One was a Doolittle Raider, Jacob Manch, who flew a B-25 off the aircraft carrier 'Hornet' and struck Japanese cities on April 19, 1942. He was killed near Nellis in a T-33 accident. Another B-25 pilot was from a unit of the OSI (Office of Special Investigation). These people were military but wore civilian clothing. This OSI officer was charged with taking a newspaper photographer from Las Vegas up to shoot some photographs of F-86s making simulated attacks on them. A flight of four students was tasked to do the simulations. An experienced pilot, a major, led them. The fighters were making passes at the bomber, much like we did on the air-to-air range making passes on a towed target. Unfortunately, on one pass the leader hit a propeller on the bomber and disabled it. The fighter was disabled as well, but the pilot ejected and parachuted to safety. The pilot of the bomber tried to land at the civilian airport, McCarran Field. He almost made it, landing on his belly short of the runway and then sliding up on the runway. There, the aircraft caught fire. A Naval fireman, who was stationed at Lake Mead Base (a nuclear weapons storage site northeast of Nellis), lived adjacent to McCarran Field and was in his backyard watering his lawn when the aircraft bellied in. He wet himself down, went over the fence and into the burning bomber and pulled some people out; all were dead except the pilot, who was burned badly. He was transported to San Antonio, Texas, to the Air Force Burn Center for treatment; however, he too died. We arrived at the site in the L-20 and landed to see what we could do. However, there was nothing we could do. There was some flap accompanying this accident because the fire engines on McCarran Field never got out of their garage.

Shortly after this accident, there was another that involved the two of us in an L-20. A propeller driven four engine transport, a C-54, carrying a number of nuclear scientists was flying from Los Angeles to Indian Springs Air Force Base, an auxiliary field about 40 miles north of Nellis. They were coming to witness an A-bomb test. They were on an instrument flight plan. However, breaking out into the clear, they had canceled this plan and proceeded visually. It looked like they had gotten into clouds again and made a 180° turn to exit the clouds. A mountain peak got in their way. Since we were airborne in the L-20, and the C-54 was overdue, we were asked to take a look at Mount Charleston, which is about 12,000 feet high. We found the aircraft. It appeared that the pilot tried to fly through a small gap near the mountain peak, pulled up, and stalled into the mountainside. When we arrived, the airplane had been burned out; all had been killed. My next door neighbor at Nellis worked in the Flying Safety Office, which was charged with accident investigations, and this one took them the better part of a week to arrive at the scene. The rugged terrain required the use of horses. We had a helicopter, but the altitude was too high for it, and there was no place for it to land anyhow.

I was flying an L-20 from Nellis to Los Angeles one time and I noticed a Greyhound bus traveling at great speed. I let down to 15 to 20 feet above the desert, throttled back and allowed the bus to pass me. On another L-20 mission, it was my job to deliver an Army liaison officer to Camp Irwin on the desert west of Nellis. The landing area there was on a dry lake bed. However, this time it was flooded. I called and asked where I should land; they told me to land on the 'company street.' Although I spent some time in the Army Artillery, I didn't recognize that term, so I asked where it was; the answer was the green spot between the barracks buildings.

Another fun thing to do with the L-20 was when I had a passenger who had not flown with me before. On the base, we had some people that had to log at least four hours of flying time per month in order to justify their flying pay. We had some flight surgeons, a navigator and an Army Liaison officer at Nellis. The easiest way for them to log time was to deadhead in an L-20. I had a prank I played with newcomers. I would fly out near the north rim of the Grand Canyon, to a place where it dropped off 5000 feet. Letting down gradually, until I was about 15 feet above the desert, I would fly over the edge. There was usually an updraft or downdraft so the airplane would respond with some turbulence and the dozing passenger would react to flying off the edge of the world. Good fun!

If an aircraft has undergone extensive maintenance, it is not released for flight right away. A designated test pilot takes it aloft with a checklist, and puts it through its paces in order to see that everything is working properly. Our Flying Safety officer was one of these test pilots. He took off in an F-86 and did his routine, then made a radio call saying that he had finished his job and was going to fly until he burned the fuel out of his drop tanks. It was unwise to land with fuel in the drop tanks because the extra weight could cause too much stress on the airframe if one made a hard landing. He was never heard from again. We shut down operations for ten days and searched for him. Some T-33s and T-28s came up from Williams Air Force Base in Arizona to help in the search. Unfortunately, a T-28 was lost in the search, having flown into a box canyon, and in an attempt to get out of it, crashed killing the two pilots. Years later, when I was stationed in France, I read in The Air Force Times, a service newspaper, that the test pilot had been found by a surveyor in the desert. The airplane had gone into a small ravine that was full of brush.

During the fifties, nuclear weapons were developed for fighters. Nuclear weapons before this time were big, fat and ugly. The things were too heavy to carry on a fighter or too large to sling under it. As the fighter weapons came on line, it was necessary to develop tactics to employ them. The Fighter Weapons School looked around for some expertise in this field. I was somewhat flattered when they asked me if I would like to join them. So, I transferred to Tactical Air Command and no longer taught in the Special Weapons School at Nellis. About this time, our fighter units in Europe were to begin transition from F-86s to F-100s. A team of three pilots was selected to travel to our bases in France and Germany. The mission of the team would be to orient pilots about the F-100. My portion of the effort was in the special weapons area. I told them how the bomb was built, the physics behind it, the fusing and firing systems and weapons effects. Also a minor part of my presentation dealt with biological and chemical weapons, which were also classified as 'special'.

The three of us flew to Frankfurt, Germany, and began our work. This duty lasted about three months. Weekends generally were free, and I tried to see as much of the countries as I could. Thinking that this might be the only time I would ever be in Europe, I suggested that my wife fly over to join me on some leave. I plotted out an itinerary, traveling mostly by train. Then I bumped into a person I had worked with at Nellis. He showed me an inexpensive small car and suggested I buy one and do my traveling that way. The price of the car was less than the train fares I had planned for. The car was manufactured by BMW from an Italian design called an Isetta. It had room for two and a small luggage space and was powered by a BMW motorcycle engine. We started our tour in Belgium and toured France, Italy and

Germany. I shipped it to Los Angeles from Bremerhaven, Germany at a cost of $100. Many of the pilots at Nellis had motor scooters to use on the base; I had the only all-weather model.

On leave in Europe in 1957, I was careful with the Isetta, breaking-in the engine strictly according to the book. When the mileage had reached the end of the break-in period, I was on an auto strada (Italian freeway) not far from Milan, so I opened it up to see what it would do; shortly the engine siezed up. I hitchhiked to a telephone with an Italian F-86 fighter pilot that helped me call a BMW dealer in

My mother and my son with the BMW Isetta, 1957, Nellis Air Force Base, Nevada.

Milan. The dealer sent help and had the machine repaired with a new engine within two days. I only had to pay for the labor involved.

While at Nellis, I competed in a highway safety demonstration. An organization came to the base and offered a $100.00 reward for anybody who could stop his car from 30 miles an hour within a certain distance. I practiced doing this on the back roads of the base with the Isetta. A friend would slap his hand against the car body when he saw an identifiable spot on the side of the road. That was the signal to stop. We would then measure the distance it took to stop. I was consistently getting results that would win the prize. The first person to try to stop within the limits was the Base Commander, General McGehee. He failed with his big Cadillac. The official who rode with me fastened a device to the front bumper, which would fire a piece of white chalk into the pavement when he was satisfied with my speed. When I heard a bang, it was a signal to stop. Well, I won. The official asked me not to claim the prize, because the Isetta wasn't a regular automobile, and it would also detract from the purpose of the demonstration, that is, highway safety. I acquiesced.

In August of 1958, when I left Nellis for good after 5 1/2 years, I drove the Isetta 520 miles one day on my way to Seattle. My next station was at the University of Washington, working on an advanced degree. I found the Isetta convenient in finding a parking place daily near the campus because of its diminutive size. I also used to commute to Paine Air Force Base in Everett, Washington, where I discharged my flying duties. I sold it in Seattle before being transferred to France.

While on TDY in Europe, my two coworkers and I decided to celebrate the Fourth of July by buying some hot dogs and buns and having a picnic. We drove up a small back road in Germany to a wooded area and built a small fire to roast our hot dogs. It took about fifteen minutes from the time we started the fire that a yeager showed up. A yeager is a forest ranger. He had us put out the fire, so we ate a cold lunch. A yeager oversees a patch of land, and he manages and protects it. When it has surplus game, he authorizes hunters to come out and shoot the game. However, the yeager owns the game and he sells it to local restaurants; thus, you can sometimes find wild boar, deer, game birds and other wild fauna on menus.

While waiting for transportation from downtown Paris to the airport after my European sojourn was over, I was seated outside a *cafe*. (Although 'cafe' means 'coffee' in French, it's primarily a bar.) The door was open, and I recognized an officer who had been our host at one of our bases in France that we had visited. Standing with him was a person that looked familiar. I remarked, "If that's not Joe Dimaggio, I'll eat my hat." I went in to greet my friend and he introduced me to Joe Dimaggio. Apparently he was in Europe to cry in his beer, having just separated from Marilyn Monroe. I didn't have to eat my hat.

In August of 1958, I left what had been my home for the previous 5 1/2 years. But before I leave the subject of Nellis, I'll relate a few incidents that happened there.

My cousin, Dale McMullen, who had followed me through pilot training and was in my unit in Korea, was also stationed at Nellis after the Korean campaign. Once, when he was going to 'drag a rag,' that is, tow a 5 foot by 29 foot nylon mesh target airborne for the air-to-air gunnery range, he telephoned me and wanted to know if I wanted to go along. So, I rushed down to the line, jumped in the rear cockpit and off we went. Our airspeed indicators never got above 80 knots. We became airborne and tried to rectify the problem to no avail. We dropped the target and flew around until the tip tanks were empty, then flew formation with another aircraft on final approach and landed. We taxied in and shut the airplane down, and then we got to looking for the possible cause of our problem. There was a gunnery meet scheduled in the near future and six T-33s had been painted a bright orange so as to be seen more easily on the air-to-air gunnery range. An inspection of the static ports, which were a series of small holes that allowed static air pressure to enter and operate some of the instruments, showed that ours was covered with masking tape. The tape had been put on to prevent paint from entering the holes. These blocked holes were the cause of our problem. An examination of the other five aircraft that had been painted bright orange showed that all but one either had masking tape still on them or masking tape had not been put on them and consequently the holes were clogged with paint. My cousin should have caught this discrepancy in his pre-flight walk around inspection and the painters should not have caused this discrepancy in the first place. Here were five accidents waiting to happen. This shows the importance of doing the walk around inspection before flight. "Kick the tire before lighting the fire."

A replacement for me arrived on the base shortly before I left. I was giving him an orientation so he could become familiar with our operations. We were in an F-100 F model (2 seats). I was in the rear acting as an instructor and he was in the front cockpit flying the airplane. This airplane has a non-skid braking system. It is well-known that a tire skidding has less friction needed for stopping than one which is just barely turning. This system was automatic if it were engaged. I never used it because I felt I could manually stop the airplane. To assist in deceleration, a drag 'chute was used also. My replacement was used to relying upon this non-skid system, consequently, when we landed, he stood on the brakes and blew a tire and we ran off the runway. Now, part of the preflight inspection calls for looking into what we called the Form 1 which is kept in the airplane. In it one can see if there are any write-ups that might affect safe flight. It is the pilot's responsibility to know if an airplane had any discrepancies. My replacement read this but forgot about it. This was another failure of not doing the walk around properly. After I left Nellis, I heard that this person crashed and killed himself.

The F-100 was our first supersonic airplane. The F-86 would go through mach one (the speed of sound) in a dive, but the F-100 would exceed this speed easily in level flight. Landing this airplane was a little different. Turning final approach to the runway, you had to decide to land or not right then because if you changed your mind as you approached touch down, you wouldn't have enough power to go around even if you lit the afterburner. The airplane had no flaps; you would come over the 'fence' at 160 knots (184 miles an hour.) This was a hot machine.

Occasionally we would get a message from SAC (Strategic Air Command) saying that one of their B-36s would be transiting our area and they would be pleased if we could make some passes on it in order to give their gunners some tracking practice. It would give us some tracking practice as well. My first pass at it was a dry one. I could not decide where to aim at the ten engine behemoth!

A fellow pilot in The Fighter Weapons School was demonstrating a slow over the top maneuver to some students in an F-86 H model and got into an inverted spin and ejected. He said his parachute, which was deployed automatically, made two swings and he hit the ground. As he sat there, the canopy hit not far from him; next, the ejection seat hit close to him, and then the airplane hit upside down, not too far away.

Another fellow pilot experienced engine failure and tried to make it back to base. However, he didn't have enough altitude and punched out not far from Nellis. The Navy operated a special weapons storage site called Lake Mead Base. It had a double chain link fence around it and sentries patrolling around the clock. The pilot landed between the two fences and proceeded to gather up his parachute. A sentry came running down the hill toward him with his guard dog, yelling at the pilot not to move. He saw no danger and continued to gather up his parachute. However, he stopped what he was doing when the sentry told him he was standing in a minefield between the two fences.

While flying on instruments in the rear seat of a T-33, we got a call asking us to check on a pall of smoke on the edge of Lake Mead. We flew over there but could not find the pilot. When our helicopter arrived, we left. Later we learned that the reason we couldn't see the pilot was because he was in the water, taking a swim to escape the heat.

Not too long after I left Nellis, The Thunderbird Demonstration Team was practicing north of the base, and due to a misjudgment on the leader's part, all four crashed into the desert. Later, a different leader of the Thunderbirds, a friend of mine, was killed in an F-100 F; the reason was unknown. While I was still there, a pilot was trying out for the solo slot on the Thunderbird team. He had gone over to the Parumph Valley west of Mount Charleston to practice alone. For some unknown reason he crashed and was killed.

At one time during one hot summer at Nellis, we had a spate of unexplained crashes. Finally, some autopsies were performed and they found that the salt content of the remains was drastically low.

This prompted a program which required pilots to take salt pills for each flight. Some could not stomach the salt pills; they would come up as soon as they went down. To solve this problem, each squadron had a refrigerator with paper cups filled with tomato juice saturated with salt. These tasted mighty good to me in the heat.

One hot day at Nellis, I was in a T-33, aligned on the runway awaiting the ground crew to attach a cable to my airplane. This cable had a banner target on it. We towed these to our air-to-air range so our fighters could fire on them. While waiting with the canopy open, I called the tower to see what the runway temperature was (it is a factor in determining the length of runway needed for a particular aircraft to takeoff.) The runway temperature was taken six feet above the surface where the engine 'breathed.' The reading was 128 degrees. That evening at home, I checked a meat thermometer I had; 140 degrees was for rare beef. I suppose I could have cooked if I'd sat there long enough.

There was a 30 gallon tank in the T-33 in which water and alcohol were mixed. This was fed into the engine on take off, increasing the volumetric efficiency.

On another occasion, I saw a crew chief frying an egg on the horizontal stabilizer of an F-100. I don't know how long it had taken, but the albumin was white.

There was a lieutenant colonel in the base maintenance section, a bachelor. One time he took up an F-80 on a test flight and came down vertically through a low overcast and impacted across the highway and railroad tracks next to the base. This was presumed to be a suicide when it was learned he had huge gambling debts in Las Vegas.

Sometimes we shut down operations over Christmas time, and people were encouraged to fly the airplanes during this period if they were around the base. The reason for this was, "you can't tell what's wrong with anything unless you use it." One Christmas there were four people who took a B-25 to the east coast to be with their families. Bad weather and perhaps other factors caused the airplane to end up in the Susquehanna River in Pennsylvania; all four were killed. During the same Christmas, two instructor pilots were rat racing in F-86s. Rat racing is done in trail formation, one aircraft behind the other, the first trying to lose the second and the second trying to stay on the other's tail. Somehow they both crashed into a dry lakebed, killing them both.

We also had a mid-air collision between an F-100 F and a prop driven airliner. The two pilots were making simulated instrument let downs out over the desert southwest of Las Vegas.

An odd accident occurred when a C-47 was making practice instrument let downs and approaches out over the desert. Applying nose up trim on final approach, the more nose up trim applied, the heavier the nose became, causing the airplane to belly into the desert. Recent maintenance had rigged the control cables to the elevator trim tabs backwards.

An instrument instructor pilot neglected to insert the safety pin in his T-33's ejection seat before climbing out of his airplane. He triggered the seat when he was getting out. Fortunately, he only suffered a broken arm.

A pilot with whom I worked had a harrowing flight once. He was tasked to fly a Las Vegas Sun newspaper reporter to Phoenix and then return him to Nellis. It was evening when he left Phoenix, and being a fan of boxing, he tuned in the airplane's radio compass to the fights. Apparently immersed in the boxing, he noticed there were no lights as his estimated time of arrival at Las Vegas approached. Somewhat disoriented, he kept flying until some lights were sighted. He circled trying to identify anything he could. His circling attracted some attention on the ground; observers thought an airplane was in distress. These observers aligned a number of cars along a landing strip with their headlights on outside a small town in Utah. The pilot landed safely, but was somewhat embarrassed by the article in the newspaper the next day. The reporter had a heyday telling of his adventure of being lost at night in a jet airplane.

So it was like this at Nellis during the middle fifties. I've already mentioned that we lost almost a student a week, and that I could count eighteen instructor pilots that bit the dust during the first 32 months I was there. Besides taking fingerprints for identification, which is not unusual, we had footprints taken for the same purpose because sometimes that was the only thing left for identification.

I hope my picture of my tour at Nellis doesn't appear all morbid. There's nothing morbid about flying; it is a delight. But in high-powered military aircraft sometimes (but rarely) it is punctuated with terror.

A delightful thing I did was write my name in the sky. The condensation trails left at high altitude are of two types: persistent and non-persistent. If I had the time, the fuel and persistent contrails, I would write my first name in the sky: (Lee). It was simple, involving four level turns. Of course it wouldn't look like the text shown here, but cursive. There were times when I did this, I'd let down and land quickly, go home for lunch and take my young daughter out into the yard to see my name in the sky. The shadow of the name could also be read on the desert floor from above.

We had to fly so much night time. One time I had an F-86 and was above a very stable layer of cloud. The sun had gone down and the top of the cloud layer was pink. I lowered the aircraft down into the layer so just the canopy was sticking out of it and enjoyed the 500-knot ride through the top of 'pink whipped cream'.

Occasionally one can see a rainbow from high altitude. These appear as complete circles, not just arcs it as you see on the ground. These are a delight to see.

I was going to log some night time in a T-33 one evening, and kidding the ground crewman, I asked him if he'd like to go along. When he answered in the affirmative, I thought, "Why not?" So I got him checked out with the use of a parachute and how to use the ejection seat, and off we went. It was a beautiful evening, a full moon was rising and I told my passenger I was going to do a roll around the moon. I told him that if he felt uncomfortable to say so and I wouldn't do it anymore. After the roll, he said he liked it and it was great. So, I did another in the opposite direction. Then, after a couple more, I asked him if he'd like to do one. He said he'd had no experience flying at all, so I told him to take hold of the stick below the handgrip and I'd talk him through a roll. After a few rolls he was able to do one by himself. Now, rolling in a jet airplane is rather simple because of lack of torque, and hardly any rudder is needed. I hope he is enjoying himself telling this story right now to his grandchildren as I am enjoying telling it to you.

Another pleasurable flight (actually three flights) was when I took my brother Glenn up in a T-33 and brother Bob later. I took my friend Stan Griffiths up once at Nellis. I think Bob especially enjoyed it because the horsepower available was more than double that of the fighters he used to fly.

Sometimes on a weekend, I would take a T-33 from Las Vegas to McChord Air Force Base at Tacoma, WA. There were times when I called my brother Bob, who lived at Des Moines, not far from McChord, to see if he could come and pick me up. There were a couple of times when I beat him there. If it were daylight, it was a delight flying from Las Vegas to McChord once I got as far as northern California. If it were clear, the mountain peaks served as guides: Mounts Lassen, Shasta, Jefferson, Three Sisters, Hood, Adams, St. Helens and Rainier. Sometimes Mount Baker was also visible.

Before leaving the subject of Nellis, I might make mention that one of my fellow pilots in The Fighter Weapons School later became an astronaut. His name was Bill Pogue. He flew with The Thunderbirds, and as an astronaut he was instrumental in resolving problems in the space lab that we had. Another fellow pilot at Nellis, who became more famous, was Edwin (Buzz) Aldrin. He had been in my cousin's

I knew 'Buzz' Aldrin, second man to step on the moon with Neil Armstrong. He, my cousin Dale McMullen and I used to play handball together at Nellis AFB. Here is a copy of orders sending myself and Aldrin to an instructor's course in Texas in 1954.

flying class, and became an astronaut, the second man to step on the moon. Buzz, my cousin Dale and I used to play handball together at Nellis. Buzz went to the Air Force Academy when it opened. Academy graduates (he was a Naval Academy graduate) on active duty were asked to volunteer to act as upper classmen because there weren't any. Later he got into the space program. To get into the space program, a person was not eligible to apply unless one was an academy graduate or had a degree in engineering. I was not eligible.

In late summer of 1958, I was landing an F-100 one day and I scared myself. This airplane had a small rudder, and to increase directional control at lower speeds on the ground, a hydraulic nose wheel steering system was installed. The procedure upon landing was to touch down on the main gear and then lower the nose right away, depress a small lever on the stick, and run the rudder pedals through a neutral position. This would pick up the nose wheel steering system and allow you positive directional control with your feet. On this particular day there was a crosswind from the left, and at touchdown I pressed the lever and went to push the rudder pedals through the neutral position; I found that my right leg would not extend. I had been having trouble with my right knee joint due to an old football injury that had torn the cartilage. I managed to get my left foot under the left pedal and drew it back through the neutral position, thus gaining directional control. In the meantime, the aircraft was weather cocking into the wind, and I was about to run off the runway into the desert. I got it straightened out and went directly up to the hospital to talk to a flight surgeon about my problem. He showed me both of his knees, which had had operations correcting similar problems, so I acquiesced to an operation. They found twelve pieces of cartilage floating around in the joint, some of which would block joint mobility at times. It took a long time to recover from this operation. Later on, in 1970 or so, I had a second operation on the knee and now that I am an octogenarian I may have an artificial joint installed before too long. My brother Bob had one and got along fine.

Chapter Eight

Graduate School

In order to upgrade the educational level of the officer corps in the Air Force, there were opportunities to apply for additional schooling. The normal tour of duty on a base was about four years, and having been at Nellis for five and a half years, I figured it was time to move on. I applied to what we called the Institute of Technology to return to school. They wanted to know where I wanted to go and I told them that all my credits were good at my alma mater, the University of Washington, and that's where they sent me. My orders were to contact an adviser, establish a goal and achieve the goal. My goal was a Master's Degree.

Here I was in Seattle, my hometown, on my new assignment. My first order of business was to find a place to live. I found a rental house near Green Lake, not far from the university campus. The second order was to go to the university and seek an adviser in the College of Education. Inasmuch as my degree was in Art Education, it was natural for me to seek an advanced degree in the education field. I conferred with an adviser and established a Master's Degree as a goal. I registered for the fall quarter and was able to arrange all of my classes in the morning hours. I was assigned a carrel in the university library, which I shared with another student who used it in the morning hours. A carrel is an isolated spot among the stacks in the university library, quiet and private. It was here that I did most of my studying.

My next step was to go to Paine Air Force Base in Everett, Washington, about thirty miles north of Seattle. It was here that I would perform my flying duties. The base had all-weather jet interceptors to accomplish their mission. They also had some support aircraft, one of which was the C-47, a twin-engine transport, which revolutionized the air transport industry in the early thirties. We called these airplanes, affectionately, "Gooney Birds." The base was responsible to provide for my flying requirements; however, they didn't feel like we students could be part of their primary mission, so we were relegated to fly C-47s and not the mission aircraft. So, I checked out in these, which flew low and slow. Our primary job was flying cargo or personnel in the northwest corner of the country.

Everett, Washington is in an area called the 'convergence zone'. It is here where the weather systems that arrive from the north pacific join after funneling through the Juan De Fuca Strait around the north and south end of the Olympic Mountains. The two streams meet and the air rises, cools and condenses. Thus, Everett finds itself having more than its share of low ceilings and rainfall. Often we would take off in drizzling conditions and low ceilings and, climbing out to the northwest, we would break out of the soup and find ourselves over a group of islands called the San Juans. These are located meteorologically in what is called a 'rain shadow.' Incoming weather systems from the North Pacific are forced aloft over the Olympic Mountains, cooling there and causing precipitation. One town on the west side of the mountains gets about 100 inches of rain annually. On the down slope, the air is warmed by compression and is able to hold more moisture. This downwind area is called a rain shadow. One town here gets only 17 inches of rain a year.

I had been in the San Juan Islands hunting rabbits with my brother and some friends in 1946. I remembered that it was very beautiful there and before I left the university on January 1, 1960, I went to the islands seeking real estate, thinking it would be a nice place to retire. I bought some land on an island before I was transferred to my next base in France, but more about that later.

It was quite a change from flying the hottest fighter in the Air Force inventory to flying an airplane that seldom went over 140 miles an hour. Contrast that with the supersonic F-100, that came down final approach at 184 miles an hour. In retrospect, I am glad I got a chance to fly the C-47, because it is a historical icon of American aviation.

The master's program at the University of Washington required a thesis. At the master's level, it is primarily an exercise in conducting research. I doubt very much if anybody ever made a major contribution to knowledge writing a master's thesis. My advisor helped me pick a subject for the thesis, and since I was a military man, he suggested I make a survey of high school seniors to see what they knew about their military obligations (the draft was in effect at this time). So, I composed a questionnaire after visiting recruiting offices in Seattle

The C-47 Gooney Bird. My 'steed' for 15 months.

to find out what the students should know about their military obligations. Compiling these data into a questionnaire, the university petitioned the Seattle school system to see if I could go to two different high schools and administer my questionnaire. After this was accomplished, the job of rendering the results into statistics to present to the College of Education was tedious and lengthy. Because I had not finished writing my thesis when my orders arrived for my transfer to France, I was obliged to register for the spring quarter (even though I would not be there, all that was left to do was to have the paper typed). My thesis would be submitted in the spring quarter and the degree awarded at the end of that quarter, which was June 1960. I had achieved my goal in about fifteen months, which included summer school. It was my turn to go overseas again, so the Air Force reassigned me to a base in France.

I sold my Isetta and moved my family to Vancouver, Washington, where relatives were plentiful. My daughter Chris had started the first grade in Seattle and continued with the first grade in Vancouver. She finished the first grade in an English speaking school on the base in France.

To occupy some spare time while in Seattle, I began to build a flying machine. It was an 'auto-gyro.' This was a patented name applied to such flying machines during the thirties; it was actually named a 'gyro-copter'. It consisted of a framework and a mast to which was attached an engine and propeller to push it forward. At the top of the mast there were two rotor blades which would rotate automatically when the machine was pushed forward by the prop. These machines flew without wings, although one can consider the rotor blades as rotary wings, the same as a helicopter has except they are not powered directly by an engine. It was unfinished when I left Seattle, so I stored it in my in-laws' basement in Vancouver.

In 1959, I read a story in the newspaper about the Chief Justice of the U.S. Supreme Court hiking along Washington's Pacific coast some 30 miles, followed by the press. He did this to advertise the fact that he was against the movement to make a highway through the Olympic National Park along the coast. This gave me the idea that it might be a good thing to do myself, so I convinced my lifelong friends, Stan Griffiths and his wife Erma, to accompany us on such an adventure. It took us three days.

Chapter Nine

Flying in Europe

My family was not allowed to accompany me to my new station in France. The primary reason was a housing shortage. There were units on base and near the base but not enough for all; one had to await their turn. To get the family there quicker, one was obliged to go into the French community and seek housing. The base had certain requirements for French housing. The quarters had to have running water, a means of heating the water and a means of bathing. This might sound odd, but in many respects, a large part of northern France was many years behind the living standards of the United States. The housing office on the base had an interpreter who would accompany one to make arrangements with landowners if one found a place that met the standards. By chance, I met a dentist on the base who had found a place and had it upgraded to satisfy the standards (principally plumbing), but when his wife arrived from the States she took one look and turned it down. He had some money invested in this house that he was not going to use, so I agreed to take a look at it and paid him what he had invested. This way I was able to have my family join me about three months after I arrived in France. When I was about to leave France, the landlord and his attorney came by and wanted to know what I was going to do about my plumbing, was I going to take it with me or what? I left it there in lieu of the last month's rent. They were happy with that arrangement.

Before leaving Seattle, I bought a Volkswagen on a tourist deal. I bought the car in Seattle and took delivery in Frankfurt, Germany. When my family arrived, I had some wheels. The house was located about twenty miles from the base in a French town called Chauny, which had about 15,000 residents. The street we lived on was on the fringe of town, and most of the adjacent houses were 400 years old. The better houses and most of the town were dynamited by the Germans when they retreated in 1918. Many of the buildings downtown had tiled entrances decorated with the French: "Dynamité par les Allemands,

1918." A family across the street had four children: two teenage girls and two younger boys. This family became good friends and the friendship has lasted more than 46 years. Since I left France in 1963, I've been back to visit five different times, and we have had some of those family members and their friends visit us on three occasions. Through the French teacher at the local high school, we made arrangements for a student from Friday Harbor to spend a summer with some of these friends and in the following year, the daughter of some of these French friends spent a summer with a family in Friday Harbor.

Over the years I've tried to keep a bit current in the French language. There is little opportunity to converse in the language in Friday Harbor and, although there is a French speaking radio station in Vancouver, British Columbia, I find they speak so fast it is difficult to understand. A thing I did for more than 30 years was subscribe to the French language ver-

Our French neighbors, minus a daughter and a son,; the boy in the foreground is my son, Mark.

Les Filles Francaises. 1963

Reunited after 46 years. 2009

sion of the magazine *Readers' Digest*, which is printed in Montreal, Canada. There was a difference between the U.S. dollar and the Canadian dollar (in our favor). For years I had been subscribing to this magazine, paying in U.S. dollars; then it dawned on me that I was getting the bill in Canadian dollars. So I wrote a letter saying I discovered the difference after 30 years and perhaps they would send me a free subscription. I never heard from them.

In May-June 2005, my daughter and I made our second trip in fifteen years to visit French friends. We communicate by e-mail now. I know I make many mistakes in writing, but so long as communication is the important thing, I'm sure they are overlooked. Besides, I can always blame the errors on the computer.

My flying in France began in the C-47 because that was the last airplane I flew on my previous base at Paine Air Force Base. I only made one flight in this airplane in Europe and that was from my base in France to Copenhagen, Denmark and return. This was a flight to reward the base's baseball team, which had won second place Air Force-wide. The flight was uneventful except for a landing. There was fog on the surface that only covered half of the airport in Copenhagen. We landed, and halfway down the runway ran into the fog bank. We had to wait for a vehicle to lead us to the ramp because visibility was almost zero.

The mission aircraft on my air base in France were RF-101s. These aircraft were configured to take photographs. The 'R' stood for reconnaissance; the 'F' stood for fighter. I was assigned to the air base group and inherited a number of jobs. My primary job was Education Officer. This involved organizing classes that could be taken by personnel on the base. I had three enlisted men and two civilians who did most of the work. Instructors were recruited from qualified people on the base. Typical subjects were mathematics, history and language. In addition to this job, I had other jobs which included special services, athletics, the library and numerous other worms in a bucket.

Shortly after I arrived at my new base in France (Laon Air Base), I was at Ramstein Air Base, Germany, and a met a pilot with whom I had been stationed in The Fighter Weapons School at Nellis. He was a pilot in an F-100 unit on one of our German bases. He thought perhaps I would be of value in his fighter unit rather than flying a desk in a reconnaissance unit. So, I met his commander and he said he would request my transfer if I approved. Upon my return to Laon, my

Wing Commander called me in to discuss this matter. He was willing to let me go if I wouldn't do just what I was doing at Laon. After about two weeks, the Wing Commander called me in and told me I could not go. The reason was that I was on a 'directed-duty assignment,' and it would take an act of Congress to change that. When I applied to go back to the university, this restriction did not exist; however, while I was in school they changed the rules, rightly so. After the time and expense of upgrading my education, the Air Force was justified by putting me in a field which related to that education.

Having had experience in the T-33 aircraft and in the L-20, I checked out in both at Laon. My flights were frequent and took me to Germany almost weekly. The following are some flights of note.

NATO (North Atlantic Treaty Organization) fighters in Germany used the T-33, a two-seated jet trainer, as a target for intercepts. I would cruise on a prescribed course and radar would direct fighters to come up and intercept me as an exercise. Usually it was necessary to refuel prior to returning to my base. On one occasion I was making a ground controlled radar approach to Spangdahlem Air Base in Germany in order to refuel, and while under radar control in the traffic pattern under instrument conditions, I spotted an F-100 less than 100 feet in front of me. This was a close one. I reported the incident but never heard why it happened.

It was common to fly to Spain, either to Madrid or Zaragotha and back, to log night time or hood time. The pilot in the rear of a T-33 would fly on instruments under a hood to simulate weather conditions, while the pilot in the front seat took off and landed the aircraft and served as an observer to stay clear visually. We would land at a Spanish base, refuel, change positions and return to home base. On one occasion in Spain, I was in the front seat; the pilot in the rear seat did a good job navigating and making his letdown under the hood, but he was a little low on his final approach. We did not land the airplane under the hood. I shook the stick and told him that I had it. Because we were a little low, I moved the throttle to add power. There was no response. I told the other pilot to add power but there was no response. We were committed to land, so I retracted the dive brakes and flaps to extend my approach. Retracting the gear would take too long and it would have to be extended again. As I approached the end of the runway I was looking at a concrete wall about 4 feet high. Some work and been done to extend the runway and the earth had not been graded up to the concrete addition. This might seem like a very thick runway and it was because we had jet bombers stationed there and they needed a strong runway to support their weight.

To get maximum distance in an airplane there is a speed called maximum lift over drag, or L/D. It was 120 knots for the T-33. I was holding this speed and at the last second I extended the flaps. This added immediate lift and also immediate drag. The lift was sufficient to clear the wall; however, one of my wheels hit a light on the end of the runway that stuck up a foot or so. I coasted off the runway onto the nearest exit, shut the airplane down and climbed out. Shortly, there was a vehicle there with a safety officer saying that he would have to write me up for a violation, having hit the light. I explained the emergency situation to him. We then opened an access door on the fuselage where the fuel filter was located, opened the drain, and the first thing that came out was water. There had been other instances of fuel filters freezing, so that explained why we had no additional power on approach. The safety officer didn't write me up. This was another close one. About the same time there was also trouble with jet fuel developing sludge caused by certain bacteria. This would also clog fuel filters.

Here is another flying episode in the T-33: To log some night time, Madrid or Zaragotha were just about the right distance. It was about two hours each way and again, the pilot in the rear seat would fly under a hood on instruments and the pilot in the front seat would takeoff, land and act as an observer to keep the aircraft visually clear. I was in the front seat going to Madrid. We landed, refueled, had a bite to eat, traded places in the cockpits and headed back to home base. Climbing out, I felt something stirring in my belly, and the higher we went the worse some gas pains became. We leveled off at our assigned cruising altitude and I could no longer concentrate on the instruments. Had I been alone, I would have had an acute problem. I became nauseous and generally quite ill. We called the controller for a different altitude, thinking that perhaps a lower flight level might alleviate the problem; this made no difference. Finally, I got to the point, knowing I had diarrhea, there was nothing to do but relieve it. I told the other pilot I was going to try to hit my helmet bag. We carried our hard helmets in a bag and, upon entering the aircraft, this bag was thrown into the bottom of the seat. In order to retrieve it, then use it as a receptacle, I had to get out of my seat belt and shoulder straps first of all, elevate myself in the cockpit to a stooped position, unzip my flying suit and pull it down and arrange the bag. While pulling down my

Les enfants (My kids in France)

shorts, I lost control. There was nothing to do then except go on 100% oxygen to avoid the odor and sit down in the mess. This came on all of a sudden. I don't believe it was anything I ate at Madrid; the reaction was too soon. I don't know what caused it, but it was debilitating. It was raining when we landed at our airbase, and I climbed out of the cockpit with nothing on but my tee shirt and boots. I walked away from the airplane where the grass was wet and sat down and scooted around a bit. I apologized to the crew chief for the mess, took my parachute and dirty clothes to my car and went home. Everyone was asleep. I got up early so I didn't see any of my family until the next evening. I had taken my dirty flying suit and other clothes and had put them in some water in the bathtub. When I got home that evening, I apologized for the mess I had left in the bathroom. The response was, "What mess?" Apparently the French lady who occasionally came to do housework saw the mess, cleaned it up and said nothing about it. I also apologized to those in the parachute loft. Fortunately, there was another pilot on board or I could have been in serious trouble, being almost completely debilitated at night in weather. I did have my ejection seat and parachute, however.

Every flight we made in Europe was under instrument flight rules. Progress was followed by radar, and air traffic controllers would be in charge. The radios in the L-20s were from old T-6s, which had six push buttons for changing channels. However, it took seven different channels to fly from our base to our headquarters at Ramstein Air Base in Germany. There were times when I was alone that I would have to change channels somewhere en route. At night in weather, this was especially challenging. I would have to get out of my seat and adjust the elevator trim tab (which was a small wheel overhead between the seats) so that the aircraft would remain level. This airplane had no auto pilot. Next, I would change position, taking a couple of steps to the rear to see what the plane was going to do, step back forward and make a trim adjustment, and after doing this maybe three or four times, seeking some guarantee that the aircraft might remain level, I would look for the crystals in the back of the cabin in order change radio frequencies. There were two plywood sheets with holes drilled to accept the crystal's contacts. One sheet had transmitter crystals and one had receiver crystals. I would have to find the ones that I was through using and pull them out of the radio and replace them with those that were needed further in the flight. Then I would make my way back to the seat and get the aircraft under control again. All this was done using a flashlight.

One time on my way to Germany, I got icing on the L-20. It had no de-icing equipment. I could look out the window at my eye level and see the thick, ugly growth on the leading edge of the wing. I was wishing I had a stick to reach out there and knock it off because it got to the point where I could no longer keep altitude. I called ahead to air traffic control and told them what my problem was. The airplane was making a gradual descent as I approached the high hills in eastern France. I almost turned around to get back above the flat level ground when the ice started to come off because of warmer temperatures at the lower altitude.

One day I had a passenger (actually two passengers) to take to Germany from our base. One was an air policeman, the other was his guard dog. As I was leaving the traffic area, I got a call from the tower asking me if I had a dog on board. I said I did and he said that he had to have the dog's serial number for the manifest file. I gave the microphone to the air policemen to transmit the dog's serial number. I was amused to find the serial number began with K9.

Another hair-raising event happened while I was working with the radio direction finding people on our base. I would fly out into the boondocks somewhere in the L-20 and contact them on the radio. They would have me hold the microphone button down for a five count, and then they would give me a heading back to base, giving me corrections en route with subsequent five counts. The radio direction finder was an aid to navigation. While involved in this process once, I suddenly saw a glider directly in front of me. Where it came from and where it went I don't know. I suppose I scared him as much as he scared me.

An amusing thing happened the first time I flew from our base to England. I was in a T-33 crossing the channel when I switched over to English Anglia Control. They advised me that they had me on their radar screen and after a few minutes asked me to make a course correction to port. At that time, not knowing port from starboard, I had to call back and ask if port was left or right. England, being a maritime nation, I supposed the terms port and starboard were left over from sailing ship days. This was new to me.

One of the tactics used by our fighters in Europe involved flying low to avoid radar detection. We would fly at 500 feet at 500 knots (575 miles an hour). At this speed, one was limited to dead reckoning or pilotage. Pilotage is determining position by observing identifiable things on the ground: cities, lakes, rivers, geographical features, etc. Dead reckoning is observing heading, speed and time, plotting these on a chart. This should show approximately where you have been, where you are and where you will be. Both of these are difficult to manage because of being at only 500 feet and going so fast. In Europe, there are hundreds, if not thousands, of towns and they all look somewhat alike. A solution to this navigation problem was found by using L'Armée de l'Aire (French Air Force) maps. In France, it's against the law to cut a tree down without a permit. For example, there was a dead fruit tree in my yard where I lived in France and I asked the landlord why he didn't cut the tree down. He replied that it was too much red tape. I was puzzled. He said a permit was required and why not wait until it fell down? A probable reason for this is that during the days of sailing vessels, forests in Europe were decimated for timber to build ships. Then, when it was discovered that iron and charcoal would produce steel, this probably ate up a lot more trees to make charcoal. So the government regulates the patches of forest that are left, and these patches are printed on the French aviation charts. The patches' shapes and sizes are stable. So by drawing a line from point A to point B on one of these charts, you can see where your course should be relative to these identifiable wood patches. Of course, this was called 'wood patch' navigation.

Chauny, where we lived, had been in the middle of WW I. There was a British cemetery in the town, maintained by a young English couple. The Union Jack flew there over that piece of Britain. There were cemeteries all over. One time I took the kids out to an open area with the .22 rifle and we shot at paper plates. After romping in the tall grass, we took a walk through the woods nearby. The ground was very lumpy there. I thought that perhaps it was due to trees being up-rooted. Emerging out the other side of the woods, I recognized the lumpy area as a battlefield. We were seeing shell craters left over from WW I. There was a German cemetery on the other side of the wood patch. It is interesting that the crosses on the German graves were made of wood, whereas those of the Allies were of masonry.

There is a place called Duomont, not far from Verdun. A vast cemetery there has 180,000 unknown. A building called an ossarium dominates the cemetery. It has a tower-shaped like an artillery shell and the only light admitted into the building comes through blood-red glass bricks.

Inside, there are lines of granite crypts with unknown soldiers laid therein. Many of the stones in the archways inside the building have names on them, sposnored by friends and relatives of those unknown soldiers who never came home. From the exterior of the building, you can look down through thick glass windows into the basement storage rooms. One room may have all thighbones stacked like cordwood, another room may be filled with skulls, and many more filled with other bones gleaned from WW I battlefields. This is a very sobering monument to behold.

Each spring, when I was in France, I would read in the local newspaper about some farmer and his horse being blown up when his plow struck unexploded ordnance in his fields. You could drive to the countryside in the spring and see rusty metal in piles along side the road that farmers had unearthed while plowing and had set aside for disposal by the government.

I'd heard that there was an historic site near the base. It was the remains of a large German cannon and emplacement that shot shells into Paris 75 miles away in WW I. There was a railroad spur that led to it, easily recognized from the air. So, one day I drove out on the abandoned railroad embankment and walked in to take a look. There was a large concrete pad called a trunion, and a blockhouse which was probably used to store shells. Another of these guns placed elsewhere was called Big Bertha. The barrels were so long on these guns that they had to have a truss affixed on top of the barrel to hold it straight.

The city of Laon was built on a butte on which there was a cathedral. Laon was the capital of France in the days of Charlemagne. Reflecting the political instability of the Middle Ages, a tunnel was built from the city to some distance northward as an escape route in case of attack. This tunnel was large enough to ride a horse through. There was an officer and his son on the base who were spelunkers. They examined a portion of this tunnel, and found it hazardous because parts of it were caved in. They also examined a WW I German bunker that had been filled with earth. Digging near the top of the fill, they came upon a large room filled with guns and ammunition left over from WW I. They took nothing because of the danger involved, covered their tracks and abandoned it.

I trust this picture of my surroundings where I was based might add to the flavor of flight in France during the sixties.

In order to give an idea what my duties were like (outside of flying) on the base in France, a sample from March 1962 to March 1963 follows:

In the Air Force, a pilot was alternately assigned to a cockpit job and then to a desk job. My tour in France was a desk job. My primary duties as General Military Training Officer, which was in the Education and Training Career Field, was mandated by a Directed Duty Assignment after achieving a Master's Degree at the University of Washington at Air Force expense. I supervised the General Military Training Section and the following training programs on the base: newcomer's orientation, moral leadership, military justice, Mutual Defense Assistance Pact (MDAP), chemical, biological and radiological orientation, small arms range activities and firing, code of conduct, Commander's Call, security, parades and ceremonies and physical training.

Additional duties performed: flying (to include both preflight and post fight tasks); graduating from the Bomb Commander's School in the 81st Tactical Fighter Wing, Bentwaters and Woodbridge Bases, England; organized and taught the Bomb Commander's Course at the 66th Tactical Reconnaissance Wing; conducted on-the-job training of non-commissioned officers in the Field Training Detachment to take over this teaching; handled Project Third Lieutenant (USAF Academy cadets on base for three weeks; a letter of appreciation from General Hatch, endorsed by Colonel Muldoon was given for the successful project); organized a Combat Support Group sponsored dance at the club, and made 100 posters to advertise this. I handled one Iranian, five Germans, three Italians and five Turks in MDAP projects; I rewrote the Disaster Control Plan and rewrote the reporting section of the Razor's Edge plan for Wing Operations; organized and published standardized exposure control procedures for the base; conducted disaster control exercises, personally constructed end-lit Plexiglas display boards, map boards and made plans for the renovation of the Base Command Post. I performed as Top Secret Control Officer for the Combat Support Group, handled the classified account for the Command Post, made signs for Command Post positions and an organizational and functional chart for the Command Post, developed a card file for alert actions for Command Post personnel, trained Command Post personnel in disaster control procedures, added improved communications equipment to the Command Post and in the Base Commander's staff car, and wrote a physical conditioning regulation.

I organized and conducted two random sample tests of progress toward 5BX and XBX goals (this was not a training function but one of personnel quality control). I wrote a plan for base spring cleanup, handled advertising for the base Red Cross drive making 120 silk-screened posters, organized and conducted a Wing review including writing a parade order and conducting two dry-runs for the review, marked the parade ground and had a reviewing stand built. I cleaned out the Command Post safe and destroyed over 600 aged documents, taught exposure control procedures to unit disaster control officers and non-commissioned officers, wrote a handbook called *Nuclear Primer for Dependents,* established an alternate Command Post in the firehouse, wrote an article for the base newspaper called "Alert Procedures for Families," devised and administered an alert questionnaire, wrote an article for the base newspaper called, "Playing the Game," and built a demonstration fallout shelter with discarded F-101 engine shipping containers and earth. I computed residual numbers for base masonry buildings, devised a form for these calculations, lectured to ninth and tenth grade children in the dependent's school on disaster control, and organized an effective writing course.

You might agree that I really had a 'bucket of worms' here. My duties for the two previous years, 1960-62 were similar.

Forgive me if the following has little to do with being airborne, but I think these paragraphs show some aspects of military life in foreign surroundings that color and supplement what the Air Force offers outside of being in a cockpit.

Part of military life was 30 days' leave each year. In the States, I spent my leave time in the northwest where I was raised. In Europe, during the sixties, leave time was spent visiting other countries. One winter we traveled to Bavaria and took in some skiing and ice-skating and went on to Austria to Innsbruck and Salzburg. The scenery was much like it is at home. The buildings were beautiful and the people were friendly and outgoing.

Switzerland has no standing army, instead, eligible males have their equipment at home and on one Sunday a month uniforms are everywhere. Military bands are playing in the towns and rifles are at hand. Military pilots in Switzerland are also the pilots of Swissair, the country's commercial airline. They rotate from one organization to the other. The country is beautiful: high mountains, tunnels, lakes, picturesque houses and lots of flowers.

Of course, we had to visit Rome and Florence, homes of some of the greatest artworks ever produced. We took in Michelangelo's Pieta, the Sistine chapel ceiling, the huge statue of Moses, and of course the architecture of the Vatican. We also saw Michelangelo's statue of David, which was in the Ufizzi gallery in Florence. We spent some time on the beaches near Pisa and in the foothills of Tuscany. On one weekend, with my Base Commander, I flew to an Italian air base near Venice, took a train from the base into Venice and enjoyed the sights. I especially enjoyed listening to a symphony orchestra on Sunday in the Piazza Di San Marco in Venice. We saw nothing of the Italian boot south of Rome.

As far back as 1943, my mother developed a habit of visiting her errant sons in the military. During the war, she went to Sikeston, Missouri, to visit my brother Bob in flight training. From there, she visited relatives in eastern Ohio; next, she came to Slippery Rock, Pennsylvania, where I was. While I was in flight training in Texas in 1951-2, she came there too. So, when I was in France, I invited her to come and visit us, offering to pay half her expenses as an incentive. She crossed the country in a bus, visited relatives in Ohio, continued by bus to New York and boarded the Dutch passenger liner, "Statendam." We met her in Le Havre and she spent some weeks with us. While she was with us, we made a trip to the Riviera and did some camping. By this time, my kids had learned French so well that they almost used this exclusively among themselves. It became a problem while traveling with Grandma in the Volkswagen because she felt left out, not understanding what the kids were saying. So, I would get them aside and explain this problem to them and they would use English. However, it wasn't long before they lapsed back into French.

I had a large army surplus tent, octagonal in floor plan, and we used this to camp in down on the Riviera. One campground was so crowded that there was little space left. In fact, some people came in during the night and pitched a tent next to ours and when we went to break camp in the morning and take the tent down, one of my tent stakes and the associated rope were inside their small tent.

Mom got seasick on the way over to France. We took her back down to Le Havre to return to the States, hoping she wouldn't get seasick again, but I believe she did, although there's no mention of it in the journal she kept which I still have.

We spent some time on the Spanish Mediterranean coast and stayed in a hotel near the beach. It was here that Chris 'fell in love' with a Spanish waiter. He had her rapt attention, preparing her dessert at the supper table. He took an orange on a fork and with a knife, peeled the orange with one long spiral peeling, then separated the sections with fork and knife. Next, he arranged the pieces in a design on her plate and sprinkled them with powdered sugar. Chris cherishes this memory today, some 46 years later.

An enjoyable experience in Spain was the Flamenco music, which I still like. Our visit to Madrid coincided with Easter. We took in the Spanish "Super Bowl." Easter Sunday produced the super bowl of bullfights in Madrid. We left the kids at the hotel and took in the spectacle. We had less expensive seats; therefore, we sat in the sun. A number of bullfights took place including one where the bull refused to fight. The bull came into the arena, walked around sniffing at the ground and when provoked, would trot off and ignore his antagonists. Finally, it was realized that there would be no fight. A gate was opened and about a half dozen floppy cows were admitted with bells jangling around their necks. These cows were trained to come in, surround the bull and herd him out of the arena. I imagine this was a disgrace for the rancher who raised this 'fierce' animal. It was an interesting experience, but I don't think I'd ever go to see another bull fight.

In connection with Easter Sunday in Madrid, there was a religious procession (not a parade). Chris and I went to watch. It began late, about midnight. There were an estimated 400,000 people in the main square and its environs. I had never seen so many people in one place before. There were horse drawn carriages transporting glass cases removed from churches, which held the remains of saints and relics. The carriages had iron-shod wheels, and a distinctive sound was made by their slow-speed rumbling on the cobblestones. There were horsemen wearing medieval armor and weapons. There were individuals with chains shackled to their legs, dragging heavy crosses over their shoulders; these chains made unforgettable sounds being dragged over the cobblestones. Many persons were dressed like Ku Klux Klansmen in white robes with pointed hoods and peepholes. No bands were playing; in fact, there was hardly any noise at all outside of the horses' hooves, chains, and iron-shod wheels. It was eerily quite silent. At one time, not far from us, the procession stopped because a woman in the crowd began singing in a beautiful voice. When she finished, there was no applause, and the procession ensued. Most of this time I had Chris on my shoulders so she could see over the crowd.

On one of our trips to the Normandy coast, we took along one of the teenage girls from the family that lived across the street. She acted as a babysitter. On another occasion, we took her sister with us to Holland. We went to Amsterdam to take in the Rijks museum in which were many famous Flemish and Dutch paintings. The kids tended to become bored. In an attempt to keep up interest, I would peek into the next gallery ahead of the kids and find something they might like. Then, before entering the next gallery, I would try to excite them about that which they were about to see. In the last gallery, at the far end, was a huge painting by Rembrandt called *The Cloth Merchants' Guild.* Now, I had a cigar box in which I used to keep odds and ends, nuts and bolts and other things that were too good to throw away but had no immediate use. On the inside of the box's lid was a reproduction of *The Cloth Merchants' Guild,* the trademark of Dutch Masters Cigar Company. So, I gave my pep talk to the kids about this famous painting they were about to witness. Coming through the doorway, Chris, then seven years of age, took one look and said, "That's nothing. I've seen that a lot of times on a cigar box."

In Breda, Holland, for an evening out, we left the kids with the sitter in our hotel. We had two rooms in the hotel. Mark and Chris were in one room and the sitter in the other. Mark was asleep and Chris, longing for company, went next door to be with the sitter. When Mark awoke he found himself alone and tried to open the door. Instead, he locked it (he was four years old). Frustrated and alone, he put up a fuss. We had the only key with us. When we returned and entered the room, Mark was missing, the window was open and a ladder was at the window. This was quite a shock. The hotel staff had reacted to the fuss and had come up a ladder, entered the room and had taken Mark next door to be with his sister and the sitter.

The house we lived in at Chauny was one of two that had running water on our street; the rest of the residents drew their water from a hydrant in the street. Across the street were open fields where people had individual gardens. In the springtime, there would be many folks spading their plots to produce vegetables and flowers. Many of the gardeners wore wooden shoes that could be bought at a hardware store in town. The reason for this was that they would stand the mud and moisture better than leather shoes. Those that could afford it would wear rubber boots. Occasionally, leaving the house in the morning, I would find flowers or vegetables on the doorstep, or perhaps on the windowsill, unsolicited gifts from my neighbors.

Across the street, there was a family of six. Although not adopted in the legal sense, we became great friends with these folks. Bruno, the man of the house, worked on the other side of town in a wire factory; his particular job was making dies through which wire was drawn to make the diameters needed. These neighbors had bathing facilities in their house, but used them rarely. On Saturdays they would go to the factory and use the showers that were available there. They had no car, so Bruno commuted to his job on a motorized bicycle. I believe his wages were about $20 a week. He would come home for lunch and return about two hours later after a little nap or a bit of work in the garden. The morning meal, or *petit déjeuner*, consisted of coffee and fresh bread. French bakeries made bread twice a day, once in the morning about 4 o'clock, and about the same time in the afternoon. As I understand it, the ingredients and procedures are regulated, as are the quality, size and prices. Sometimes the coffee is served in cups; however, the cups tend to be larger than we're used to. Sometimes coffee is served in bowls with milk added (*café au lait*). Children, as well as adults, have this dish, and at around noon the large meal of the day is eaten. Something light, like soup, is eaten around eight in the evening. In the afternoons, around 4 o'clock, you might see most of the children outdoors, looking like they're playing harmonicas. However, what they're doing is having a snack or *gouté* consisting of a piece of bread sliced lengthwise made into a sandwich that contained cheese, *paté* or thin wafers of chocolate.

Whenever the neighbors were celebrating, they did so by feasting.

For example, a child's first communion would be cause for celebration. The meal might start at one or so in the afternoon and one might get up from the table around 6 or 8 o'clock PM. Men would take a stroll to the nearest *café* and have a libation. The women cleared the table, did the dishes and prepared to serve the same courses in the same sequence again, using the leftovers. There were times when the feast wasn't over until one or two in the morning. When we were invited to these affairs, being the male member of the guest family, I was always served each course first. There were some unfamiliar foods sometimes; however, it was not polite to pass them up. It was common courtesy for dinner guests to bring flowers to the hosts. However, I substituted wine and champagne, and my French hosts seemed happy with that. In a French household, eating is done with both hands on the table. If there was any misbehavior at the table, Bruno had within his reach, hanging on a nail behind his seat, an instrument that was sold in hardware stores to train dogs. It was called a *martinet*. It looked like a miniature Cat O'Nine Tails with a wooden handle and many rawhide strips attached to one end. It immediately commanded respect when taken from the nail and slung over Bruno's shoulder, ready for use.

My neighbors raised vegetables, especially potatoes. Besides a large garden in the backyard, Bruno had some property nearby down the road dedicated to potatoes. Many of these potatoes were used to feed pigs, which they would either sell or butcher. The potatoes had to be cooked for feeding the pigs, and I'm not quite sure why. Often the cookstove would be active in the evenings boiling potatoes. My neighbors also raised rabbits for their own consumption. One time when the neighbor boy was going down the street to gather straw for the rabbits, he asked Mark if he'd like to go with him to get some *paille*, (pronounced 'pie'). Mark mistook this French word for the English word 'pie' and was eager to go along. He was somewhat chagrined when he found out that he was not going to have any pie.

Catholicism is the state religion in France; however, it was not strictly practiced where I was. People only attended church when there was some ceremony involving the family, for example, attending a wedding or a first communion. Incidentally, one weds twice in France (to the same person): once in the church and once in the city hall.

Elections are held on Sundays. Our neighbors would make a holiday out of an election. They would dress up and walk solemnly as a family unit to the polling place. After casting ballots, the entire family would retire to a *café* and have a libation. I believe part of this was to see and be seen.

I found the people in northern France much more class conscious than those of other parts of France. Perhaps because in northern France, the farms are very large, mostly wheat and sugar beets. Thus, there was a tendency to become 'haves' and 'have-nots'. This contrasts with other parts of France were farms are smaller and more individually owned. This would tend to make people more equal.

There was a *café* (bar) at the end of our street. I was having a beer there on my way home from work. I was in uniform. There were a number of mill workers there who seemed curious, and they asked me if I was from the base. Then they asked me what I did at the base. I told them I was a pilot. Next, I was asked if the insignia I had meant that I was 'grade' (that is, graded, other than a common soldier). I told them that I was a captain. They reacted as though I had told them I was the Pope. There was no further attempted conversation except on my part. They seemed to be overwhelmed by the assumed social difference.

I saw some samples of class distinction among my neighbors as well. There was a Frenchman who lived nearby who served as an interpreter in the housing office on the base. He rode to work with me and although he had a car, he only used it about once a week on his days off. He had been riding the train back and forth to the base to save money, and riding with me helped him save more. I was talking to him in front of the house on the street one time, and an old man came by on a bicycle, stopped and waved an envelope at me. The interpreter took the letter, glanced at it and gave it back, dismissing the bicyclist with a wave of his hand. Later one day, I was riding my bike out our road and I recognized this elderly man and he waved to me to come into his yard, asked me in, and served me some powerful plum brandy. He produced his letter, which was from his son in New York. All he wanted to do was identify a bit with an American. The interpreter wore a necktie and white shirt on the job and considered himself several rungs higher on the social ladder than this elderly man. I didn't like what had happened on the street; however, one should be cautious about ridiculing cultural differences, especially as a military foreigner.

On another occasion, with the same interpreter, we stopped in a *cafe* in downtown Chauny to have a beer on the way home. There were three gentlemen sitting at another table and they obviously recognized my uniform and waved us over to have a drink with them.

I had difficulty understanding them because my French was rather primitive and my translator friend would hardly open his mouth to help out. After we left there, he pointed out that we were associating with some pretty high company. I asked him how so. He said one of them was the druggist in the town, and the other two were merchants as well. It seemed that my translator was so intimidated by these higher-ranking people that he couldn't get his mouth open.

Meeting a Frenchman (or woman) for the first time, it doesn't take long for them to ask you what you think about the political situation. These things are discussed more openly and more often than they are at home. I found that the best response when asked what I thought about the political situation was to respond with, "*Pas grand chose*," meaning, "Not much." I listened, but didn't participate much in political discussions.

One time a Frenchman asked me if France wasn't more free and democratic than the United States. I said I didn't think so and he asked me why. Well, there is a tax in France called 'the right to occupy quarters.' I was obliged to pay this as part of my rent. I brought this up to my interlocutor saying that if one paid taxes one should be allowed to vote. Then I told him I paid this tax, but was not allowed to vote. He agreed that this was not just. I also told him that I could circulate freely in my country as I pleased. However, in France, when you move into a town you're required to go to the town hall and register. If you move, or leave as I eventually did, you must go to the town hall and sign out. I found evidence of this in Germany as well. The third item I offered was that at home, I could possess and carry a firearm almost anywhere I pleased, and in France, you're not allowed to own a pistol nor a high-powered rifle. Shotguns and .22 caliber rifles are okay. I can see the ban on high-powered rifles because even when one would hunt in a wooded area, the patches of wood are so small and the towns are so close together, it would be hazardous to community health. Shotguns are allowed because of their short range. I think these three things convinced my questioner that we're more free and democratic.

Not long after my family arrived in France, I came home one day and Chris told me that she had found a 'head bone' in one of the concrete rabbit hutches in the backyard. She showed it to me; it was a human skull, complete with a detached jawbone. I acted nonchalantly, not wanting to frighten Chris. I put it aside and was going to ask the landlord about it the next time I went to pay the rent. Being facetious, I asked him if it were his first wife. He said his son went to school in Paris to become a fireman and such an object was required as a training aid in their first aid lessons. Apparently, skulls are plentiful in old countries such as France. When I related this jest to the neighbors, they told me that he was seen chasing his wife across the garden plots once with a meat cleaver in his hand. I took this skull and gave it to the school on the base with the permission of the landlord.

Shortly after the family arrived, the kids' mother wanted to go downtown and have her hair washed and set. So, I mustered my best college French and made up exactly what I was going to say when at the hairdressers. Upon arrival there, I asked first of all if anyone spoke English. One woman did, thus I was relieved of my feeble French approach. That evening, the interpreter was at the house and asked how my French was coming along. I told him of my unused composition at the hairdressers. He said he wanted to hear it so I recited what I had prepared. He about split with laughter. Unknown to me, there are two words for hair in French. One is *cheveu*, the hair on the head; the other is *poil*, body hair. I was about to ask that madam have her body hair washed and set! Another language boo-boo happened when I drove the neighbor girl across town to the dentist. That evening, her father, Bruno, thanked me for the favor and I mentioned taking her to the dentist was nothing. At that point, Therese, Bruno's wife gasped and corrected me, saying one takes a cow to a bull but you don't take my daughter to the dentist, you take her to the dentist's place, *chez le dentiste*. Another gaff was at the dinner table. I had been reading in French about a young man in Chicago after WW I. His name was Studs Lonigan. I suspected there was some slang in the story, but had no idea of the translation. One such passage used the phrase *La Ferme*, which literally means 'the farm'. From the context, I thought it an innocuous term used when someone interrupted your conversation. So we were at the dinner table and I was interrupted and said, "*La ferme*." Now, *fermer* is a French verb meaning to close; for example, *fermez la porte* means close the door. What I said really meant, "Shut your damn mouth." Nobody ever got on my case for making language gaffs; quite the opposite, they appreciated the effort to learn the language. It's not easy.

I was sent on TDY to England for a couple of weeks. I drove the Volkswagen and took a ferry across the channel. Now, the British drive on the wrong side of the road, that is, on the left side as they do in some other commonwealth countries as well as Japan. Leaving the ferry, I was very conscientious of this fact while driving on a freeway.

However, after entering London I came to a stoplight; my next turn was to the left, and I automatically swung over to the right side of the street. Horns blaring and lights flashing let me know of my mistake.

I made several trips to Germany by airplane as well as by automobile to our headquarters, located just across the German border at Ramstein Air Force Base. Several trips were made on business. We also had a base at Wiesbaden (White Springs.) It had been a popular place for people to go and bathe in the mineral waters. In Germany, there is a pre-Lenten celebration called *Fasching*. *Fasching* season begins at eleven seconds after eleven minutes after 11 o'clock PM on the eleventh day of the eleventh month. Children can be seen in the streets with lanterns and fireworks at this time. Subsequent to this date, celebrations take place until Lent. The celebrations grow in size and participation as Lent approaches. Dancing in the streets, singing in *gasthauses* and masked balls marks them. The celebrations are more predominant in the Catholic sections of Germany. During this season, we were having a meal in a restaurant in downtown Wiesbaden. Two young men at an adjacent table, who had finished eating and were drinking some wine, sent some wine to our table and then left. However, they were waiting for us outside the door. They took us by the arms and walked toward the center of town where music was blaring from a music store. As we arrived there, people had begun dancing on the sidewalks and in the street. Within about twenty minutes, the intersection was crowded with dancers and police had blocked off traffic to assist the celebrators.

In a *gasthaus* (tavern), we were seated, as others were, around the periphery of a room, having a beer. A band came in and when the music struck up, patrons locked arms with us, singing and rocking to and fro to the music's tempo. All this was spontaneous.

I attended one of the masked balls as an observer. There were costumes that must have taken all year to prepare. Those of the Wild West, that is, cowboys and Indians, were amusing because they didn't look like our concept of the Wild West denizens. The ball I attended was in the *Kurhaus*, the main structure of the mineral water baths in Wiesbaden. The building was very large, big enough to have three or four bands going in different corners at the same time. It was quite a spectacle.

One time during *Fasching* a man dressed in a polar bear suit captured us. You could see his eyes through the grinning mouth. After the bear's companion took our picture with the 'bear,' they went away, doing the same thing with others.

Nearby was the city of Heidelburg, on the Neckar River. It was here that Sigmund Romberg wrote his operetta, *The Student Prince*. I visited the 'The Red Ox,' the *gasthaus* where he had hung out. Again, it was here that I witnessed more spontaneous singing by the patrons.

An interesting thing happened when motoring near Stuttgart. I had turned off the main highway looking for a suitable spot to empty my bladder when I came upon a trash dump. Lying among the detritus were two blue enameled French street signs. One said, "Avenue Georges Clemenceau," the other was named after a French admiral whose name I don't remember. Now, Clemenceau was the architect of the severe Versailles Treaty laid on the Germans after WW I. Why were these signs there? A plausible answer is that a vindictive German soldier took them home in WW II as souvenirs, then seeing Germany losing WW II, decided that these signs weren't such good souvenirs to have in his possession and dumped them. I still have the Clemenceau sign as my souvenir.

I flew to Morocco one time but never got off the base. While filing my flight plan to return to Madrid, I looked out the window of base operations and saw an Arab going through the parking lot, trying all the car doors. I pointed this out to the clerk in charge, and he said that was normal: if you left your door unlocked, it was an invitation to enter.

While talking about North Africa, one my fellow pilots with whom I traveled to our bases in Europe on temporary duty in 1957 had been previously stationed in Germany. For lack of real estate, there was no practice gunnery range in Europe. Consequently, fighter pilots would go to North Africa where there was ample space. We had gunnery ranges in Libya at that time. My friend had become acquainted with the Arabs that maintained the ground targets on the gunnery range, so they invited him out to their tents for supper one time. Being the guest, he was served the dishes first. My friend was left-handed. After he had helped himself to two or three dishes, the dishes disappeared. Then one of his hosts took him aside and said that water was very scarce in the desert and that they only washed one hand; he was using the wrong hand to eat with.

I had contacts with military people from several other countries. The United States had a pact with certain European countries called the Mutual Defense Assistance Pact. This provided training that was needed by European members of the pact. The idea was to provide training in Europe instead of having people come to the States, which would be more costly. Each year on every American base in Europe, an inventory would be made of possible training facilities available on their individual bases. Then, the European countries could look at this inventory, and if some of the facilities matched training that they needed, it would be arranged for them to visit these facilities. So, one of the additional jobs I had in France was to meet and greet these people, take them to the French community to arrange for postal services (since they were not allowed to use our system on base) and generally see that they were taken care of. As each batch came to our base, I would invite them to my house for dinner and a *soirée*. At these events I would also invite my French neighbors that lived across the street.

Twice a year, in the fall and spring, I would have groups of young German officers who had just graduated from engineering schools. I didn't know what the reaction of my French neighbors would be to these young German officers, having been ruled by the Germans in WW II and been deadly enemies in WW I. However, the generation gap provided a cushion against any overt hostile feelings.

The Italians turned down my invitation. However, I had two Dutch officers to dinner at the house one time. One of these was very outgoing, the other rather reserved. We entertained the outgoing officer and his wife, both of whom had been in the underground during WW II in Holland. On a subsequent visit to Holland, we visited them in their home at Breda. Incidentally, this officer, Peter Kappelhof, had a famous cousin whose name was Doris Kappelhof, otherwise known as Doris Day. She had gone to school in England and subsequently ended up in American movies. Peter had two daughters, one of which looked very much like Doris Day.

While on a visit to Breda, Peter took me to the base where he worked as an aircraft maintenance officer. He showed me around and we ended up in his officers' club for a beer. While at the bar, he pointed out the chandelier and said that it had cost him a lot of money. Curious, I asked how. He explained that at a party one night, they were taking turns standing on the bar, and then jumping to catch the swinging chandelier. Then, hanging by the knees, they would drink a bottle of beer. He said it was unfortunate that the chandelier fell from the ceiling while he was enjoying his beer. He was responsible for the repair of the chandelier.

One winter I had four Turks on the base. They were photo

interpreters and were studying how their counterparts did their work on our base. There were two men and two women, all lieutenants in the Turkish Air force. One of the women was married to a lieutenant in the Turkish Air force, but he was not with the group. She was quite pregnant, close to eight months along, when she slipped on some ice on the base and fell. Her child was born prematurely at the base hospital. This posed a question: was the child Turkish, French or American? Our French liaison officer on the base did not know, so he queried his superiors in Paris and found out that the child had dual citizenship: both French and Turkish, and at age 21 could make it its own decision.

This story of dual citizenship reminds me of an incident that took place at my following assignment after leaving France. This took place at Montana State College, in Bozeman. It was June, the time of graduation and commissioning. A few days prior to commissioning, a student came into my office quite pale and said he had a problem. He had a letter from the Chilean government asking him why he had not reported for the draft. His parents were missionaries in Chile and he had been born there. We didn't have the solution to his plight, so we queried the State Department. Since he was born of Americans in Chile, he too had dual citizenship, American and Chilean, and since he was 21, he could make a decision. He was quite relieved to know that he had a choice in the matter. Foreigners cannot be officers in the United States military; however, non-citizens can be enlisted.

During my tour on the base in France, there was a program command-wide to cut down on the number of automobile accidents. Some of the hazards that drivers were not used to in Europe were narrow streets, cobblestone paving and trees that bordered the highways. There were an inordinate number of Volkswagen accidents that were attributed to the rear engine installation. On a wet surface, in a tight turn, there was a tendency to jackknife the car, spinning out. To make personnel aware of the grisly results of these accidents, and as a reminder to take it easy, wrecked vehicles were parked just inside the main gate in plain view. Another effort that came down from our headquarters mandated that everyone view a film. I attended the first showing. Looking around at the audience, I found many either asleep or not looking at the screen because it showed the aftermath of many accidents, including corpses and mangled bodies. Before the second showing, I had a photographer come, and in the middle of the film step out from behind the curtain and take a flash picture of the audience.

I forwarded a copy of this photo to headquarters as evidence that the grisly film wasn't doing what it was intended to do. People were not looking at it.

The Base Commander had an MG sports car that he managed to roll. He escaped unhurt, had a wrecker come from the base, pick the car up, put aboard a C-47, and flown off to England for repair, thus removing the evidence of the accident scene. The same commander had a dirt bike and used to ride it inside the BOQ (Bachelor Officers' Quarters), up and down the stairs and through the halls. One night when he was unconscious (from drinking) some pranksters took his clothes off and painted the bottom of his feet and his buttocks with purple paint. Then they elevated him upside down in the club by standing on the billiard table and put his footprints and butt print on the ceiling. That same commander was death on two things: one was long grass. It had to be mowed constantly and kept tidy. The second thing was that he didn't tolerate dirty hats. He would come into the officers' club and examine the hats in the cloakroom. If he found a dirty garrison cap (the round one with the visor), he would puncture the top with scissors; if the hat was a dirty overseas cap, (the flat one) he would cut it in two.

This commander's successor was scheduled to go on leave to Italy with his family. Before he left, the base was put on alert, which usually was an exercise of combat readiness. He checked into the command post and then went on leave. When he returned, he had no job. He had an empty desk, but no job. He spent a couple of months going around the base looking through files, trying to find evidence that he had been doing his job and doing it well. He came into my office and did this; however, he had been fired and left the base. I don't know what happened to him.

We had a physical training program called the 5BX. This acronym stood for five basic exercises. These were to be done on one's own, and tests were scheduled for the future. One had to do some warm up exercises, pushups, sit ups, a back arching exercise and run a mile under eight minutes. This was a brand new program, and since it fell in the training category, it was handed to me. After a week or so at the commander's call (a monthly meeting of the officers), the Wing Commander brought the subject up. He said he was doing his exercises and it was killing him. He gave a warning that at the next meeting he would choose an officer at random and have him do his pushups and sit-ups on a table. He did this, choosing the

Communications Officer, who appeared to be overweight and a bit unsightly in uniform. The Communications Officer failed miserably and was greatly embarrassed. The back exercise was later eliminated because it tended to cause some back problems.

Another training item I oversaw was small arms qualification. The squadron units on the base had responsibility to train and record the scores of its officers and men. The range was scheduled and supervised by a Technical Sergeant who worked for me. There was one officer, our meteorologist, who just couldn't hit the target. We fired with .38 caliber pistols. This weather officer was of slight build and would flinch or look away when he fired. I challenged him by betting I would beat him by shooting a bow and arrow. I did this, but it was no incentive to him. The Air Police Squadron on the base had their own training program. They had some people who had difficulty shooting also. However, someone had developed a program whereby the cartridges would be opened, most of the powder removed and the projectile put back in. These were fired and made only a fraction of the noise and recoil of a regular cartridge. When the shooter mastered the depleted rounds and was scoring on the target, the cartridges would be gradually increased in power until the shooter was firing like everybody else. We sent our problem officer down to the Air Police Squadron to go through their program. The enlisted troops on the base didn't fire pistols; they fired .30 caliber carbines.

One day I received a letter from a Congressman. It was from the Honorable Mike Mansfield of Montana, Speaker of the House. The letter was an inquiry into why I was discriminating against one of his constituents. The man concerned was a photographer in the Base Photo Lab.

The runways were being re-paved on our base, so the mission aircraft had been moved to Toul Air Base. One additional photographer was needed to accompany the aircraft, so the Headquarters Squadron Commander and I had to choose someone to go to Toul. This was just before Christmas, so we decided to send a man who had no family at the base; all the rest of the photographers did. This man didn't like the idea so he complained to his Congressman, saying that he was being discriminated against. When you get a letter from a Congressman there is a regulation in the Air Force requiring that the response be immediate. The Headquarters Squadron Commander and I generated a letter, admitting that we had discriminated against him for cause, and we pointed out why. The man's chief complaint was that working in an air-conditioned trailer at Toul would aggravate his arthritic legs. I had him come to my office for an interview after receiving the letter. He had come from the Base Photo Lab on his bicycle in the rain and was soaked up to the knees. We got the letter off to the Speaker of the House and never heard any more about it. This man heard more about it, however. There is an Air Force Regulation that requires a copy of correspondence to a Congressman or Senator to be provided to the Commander so that an immediate response can be made. This man violated this regulation. I don't know if this infraction was pursued or not.

On an air base, there is a rated (meaning pilot) officer on duty during off duty hours. He is in charge of the aerodrome and is called the AO, or Airdrome Officer. This duty is rotated among the pilots on a roster. He meets and greets the crew of incoming aircraft, arranges for transportation and quarters and, if needed, helps the aircrew in any other way he can.

One time when I was AO, we had an inspector coming from San Bernardino, the headquarters of the Air Force Safety Office. I was on the ramp with a vehicle awaiting the aircraft, and so were the Wing Commander, Base Commander, Director of Operations and the three Squadron Commanders. The four-engine aircraft shut down, a door opened and the crew chief arranged a ladder for dismounting. A colonel appeared in the doorway, looked out, looked around, spotted me, and in a loud voice said, "Brewer, what in the hell is a fighter pilot like you doing in a Recce (Reconnaissance) outfit?" I then recognized him as Colonel Hagerstrom, who had been in 5th Air Force Headquarters in Korea and who came to my squadron to fly F-86 combat missions with us. He had become an ace in the Korean campaign. When he came down the ladder, he bypassed all the brass standing there to receive him and walked directly to me, shook my hand and carried on an animated conversation. I could see the brass breaking ranks and wandering toward us. Eventually, he acknowledged them and left to go to his quarters. It was common for the AO to eat the evening meal at the club so that's where I was when the inspector came in. He walked right by the Wing Commander who was courteously waiting by the bar for him. The inspector sat down with me and we ate supper together and talked of old times. The Wing Commander quietly left.

There is a decoration in the Air Force called the Air Force Commendation Medal. It is given for a particular performance of duty outside of combat, or for a long sustained performance of duty.

I was awarded my second one of these when I retired from the Air Force for the years I had put in. When I left France and arrived in Montana, I learned that I had been awarded my first one of these for my three-year performance of duty in France.

In March 1963, my tour in France was up. What was next? Each year around one's birthday one was called into the Personnel Office to make sure records were correct and up to date. In the process, one is allowed to make a 'statement of preference.' The normal tour of duty at a base was about four years, three years if overseas. In order to determine where one's next base was to be, one filled out this 'statement of preference.' You could specify which section of the United States you would prefer, the command level at which you would like to serve, the type of job you would like, and the foreign country of choice. If the needs of the service coincided with your choices, there was a good chance your druthers would be honored. Being from the northwest, I naturally chose that area. There was a requirement for all officers returning from overseas to apply for ROTC duty. One was allowed to say if one volunteered or not. My next station was to be in Bozeman, Montana, as a professor of Aerospace Studies at Montana State College. I never considered Montana to be in the northwest, but I guess it is.

A sad goodbye was said to my French friends. My boss had me and my family driven to Paris in his staff car to fly home.

Just before boarding the airplane, I was presented with a set of orders appointing me as a courier. There was also a sergeant who was appointed to assist me. He was armed with a pistol. I had a bag of documents to deliver upon arrival in Washington, D.C. The sergeant and I had to witness this bag being locked in the baggage compartment of the airplane. We landed in Scotland to refuel and then continued on to Labrador. We were delayed for some mechanical reason at Labrador. While on the ground, the sergeant and I had to stand guard outside the locked baggage compartment of the airplane. It was bitterly cold, so we rotated the duty, and the pistol, every twenty minutes. After a couple of hours we were told that we were going to stay overnight until the aircraft was repaired. So, we had a problem with the documents. What to do with them? I finally settled on having the Air Police lock them up in one of their cells, with the key in my possession. We continued on to Washington, D.C. the next day, and I turned the bag over to the proper authority.

Next, we boarded an aircraft bound for Portland, Oregon. This was a jet, the first jet transport I had ever been in. My brother in law had prepared my stored automobile, a 1948 Lincoln Continental, so it was ready to go when we arrived. Next, we headed for Seattle. I was on leave; however, Chris had to get back into school right away since this was the month of April. So we headed for Montana.

Chapter Ten

Professor of Aerospace Studies

During the Civil War, there was a dearth of young officers; leadership was lacking. So, after the war, Congress passed a bill called The Morill Act. This legislation has been covered earlier in this writing.

The bulk of the military officers in the United States come from ROTC. A minority comes from the military academies such as West Point, Annapolis and the Air Force Academy. This is a good system because leadership is drawn from all parts of the country and from many disciplines. For example, a music major as well as an engineering major may participate in this program. Many countries, for example, France, has one institution (St. Cyr) that produces officers, thus they tend to become of one mind, not having the diversity we enjoy.

When I went to the University of Washington in the fall of 1942, the state required that I take ROTC. My assignment was in the Army Coast Artillery Corps. I took the subject for one quarter before entering the Army. After the war when I reentered the University, I was exempt from ROTC because of my wartime experience.

Montana State College (now Montana State University), is located in the Bridger Mountains, not far from Three Forks, the headwaters of the Missouri River. Lewis and Clark passed by there in the early eighteen hundreds. The population of Bozeman was about 15,000, about the same size as my home in France, Chauny.

The primary problem on arriving in Bozeman was to locate housing. An officer with whom I would work had bought a house from a particular builder and was happy with it and recommended that I contact this builder who was just finishing up a new house. Though some things were not finished (the concrete porches had not been poured yet, nor was the house painted or any landscaping been done), I agreed to do the painting and landscaping myself for a discount. Having found a place, I could then contact the Air Force to have my household goods shipped to me.

One of the things that had to be done right away was checking into my unit. Of course, I had to get my daughter enrolled in the public school, and I had to travel to Malmstrom Air Force Base at Great Falls, 210 miles from Bozeman. This was the nearest Air Force Base and it was there that I would accomplish my flying duties. When I checked in at the base, my medical records were perused and I was told that I should not be flying. This was puzzling. Although I had had some sinus trouble, I was never designated DNIF (Duty Not Involving Flying). The flight surgeon said the reason I was DNIF was that I had been diagnosed, while in France, of having polyps in my nasal passages and they would have to be removed in order to stay on flying status. The flight surgeon told me that I could have this work done by a civilian surgeon in Bozeman at government expense. The operation was accomplished and wasn't very pleasant. To ward off any infection, I was injected with penicillin. Almost immediately, I had an allergic reaction. Muscles would develop knots. For example, I began to paint the house and after fifteen or twenty minutes, the muscles of my forearms would knot up. I would also get lumps on my scalp and on the soles of my feet. On a trip back to the flight surgeon at Malmstrom, I had this problem put on my military record. While there, the doctor told me they had a substance that would get rid of the rest of the penicillin in my system; it was called penicillinase. He told me that, in rare cases, some were also allergic to this. Therefore, he told me not to leave the base for three or four hours to see if there would be any reaction. After this time had elapsed, I set out for Bozeman in my Volkswagen. About halfway home, I started to get allergic symptoms. This time the symptoms were more severe. It took several months for them to disappear. Needless to say, I have never had a penicillin shot again.

The civilian doctor in Bozeman prescribed radiation treatments for my nose and sinuses. This was to preclude polyps from returning. Much later, I learned that this radiation really wasn't needed and was a hazard to my health. I had been exposed to some radiation before while at Nellis Air Force Base in the fifties as an eyewitness to two nuclear weapons tests on the Nevada desert. Many years later I received a letter from the government which wanted to find out if I had suffered any results from radiation exposure. I was to produce copies of the orders that sent me to the bomb tests to verify that I had been exposed. I did this and reported no maladies associated with exposure. The government deemed that if something were to occur health wise, that would have been within a certain time limit. After this limit the government had no liability, and this is the way it worked out. In the special weapons school at Nellis, from time to time I handled Uranium-238. The bomb material was a different isotope, U-235; however, the metal itself in any form is radioactive. It 'rusts'; that is to say, it develops an oxide on the surface, which can be rubbed off on the hands. We were cautioned not to smoke, eat or drink after handling this material and, after handling it each time, we washed our hands thoroughly. We wore a small device around our necks on our dog tag chains called a dosimeter. This device measured accumulated exposure to radioactivity. Periodically, it was read by machine to see what dose, if any, one had accumulated.

Every instructor in the ROTC system had to attend the Academic Instructors' School before assuming teaching duties. This course was taught at Maxwell Air Force Base in Montgomery, Alabama. So, having settled the family in, I went to Alabama.

While in France, I bought another car, a 1962 Volkswagen Karman Ghia. I shipped this car from Bremerhaven, Germany to New Orleans, Louisiana, knowing I was going to be close by in Alabama to pick it up later. So, on a weekend I went to New Orleans and drove back up to Maxwell. After finishing the school, I drove this car to Bozeman. Now I had three cars: the VW, the Ghia and the old Lincoln.

Since we didn't teach any classes during the summer months, a good deal of free time was available. I spent quite a bit of this time painting the exterior of the house and landscaping the yard. I had also retrieved my unfinished flying machine from my in-laws' basement and moved it to Bozeman. Tinkering with this also took some time. Exploring the fishing streams around the area was good recreation, too.

The Volkswagen was my car of choice for driving to and from Great Falls Malmstrom Air Force Base in the winter. Montana has severe winters. It is not uncommon to be 20 degrees below zero or lower. It was 210 miles from Bozeman to Great Falls. Each winter in the local newspaper you could read about some unfortunate soul freezing to death on a highway. So, when driving this distance in the winter, I took along survival gear: my flying clothes, parka, boots, gasoline, other warm garments, food, water, my .22 rifle and sleeping bag. Sometimes I also carried my deer rifle along.

One time between Three Forks and Townsend, I encountered what Montanans called 'black ice.' This is their description of clear or transparent ice on the blacktop highway. I slid off the highway into

what Montanans called
the 'borrow pit' (this is the
shallow ditch on either
side of the road from
which material was taken
to elevate the roadbed;
the earth was borrowed
and it left a pit). There was
about 6 inches of snow,

and regardless of how I tried, I couldn't get the bug back on the road.
Finally, I got the bug perpendicular to the road, jacked up the rear
and put the chains on. I managed to get out of the ditch. All the time I
was putting the chains on the bug, an antelope (pronghorn) across the
road was watching me. Occasionally, I would stop what I was doing
and talk to him. He would just stand there and watch. When I started
the engine, he took off running.

Coming back from Great Falls one time along the Missouri River,
a herd of about seven deer came up out of the river bottom and I
hit one of them. The collision broke my headlight and the deer was
thrown up over the car and hit the pavement behind me. I stopped
and got out to assess the damage and about that time, a semi came
around the bend and stopped. The driver offered to dispatch the deer
with a knife. The poor creature had bones sticking out of its legs. I
turned down his offer and told him I had a .22 that would take care of
it. It was common practice to report fresh road kills to the Sheriff, and
if it were feasible, he would pick these up and take them to the loony
bin (state mental hospital) for sustenance.

Returning from Great Falls one night, possibly at the same location
as my deer collision, a car came from the opposite direction around
a bend and blinked his headlights. I blinked in response to show my
lights were on low beam. He blinked again and then two or three times
more. Then I realized he was trying to tell me something, so I slowed
down. Around the bend, the highway was covered with cattle.

There was a procedure for cold weather starting in the L-20. No
doubt the same procedure was used for many other aircraft operated in
severe cold conditions. The operator's tech order for the L-20 showed
a system whereby you could dilute the engine oil to aid starting in a
cold morning. With the engine idling, one would press a button for X
number of seconds, which would direct gasoline into the crankcase.
The number of seconds depended on the temperature of the air. I

adopted the same system for the Volkswagen when I went to Great Falls in the winter. At home, I had a garage. However, at the air base, the car had to sit out all night. So, I would carry a small can of gas and a cup, measure about two thirds of a cup and pour it into the oil filler pipe while the engine was idling, let it run for three minutes or so and then shut the engine off. In the morning, the engine would start easily. Then, allowing four or five minutes at idle, the gas would vaporize and I was ready to go. This procedure worked quite well.

After flying, I was on the way back from Great Falls to Bozeman. I was about halfway home on a two-lane highway when I noticed a semi approaching in the distance. I watched him begin to cross the center-line and then it got worse. I slowed down and was on the shoulder when he went by, squarely in my lane. I did have about 12 feet more to escape into the borrow pit, but there was a small embankment beyond that. As he went by, I looked up at the cab and saw his head come up and his arms grabbing the steering wheel. I looked in my rearview mirror as he went down the highway, thinking perhaps the driver had had a heart attack, but he was back in his lane and going on his merry way. Just a week before, I had read in the newspaper about the Greyhound Bus Company burning their headlights in the daytime, as well as at night, and they claimed their accident rate had dropped because of this procedure. I had adopted this procedure for myself. Perhaps the driver was falling asleep, and perhaps my headlights got his attention. I'll never know. Another close one.

Another time when I was in Great Falls flying, it was a Friday and it was 92°. On Saturday I drove to Bozeman. My mother, the kids and I headed for Washington on Sunday morning. Passing through Butte, it was 32° and the ground was covered with snow. This was on the twelfth of June. The first snows would come in September.

Malmstrom Air Force Base at Great Falls was a missile base. Scattered around Montana were intercontinental ballistic missile sites. These rockets were stored in underground silos, the lid of which weighed 80 tons. On the surface of the sites were radar detectors, which sometimes would be set off by birds. The silos were interconnected with cables to missile control centers, which were also underground. These too were scattered widely. There would be a crew underground to monitor the missiles and launch them if they had to. These crews would be rotated. Carrying new crews to the sites and bringing the old ones back to the base was part of my flying job. The base had some L-20s and we used these to shuttle the crews back and forth to the control sites. This airplane had no deicing equipment and there were times like blizzards when the crews could not be changed; this was bad for morale, not only for the crew members, but for their families. Later on, helicopters were substituted for the L-20s.

There were a variety of other flights. I had to take a Navy pilot from Malmstrom to Butte in an L-20. He was to be the speaker at a luncheon there. Some people picked us up at the airport, and on the trip into town one of them told an interesting story. This was the old pilot who told me about being the first to take a horse up in an airplane. I saw quite a bit of Montana from low altitude in the L-20, later designated as a U-6A. Occasionally, I would bring one down to Bozeman and take my students on orientation flights, letting them get a little piloting time.

The last flight I made in the L-20 was taking it to the bone yard in Tucson, Arizona. It took me three days, stopping overnight at Ogden Air Force Base in Utah, Nellis Air Force Base in Las Vegas, and finally the bone yard at Davis-Monthan Air Force Base at Tucson, Arizona. I returned to Montana via commercial airline. Over the years, I logged about 800 hours in this venerable bird.

My second two years in Montana I flew a different airplane: the civilian designation was a Cessna 310. These air-planes were not owned by the Air Force but leased from Cessna. They were all painted blue and white in Cessna colors. We called them 'Blue Canoes.' This was a twin engine airplane with four seats.

U-3A (Cessna 310) with two of my Montana State Students

One time the weather was so severe around Montana, we had to take one to Cheyenne, Wyoming, to log some flight time; we used National Guard facilities at the Cheyenne Airport.

Landing at Laramie, Wyoming, one time on the way to Cheyenne, I had made my final approach and was about to touch down on the blacktop runway when I saw two antelope (pronghorn) lying on the runway. I didn't have enough time to stop, nor did I have enough speed to go around (which is to take off again without landing). Both animals got up when they saw me approaching. One ran off the runway, but the other slipped on the blacktop surface and fell down. I thought I was going to hit it, but it managed to get clear. I called the tower and told them that they had antelope on the runway. The answer was, "It's not unusual."

On landing at Bozeman one night, I turned on final approach and turned the landing lights on just in time to see a flock of ducks rise in front of me. I hit one of them. The damage was slight. The duck had gone through the propeller without touching it and hit the outside edge of the engine cowling and put a small dent in it. This was my only mid-air collision. This airplane had no de-icing equipment either, and had some limitations in severe cold weather. The oil temperature had to be at least 140 degrees before takeoff. So, an inventive crew chief figured out a way to warm the engines before flight. The airplane was kept in a warm hangar and the crew chief would cover the engine cooling air intakes on the cowlings with cardboard and tape. The plane would be wheeled out, the engines started and the oil temperature would come up to 140 degrees nicely. Then we would shut the engines off. The cardboard and tape would be removed, the engines restarted and we would taxi out to take off. If one taxied too slow, the temperature would drop below 140 degrees, and if one taxied too fast, more cold air would affect the engines and the temperature would drop below 140 degrees. Taking off with the oil temperature at 140 degrees, one would circle the airport to make sure the oil temperature stabilized at or above 140 degrees. This procedure was nonstandard. There was no mention of it in the technical manuals. Once headquarters discovered this procedure, the base caught hell from Strategic Air Command, the parent unit. The 310s (later designated U-3s) were grounded. Unless the ambient temperature was at least up to -20 F, they would not be flown. There were times when I went to Malmstrom to fly and the temperature would be below -20 degrees F. I would check in the morning, and as the day warmed up, the temperature would climb to its maximum around 2 o'clock in the afternoon. If it wasn't above -20 degrees F, then I would check in again the next morning. Since my boss only allowed me to fly on weekends because of my academic duties at the college, my trips to Great Falls were sometimes in vain and quite frustrating because I would not get to fly.

My academic duties at the college were mostly with seniors. I taught courses in leadership, military justice and other Air Force subjects. For those seniors who were going to go on active duty and were qualified for pilot training, we would arrange through a fixed-based operator at the local airport to give the students flying lessons.

Wood and cardboard float in a Bozeman parade built by ROTC cadets in my garage, 1966

If successful, they would earn an FAA private pilot's certificate. Of course, they needed to pass the FAA Ground School Examination too. This portion of pilot training was conducted as a regular college course. I taught this course and enjoyed it. Any student in the college could attend the course. As with any assignment, there were more jobs than people, so we would have additional duty jobs such as Education Officer, Administrative Officer, Commandant of Cadets, etc.

One of the pleasant additional duties I had was being faculty adviser for a group of marching girls that was called *The Angel Flight*. They were associated with our Air Force ROTC Detachment. There were times when they would assist in social functions, but their main *raison d'être* was to represent Montana State College in intercollegiate competition, just as a football team represented the College. There were 21 girls on the team and, of course, some substitutes in case of illness or pregnancy, both of which happens from time to time to college girls. I had one junior and one senior cadet who oversaw the operation of this group. I stayed in the background as adviser.

There were usually four trophies up for grabs at these competitions. One would be awarded for best regulation drill (the same sort of close

Four trophies won at a intercollegiate meet by the ROTC sponsored girls marching team.

order drill new recruits learn in basic training). Another category was fancy drill, essentially an unlimited performance except for the time factor. Usually another trophy was given for the best commander and a fourth for overall performance of the team. We were in the habit of winning all four trophies. This organization had a good reputation on campus. This was very popular and good PR for the ROTC Detachment so long as they were winners. It has been 46 years since I left Montana State and occasionally I think about those girls and wonder what kind of a life they have led.

In Seattle in 1958-9, I had begun to build a flying machine that was called a gyrocopter, or autogyro. Horizontal propulsion was provided by a four-cylinder two-cycle engine with a propeller. The forward motion would cause two rotor blades to rotate automatically. The machine looked like a helicopter, but the blades were not powered. A component of force from the rotor blades provided lift. If a helicopter's engine fails, the pilot, instead of driving air down with the rotor blades, arranges it so air comes up through the blades

Gyrocopter I built, Bozeman, 1967

as the machine descends. This regime is called auto-rotation; an autogyro is in auto-rotation all the time when flying. I finished up this machine while at Bozeman, took it to the airport and tried to fly it. It was in the summer of 1967. The temperature was hot and elevation high. It didn't perform well. I doubt if I ever got higher than 15 feet off the runway. Eventually, I traded it for a motorcycle when we moved to Friday Harbor.

One of my neighbors was the football coach, Jim Sweeny. Later on he coached at Washington State University and San Jose State University in California. Roger Craft was our basketball coach, and one fall he was walking from the gymnasium to the field house, cutting across the football field. Sweeny had his football players practicing nearby. Roger noticed two young men on the football field, one holding the ball and the other kicking it through the uprights in an odd fashion: the kicker was using the side of his foot as one does when playing soccer. He watched this fellow put the ball through the uprights repeatedly then went over and told Sweeny he had something to show him. He was busy and told Roger to take care of basketball and he'd take care of football. So that was that. However, the next day Roger was doing the same thing, crossing the field, and the same two young men were out there doing their thing. This time Roger took Sweeny by the arm and brought him over there to look. So Sweeny asked the young man if he'd like to turn out for football. This young man's name was Jan Stenerud, and was there on a skiing scholarship from Norway. He did well in football as a kicker, and in his second year he broke the NCAA record for kicked points. Later, he went on to play professional football. He was with Kansas City for a long time, and I believe Minnesota too. Now all kickers use this soccer technique. He was a pleasant young man and used to come down to our unit on the campus just to visit.

Chapter Eleven

Instructor Pilot

In June of 1967, my four-year tour of duty at Montana State College was finished. A set of orders arrived directing that I attend a helicopter school in Amarillo, Texas, and upon completion of the course, I was to go to Vietnam. It was normal for the Air Force to rotate a flying officer from a desk job to that of a cockpit job. In the desk job one had to maintain proficiency in flying, of course. The cockpit job might be anywhere. The war was still going on in Vietnam, and apparently it was my turn to go. So, I had a problem. Having sole custody of my children, where was I going to put them? I contacted every boarding school in Washington, Oregon and British Columbia; these locations were near my home of record and my relatives. All the boarding schools I contacted were affiliated with some church and expected one to pick the children up at Christmastime, Easter holidays and, of course, the summer months. These were of no use to me.

I assessed the possibilities of leaving the children with my relatives. My mother lived by herself in a small apartment and she had no space to raise kids; and she was getting along in years. My older brother had two adopted children and his wife had a faulty heart. She'd already undergone major heart surgery, and later, she submitted to two more operations on her heart before she died. My younger brother had four young children and was a struggling young architect. He could hardly take on two more children. The children's mother had been judged unfit by a Montana court, so she was out of the question. So, what to do?

Now, the Air Force realizes that problems like this exist, so they have a regulation that provides for a compassionate transfer. However, it is assumed that within one year's time you will have solved your problem. So, my orders were changed. I was reassigned to Air Training Command at Keesler Air Force Base at Biloxi, Mississippi, to a unit that was teaching Vietnamese students how to fly.

I sold the house. The movers came, packed up my household

goods and shipped them to Gulfport, Mississippi, near Biloxi. We went to Washington on leave and came back through Bozeman on our way to Mississippi. I had driven the Lincoln to Washington, pulling a trailer with my flying machine on it. I stored my flying machine at my in-laws. At Bozeman, I picked up my Volkswagen and towed it behind the Lincoln. Off we went. The trip was uneventful except for having a flat tire on an overpass in Dallas, Texas, near where President Kennedy was assassinated.

I had been at Biloxi once before when I transferred from the Artillery to the Air Corps during WW II. I spent a few weeks there awaiting assignment elsewhere. I was familiar with the town, base, and the environment. Biloxi is right on the Gulf of Mexico. The water extends behind the town to a back bay. It is hot and sticky in the summertime. We were arriving in September and it wasn't too bad. However, September is one of the hurricane months for this area.

The kids again were in a new environment, new school and had new classmates. Chris was about fourteen at this time and Mark ten. We were provided a house in a base housing area adjacent to the base. It was a brick structure, three bedrooms and a carport. When I say that the house was provided, this doesn't that mean it was free. If they could not provide one, I would draw a housing allowance. When housing is provided, there is no allowance.

Our mission on the base was to teach Vietnamese young men how to fly the 750 horsepower, single engine, low wing airplane called a North American T-28 Trojan. These were rather powerful airplanes for one just beginning; however, these students were rather handpicked in Vietnam and were quite bright. Some spoke French because Vietnam was once French Indochina. The students had hardly any mechanical experience. They were familiar with bicycles and one of them had an uncle who had a motor scooter. None had ever driven a car. They did well in academic subjects that had to do with aviation, but applying their knowledge to a powerful machine was challenging for them.

At Keesler, it was our mission to take young Vietnamese men and turn them into pilots. My first assignment was to make or break two students who were having difficulty. I was going to lead them through the program or put them up for elimination.

These students were very sensitive to criticism. After a flight, I was debriefing and critiquing one of my two students. I was telling him what he had done correctly during the flight and what he had done wrong and what to do about it next time. After a few minutes of this normal procedure, the student got up and walked out of the room. After about fifteen or twenty minutes, I sent the other student out to look for him. He returned and I asked him if he had found Mr. Tong. He said he had. I asked him where he was, and he said he was out in the hallway. Then I asked him what he was doing. He said he was crying. The critique had been emotional for him. I had not raised my voice nor made any fun of him. I realized that sooner or later he would get control of his emotions and return to duty. This happened and things were normal again. On a subsequent flight I had trouble with the same student. On each flight, other than instrument or night flights, we would require the student to climb to 6000 feet and put the airplane into a spin and then recover. (This was to insure that he knew how to recover if he were solo.) The student made a sloppy recovery, so I made him climb back up to altitude and try again; he was still sloppy. Again, I made him climb back up to try another. This time when I told him to put it in a spin, he did nothing. It seemed like he could not hear me over the interphone. So I checked my wires and my connections and called him again; still no answer. Then I asked him if he could hear me; he shook his head. Obviously, he had heard me or he wouldn't have shaken his head. Realizing that he was emotionally upset, there was little use in continuing the lesson, so I flew back to base and landed.

We had a Vietnamese captain who acted as a liaison officer. He had his office in the hangar that we operated out of. This hangar had partitions, but no ceilings in the offices. So, with little effort, one could hear what was going on inside an office. Walking by one day, I heard the captain shouting at some students, and I heard what sounded like slapping blows. The students accepted this kind of criticism unemotionally, but not that of a more subtle nature.

Once we got into the instrument flying phase of our training, Mr. Tong excelled. Eventually, I was able to solo both of these students and they completed the course. My second student was quite upset for a few days because the North Vietnamese had overrun his hometown and he knew nothing of the fate of his family. I know nothing of their behavior after they left the base and went back home. I trust that they did well.

We'd had a series of unexplained accidents in the T-28, and it wasn't until one of our pilots, on his preflight walk around inspection, noticed a crack in the horizontal stabilizer hinge. The fleet was grounded, and more cracks were found on other airplanes. Our operation was interrupted for awhile while these were fixed.

For recreation, I bought a small sailboat, sloop rigged, 16 feet long. I also bought a small outboard engine for it and taught myself how to sail on the Back Bay of Biloxi. There was a launch site on the base and I would take the boat and trailer there and go sailing. Sometimes I would take the kids and their friends. On Fridays, I would often sail to the west end of the Back Bay where there was a bridge. If I wanted to go any further, I would have to have the bridge opened, and so as not to impede road traffic, I never went any further. At this location there was a tavern, and on each Friday, they would have a free fish fry. Those local people, who had been fishing during the week, would save their catch, principally catfish, and give it to the tavern. They would serve fried fish and bread at no cost. Of course, they expected you to buy their beer.

Once Mark and I took the boat and launched it in the Gulf. We were sailing along nicely, then all of a sudden we ran aground on a sandbar. Sandbars came and went, depending upon the weather. There were some offshore, one of which had the remnants of a British fortress made of brick which was gradually being inundated. The sandy island was shifting to the east, the west end disappearing. One of the offshore islands disappeared entirely in a hurricane later.

One time when I was alone, sailing on the Back Bay, the wind picked up to the point where I felt I had to douse the sails. In the process, the boat drifted to a muddy island that was covered with tall grass. These were scattered throughout the Back Bay, which was quite shallow. I stepped ashore and managed to get the sails down, put the outboard in place, then shoved off, started the engine and went back to the launching ramp. When I was on the grass island, I noticed someone on the opposite shore, waving and yelling at me. I wasn't able to understand what they were saying because of the wind. Later I learned that I was at exactly the same spot where a person had put ashore the year before and had died as a result of multiple bites by water moccasins.

As you probably know, a tornado over the water is called a waterspout. We had one hit Biloxi during the night which scattered lumber all over town when it hit a lumberyard. It uprooted large oak trees that lined the road on the Gulf waterfront. It also hit a small boat storage facility near the bridge mentioned above. This was a large building that stored small boats in pigeonholes like those in the post office. Boats were scattered over a large area. The base suffered no casualties or damage. This storm caused flooding in our housing area. Base personnel came out and placed sandbags around our doorstep and elevated household furniture on sawhorses inside to prepare for the worst. The water rose to within an inch of our floor. Mark had a great time riding is bicycle down our driveway into the flooded street until he saw a large snake there.

Chapter Twelve

Retirement and Second Hiatus in Flying

The year went by quickly in Mississippi. Actually, it wasn't a whole year, it was from September to June. The compassionate transfer I received, sending me to Mississippi rather than to Vietnam, assumed that the problem I had would be solved in a year's time. June would be the date that this year would expire and I still had my problem. The only choices I had were to abandon my children or retire from the Air Force. Since I had the required time in the service to be eligible for retirement, I made application. Technically, being a regular officer, my application could have been refused. I was entitled to a ceremony and turned it down. I had a nice chat with the General, and the Squadron Commander awarded me my second Air Force Commendation medal prior to leaving.

Since I had two cars, I drove my Volkswagen to Seattle and left it with my brother. I flew back to Biloxi, and about this time I traded my old Lincoln for a more modern one. My household goods were picked up and stored in Gulfport, Mississippi. They would be kept for a maximum of two years at government expense. So the kids and I hooked the boat and trailer up and headed west. We passed through Bozeman, and briefly visited some old acquaintances and the kids looked up their former schoolmates. Then we left for the northwest. Thinking I might retire in the San Juan Islands, I looked briefly for housing there when I had taken the Volkswagen to the northwest. After visiting relatives in the northwest as a retiree, I went back to the San Juan's searching in earnest for housing.

I found a place to live. It was an old house about four miles from town. In the meantime, the kids and I went up to Bellingham and looked for property. We also looked at the university campus and local public schools with the idea that perhaps we'd settle there. I could perhaps teach at the college. We also made a trip to Victoria, British Columbia, and scouted out housing and schools near the University of Victoria. We also looked at a small island that was for sale in a place called Saanich Inlet. This was too remote, and besides, a young couple had just bought it.

Since we arrived in Friday Harbor in the summer, the kids had no immediate school problems. Twice a week I would visit the real estate offices in Friday Harbor, looking for suitable property on which to build. School buses didn't cover the entire island, so there was a restriction there. I looked at several places and finally settled on one in town. It was one square block in size, consisting of four lots, mostly in a forest. The streets were 'vacated', meaning the town didn't maintain them, although they were within the town limits. I bought a city block and went to work. We arrived on the island in July and I began building in October. I cleared a building site by hand and was ready to pour concrete for the foundation in November; however, the winter of 1968-69 was severe and I couldn't pour concrete until February in order to avoid freezing weather.

There was only one cable bringing electricity to San Juan Island and the demand was so great for power in the cold weather that the cable blew out underwater between Lopez and San Juan Islands. We had no power on the island for 13 days. The power company had some large diesel generators that had been prepared for storage and had no coolant in them. When it came time to use them, they couldn't do it because there was no anti-freeze on the island. The house I rented had an oil heater in the living room, but there was no electricity to operate its fan; consequently, it put little heat out in this cold spell. Then I got the flu. To escape the sad situation on the island, the kids and I went down to Seattle and moved in with Grandma for a few days.

On returning, I found the galvanized pipes in the house had burst. Part of the agreement I had with the landlord was that, if the house needed anything, I'd take care of it. So I took the sidewall shakes off part of the house, sawed a hole through the sheathing to expose the pipes, cut them out and replaced them. The pressure tank in the well had cracked, but this operated without repair. The trap under the lavatory in the bathroom had frozen and lifted it right off the wall, and it was lying on the floor.

I did all the labor on my new house with two exceptions: I hired a man to help me pour concrete for the foundation, and I hired a man with a crane to put two large beams in place. I managed to get the house nearly completed by the time I had to get my household goods out of storage in Mississippi. The house was of my own design, three bedrooms, one of which was upstairs with its own bath. It may be interesting to note that the town didn't require any permits to build, nor to plumb or wire. In fact, having put my telephone, electric wires and plumbing pipes from the corner to the house in a trench, I went down to the electric co-op and asked the man in charge if he'd like to come and take a look at my trench before I filled it up. He asked me if it looked any different from anybody else's. I told him I didn't know...he said to cover it up.

I already owned land in the islands, but it was on a non-ferry-served

Front entrance to the Friday Harbor house

island and it would be impossible to build there because the kids needed to be near schools. I had money in trusts for each of the kids set aside for college. I was required to turn over the sums by law when they reached age eighteen. Chris was eighteen in October of 1970. She had met the love of her life and they were to be married. Chris wanted marriage to be her own decision, so they were married after her eighteenth birthday. I asked her if she wanted her money; she wisely asked me to sit on it a while. They looked at some property, and on three occasions they came and got me to look at what they were considering to buy. In each case it didn't work out. They did buy a small parcel just outside of town that had some old buildings on it that we tore down; they installed a mobile home there.

Chapter Thirteen

Civil Flying

After retirement in 1968, there was another hiatus relative to flying for a while. Again, it was first things first. I busied myself for the first two years building a house. When I was nearly finished with the house, I began sailing more in my sixteen foot sloop, and later in my fourty foot schooner. Flying and sailing are somewhat alike in that you are dealing with Mother Nature on her own terms. There's an element of risk and adventure in both, though the speeds are quite different: 900 mph for jet fighters I flew compared to 7 mph for my sailboat. I tended to sail solo, just as I had flown as a pilot.

During the late seventies, I undertook some flying with a student's certificate. I soloed out and infrequently would rent a light aircraft to fly, but I didn't have any particular place to go. Then I undertook the procedure to get my private pilot's license. Studying the literature, I took the written examination (which I used to teach) and passed. Then, under the tutelage of a local instructor, I got my license. In 1984, I bought a single engine, two place airplane called a Cessna 150 and used it for little over a year.

On one flight in the Cessna, I passed over Arlington Airport and saw some vintage aircraft outside a large hangar. I landed and took a look. Among the aircraft was a Ryan PT-22, a pilot trainer used in WW II. I had always admired the looks of this aircraft. It had an all-metal fuselage with a bullet shaped nose, a five cylinder radial engine, fabric covered wings and tail surfaces, painted up in wartime trainer yellow with Air Corps insignia. This machine was for sale, so I hired a mechanic

Ryan PT-22

My Ryan PT-22 over the San Juan Islands, 1985

from Friday Harbor and we went in the Cessna to perform what was called a 'mechanic's survey.' The aircraft appeared to be airworthy, so I bought it. Shortly after I bought it, a pilot in Friday Harbor bent his Luscomb airplane in a minor accident and needed a replacement. I sold the Cessna to him. The fuselage on the Ryan had been painted silver, and as I started to remove the paint, I found a gunmetal blue paint under the silver. It took quite some time and a lot of elbow grease with nasty paint remover to get down to the bare metal. Then I polished it.

At this time, a friend of mine bought a Fairchild PT-23, a different WW II trainer. We attended many fly-ins and other aviation events together, almost always flying in formation. This friend, Ken Morley, had been in the Hawaiian National Guard and had also flown for Northwest Airlines. We would take friends and visitors for joyrides and occasionally we would volunteer our services to nonprofit organizations like the Animal Protection Society, Boy Scouts, the local car club and others. We would donate flights to the winners of their raffles, or other prize-giving activities.

Here is an account of some more memorable aviation events: Each year, around the Fourth of July, the Experimental Aircraft Association chapter at Arlington, Washington, has one of the country's largest aviation events. Aircraft of all types gather and a large audience comes to take in the spectacle. It seemed to us, however, that each year, the operation seemed to become more mercenary. The last time we attended, there was a fence between our aircraft on display and the concessionaires' tents. One was free to go through a gate to the tents, but admission was charged to come back to our own aircraft! We thought this was unjust, having gone to all the trouble to bring our flying machines to the event, which was part of the attraction to the public, and then be denied access to our own airplanes. A partial solution on our part was to buy one ticket and pass it back through the fence to others of our kind in order to have access to our airplanes.

Another place we visited several years in succession was Abbotsford, British Columbia. This event seemed to be more and more of a commercial nature and have less and less interest in vintage airplanes. We brought our flying machines as part of the attraction to the air show. Finally, one year they had us park our aircraft where the spectators could only see them at a distance on the other side of a fence. That was our last visit there.

One annual gathering was at Evergreen Airport in Vancouver, Washington. Here we were always treated well. For example, as I shut my engine down, there would be a person greeting me and handing me a cold beer. Limited free fuel was also provided. Most of the time at these events, I would take along a small tent and sleep on the ground underneath my wing. This event was for antique aircraft.

There was an air show in Sidney, British Columbia commemorating the 50th anniversary of the Victoria Airport. Our arrival was recorded with a video camera. The cameraman visited us at our airplanes and asked if he could take some footage from our aircraft in flight. We agreed to this and he did his shooting from the rear seat of Ken's Fairchild. At the same time, I gave a joyride to the pilot of a visiting Air Force C-5. Unknown to

Ryan at a 'fly-in'

us, this fellow also shot some footage of us departing the airfield at the end of the show. A few weeks later, both Ken and I received a copy of a VHS tape in the mail. Unknown to us, our video recorder had produced a full-length tape of the Victoria air show, showing all phases of such an operation, including our formation flying. This was his way of saying, "Thank you," for our cooperation. Occasionally, I review this tape and relive that 1989 experience.

In July 1968, there was an event in Seattle called The Goodwill Games. Some representatives of the Soviet Union attended these festivities. My flying partner, Ken Morely, his wife Linda, my brother Bob and I were invited by the Museum of Flight in Seattle to attend some of these festivities. The Russians had come over in a large jet transport called an IL-62, flanked by two Soviet fighters called Sukhoi 29s. An arrangement had been made for the Soviet aircraft to arrive from Vladavostok, Siberia, to Alaska on the 22nd of July. These aircraft were intercepted by our F-15s and had them land at Elmendorf Air Force Base in Alaska. They sat for 48 hours, awaiting State Department clearance. This delay was caused by the fact that they had left Siberia on the 22nd, as arranged, but in Alaska it was the 21st; the International Dateline was lying between the two countries.

We had our old crates on static display at Boeing Field. We had been invited by the wife of one of Ken's former fellow Northwest Airline pilots. She worked at the Museum of Flight and made some arrangements for the festivities. Once we were there, Ken, being an outgoing type, became acquainted with some of the Soviet crewmen. Two of these were test pilots and trained cosmonauts, although neither had been in space yet. Ken got the idea that perhaps we could take them for a flight around the traffic pattern. Ken came to me and asked me what I thought about this and I said okay. The senior Russian pilot, whose name was Victor Zobolotski, chose to fly with me, the other, Yuri Sheffer, was to fly with Ken. Before the flight, I explained to my guest the necessary air speeds at different points in the traffic pattern. I did this by pointing to the numbers on the air speed indicator while indicating, with my other hand, position and attitude needed throughout the pattern. So, off we went. No sooner had I lifted off the runway than I felt Victor at the controls. Our two guests flew some formation in the pattern, then I had to decide whether to let him land or not. I decided to allow him 5mph on either side of the speed I had indicated for final approach, and if he didn't stay within these limits, I would take over. Coming down final approach, he was right on the number. His touchdown was good, but then he almost ran off the runway. I took control, straightening the plane out and taxied in. Upon dismounting, Victor came to me and said, "You, my instructor." I believe his landing error was caused by his short stature and we had not adjusted the rudder pedals to his leg lengths before flying.

My son Mark and grandson Tom had flown up from Oregon for

a visit. The two were at Boeing field and observed our flight. Mark seemed puzzled and said, "You've been telling me all my life that these Soviets are sons-of-bitches and now you're friendly with them. What gives?" My answer was, "The more you know about your enemy, the better off you'll be." He seemed satisfied with that philosophy. Mark and Tom flew back to Oregon that afternoon, and later Mark told me that Tom had flown almost the whole distance on instruments and did a good job. Tom had a great deal of experience in an inexpensive simulator in the form of video flying games.

The Museum of Flight put us up in a hotel where the Soviets were staying. One of their number, Boris, an aircraft designer, was invited to stay with Ken's airline pilot friend and his wife, John and Cindy Upthegrove. They took Boris into downtown Seattle and ate Chinese food; he liked that. On the way home to Burien, Cindy needed some things at the grocery store so they stopped at a Safeway supermarket. Boris was curious so he went in too. A 15-minute stop turned into over an hour stop because Boris was incredulous regarding what he saw. It was late, about 9 o'clock and there were very few people in the store. The quantity and quality of the stocks on the shelves overwhelmed Boris. Examining many items carefully, he finally said, "This is Hollywood. You have done this for me." He was irate, believing he had been 'set-up.' Denying this, they offered to stop at any number of other stores on the way home. Boris finally believed what he saw was not constructed to deceive him.

The Morleys, Bob and I were put up in the same hotel as the Soviets by the Museum of Flight. We were invited to one of their rooms where they were celebrating some Soviet holiday. There were perhaps eight or ten of them, one of which had a guitar, and most were singing. We were offered some black bread, black hard sausage and brandy.

My brother Bob somehow struck up a conversation with the navigator of the crew and told him that I had been a navigator during WW II in B-29s. He came over and introduced himself and said he would like to 'speech' with me. So, I followed him out of the room, up to another floor and into another room. He offered me some more bread and sausage. We hadn't been there five minutes when the telephone rang; he looked at it, hesitated, it rang again, looked at me and said, "Trouble." He answered the phone and spoke to someone for a short while. Then, he looked at me again and said, "No trouble." Back where the party was going on, it had been easy to determine who was in charge: a political officer. When my navigator friend said 'trouble',

I immediately thought that he had been seen leaving alone with me, and perhaps that was not permitted. He then told me that he had heard that America helped other countries over Radio Free Europe and also from some other 'pipple' (people). I verified this, then he said he had eleven brothers and sisters and they had many children, but there was no milk and they needed help. At the moment, I was wondering if he expected me to get my wallet out and make a donation, however that was premature on my part. He gave me a book and said that before he left home his wife told him if he found somebody he liked to give him this book. The book has to do with Soviet MiG (Mikoyan-Gurevich) aircraft, some of which I fought against in the Korean War. It's a nice book, but being in Russian, I'm not able to read it. This was a nice gesture on the navigator's part.

We went back to the party and Ken, Bob and I offered a song of our own; it was an old ribald fighter pilot's song called, "Sally in the Alley," which although I hesitate to reproduce it here, I will. It goes like this:

Sally in the Alley, sifting cinders,
Lifted up her leg and
Farted like a man,
The wind from her bloomers
Broke six winders
And the cheeks of her ass
Went Bam-Bam-Bam.
(These last three words are emphasized by stomping on the floor with the foot or pounding on the table if seated.)

Breakfast in the hotel was a buffet. The Soviets gorged on fresh fruit, especially strawberries. Victor's wife, seated next to me, explained that fresh fruits hadn't reached Moscow from the south yet. (This was the third week in July.)

I was able to converse with Victor's wife because she spoke some French. She told me that she was a pilot, but only flew ultra-light aircraft. She said the range was quite limited so she couldn't fly very far.

Ken tried to get the Soviets up to the Islands for a day. This was denied, and they left suddenly for home. While waiting in the hotel lobby for transportation, Bob was sitting on a sofa with Boris. Newspaper headlines and the TV showed something was going on in the Soviet Union. This was the end of July 1968, and the advent of the breakup of the Soviet Union was in progress. When Bob explained what was happening, Boris looked around and quietly said, "Good." Boris was an outstanding aircraft designer; however, he had refused to join the Communist Party, and as a result, he was forced to do his work in a city called Irkutsk, in Siberia, on Lake Baikal.

Many of the same group that we met at Boeing Field were scheduled to return to Everett, Washington for an air show two weeks later. We heard nothing of this, and wondered if they would show up. There were posters and news releases about the upcoming event, but we heard no news. They did arrive at the appointed time, however, with the same three aircraft: the jet transport (an IL-62 and the two Sukoi jet fighters.) The two cosmonauts that we had met returned again. As the Soviet contingent of airplanes approached Everett, Victor told the navigator he wanted to cross the San Juan Islands at minimum altitude for Brewer and Morley!

Apparently it was quite a sight: the transport was flanked by the two Soviet fighters, outside of these were two of our Air Force F-15 fighters escorting the Soviets from Alaska, and outside of the F-15s were two Canadian CF-18 fighters acting as escorts through Canadian airspace. Morley and I didn't see this because we were out flying; however, many did see this and were impressed.

Upon arriving at Everett, Victor and Yuri telephoned Morley, but no one was home. They then found a person who flew them to Friday Harbor Airport, and they walked around looking in hangar door cracks for our airplanes. Of course, they didn't find them because we were flying. Disappointed, they returned to Everett and contacted Morley later by telephone. The air show at Paine Field was on Saturday and Sunday, and Ken managed to drive down and bring them up for a day. We took them up in our airplanes again and then out in my boat. They had brought an interpreter with them. There were six of us on the boat. We brought champagne, sausage, cheese and crackers for snacks. While near the shoreline, the interpreter asked if those houses lining the shore were 'state houses.' I told her they were private residences. Then she asked how large a parcel one was allowed to have. I told her that depended on how much money one wanted to spend. She asked us why we wanted to own property, and I asked her, "Why not?" Also, while conversing, the subject of great change in the Soviet Union was brought up. Victor acknowledged this and added that they didn't want to change the social order however, meaning they still wanted to be Communists. He, himself, was a member of their Duma, the Soviet parliament.

The air show at Everett was on Saturday and Sunday and their visit to the islands was on Thursday. When asked what they were going to do on Friday, the interpreter said that they were going shopping. Asked what would make a good souvenir, she said it might seem odd, but they were going to buy shoes and boots. When told that these were not cheap, she acknowledged that and added that shoes and boots were not available at home and said that their farmers worked barefoot in the fields.

After sailing, we returned to Morley's for a barbecue and a game of croquet on the lawn. Incidentally, to give you another idea of what these folks are used to at home, relative to authority, at the airport before we took our guests flying around the islands, the interpreter asked if we didn't need to notify the authorities. I explained to her that we had two types of airfields: controlled and uncontrolled. Those that were controlled had a tower on the field that controlled traffic on the ground as well as in a zone in the air over the airport. I then explained to her that Friday Harbor Airport was an uncontrolled airport, which had no tower, and we flew when we pleased; the responsibility for regulating traffic on the ground and in the air was that of the pilot in command of each aircraft. This freedom of operation seemed to be foreign to her.

After our guests returned to Everett for their weekend air show, I never saw them again. However, we were invited to come to the Soviet Union and be their guests. The Morleys and the Upthegroves could fly at no cost because of their former employment with the airlines, so Ken, Linda, John and Cindy made a trip around the world, stopping in Moscow to visit those whom we had met here. They took along some presents, the most valued of which turned out to be condoms. Other things in short supply, besides shoes and boots, were toilet paper and light bulbs. Many Russians lived in high-rise apartment buildings whose stairways were not illuminated because tenants would steal the light bulbs for their own apartments.

My friends got to go to the Bolshoi Theater for the Russian ballet. This was arranged through one of the host's friends who worked there. Both Ken and John, being pilots, were taken out to the Gromov Flight Test Center outside Moscow where Victor and Yuri worked and were treated to fly in some of their aircraft, Yak-52s. There was a low ceiling so their flight was restricted somewhat. On the way back into Moscow,

Victor stopped the car near a large gray concrete building, excused himself, saying he'd be back in a few minutes. When he returned, he gave both Ken and John a small blue book. These were Soviet pilot's licenses, numbers 20 and 21. Victor had the authority to do this, being the equivalent of an FAA Flight Examiner in our country.

After the Moscow visit, my friends headed for Siberia to visit Boris in Irkutsk. From this point on, a Soviet colonel accompanied them, most likely for security purposes. En route, Ken went to the cockpit to observe. Flashing his new pilot's license, the pilot got up out of his seat and invited him to fly the airplane!

There was a military base near Irkutsk and arrangements were made to give Ken and John a flight in a Soviet helicopter. Apparently they were not allowed to go to the base, so they were driven to a non-descript spot along the highway. Soon, a large helicopter arrived and they flew up into the mountains and landed on a gravel bar in a river. The crew got out and busied themselves fishing. As they prepared to return, Ken again flashed his new license and again he was invited to occupy the pilot's seat! Never having flown a helicopter, Ken declined.

One evening in Irkutsk, there was a group of young men seated near my friends who seemed curious about the American visitors. They approached and struck up a conversation as best they could. Eventually, one of them asked why the United States had nuclear missiles pointed at them. Ken said it was because the USSR had nuclear missiles pointed at us. The young men denied this. However, later in the evening, after discussing this amongst themselves, they returned and told Ken they believed him.

Later, after the Morleys and the Upthegroves returned home, Ken got a message from Boris saying he needed so many pair of shoes that he could sell at home. There was no mention of how he would pay for them. Russians, having been given things by the State for 70 years or so under Communism, the requirements of a free market escaped him. In another apparent attempt to become a capitalist after the collapse of the Soviet Union, Boris again contacted Ken, wanting him to make an appointment with the Boeing Company president to discuss purchasing aircraft for his proposed airline at home. Boris said this meeting was to be at such-and-such a time on such-and-such a day when he would be in Seattle. Boris didn't know that this wasn't the way business was conducted here.

Both Victor and Yuri were mum about what their future roles

were to be in the Soviet Space Program. However, in a recent (2005) issue of the Smithsonian's *Air and Space* magazine, there was an article about the Soviet Space Shuttle, complete with a photo of their "Buran," as they called it, and a picture of Victor. He was to have flown this machine which looked almost like a carbon copy of ours. Whether it was copied after ours or the appearance was delineated by design parameters, I don't know. Their shuttle was only flown once, and without a pilot, being entirely flown by signals from the ground. The enormous costs of a shuttle program have relegated their "Buran" to a Moscow park as a monument. While here on my boat, the interpreter mentioned that they were very proud of their "Buran."

So much for the Russian connection. Getting back to flying, I had my Ryan PT-22 and Ken Morley had his Fairchild PT-23. Another friend, Craig Nelson, bought a PT-22. He had never flown formation before but he worked his way into it and did a fine job. So the three of us used to fly to things called 'fly-ins,' which are basically the same sort of thing you find in kindergarten called 'show and tell.' You bring your airplane as others do, look, kick tires and tell lies. During the summer, there's a fly-in or an air show somewhere in the Northwest each week. We would attend all these that we could.

Paul Whittier, one time resident and benefactor of Friday Harbor, is shown here on his 85th birthday with myself and fellow pilot, Ken Morley. We had made a couple of passes down the harbor in formation over his home in our old crates (Ryan PT-22 and Fairchild PT-23) in his honor because he had been an early pilot. In

fact, his pilot's license was signed by none other than Orville Wright. He told us of flying down the Potomac River in a National Guard Boeing P-12 when President Roosevelt was inaugurated in 1932.

When he learned I used to fly F-86 jet fighters, he told us about a friend that had found inexpensive F-86 jet engines in Mexico and wished he had an F-86 to put one in. Paul said he'd give him one. He didn't say how he'd come by them. He did say that he'd given one of them to a Mexican employee who used it as a playground object for derelict children he would bring home from Los Angeles streets. When his friend finally believed Paul had a second F-86 in his barn, he knew that such things were available, but they were demilitarized by cutting all the electrical wires and hydraulic lines in them. Paul told him this one had not been cut because he had crawled through it and saw that it had not been cut. I don't know how this story ended. His philanthropy here involved a million dollars for the Port of Friday Harbor (used principally to modernize the airport), a half million toward building the performing arts center (if the citizens matched the sum), tennis courts at the high school, land for the Boy Scouts, land for the wildlife rehab center and perhaps other donations that I don't know about. I believe a new library, firehouse and swimming pool were in the offing when a vocal minority challenged airport modernization, saying they didn't want noisy jets on the island. This may have caused cancellation of these additional gifts.

Sometimes the ferry schedule would be such that my daughter or Merri Ann (MA), or both, who worked on the ferries, would have to board a ferry as a passenger, deadhead to Anacortes, begin their shift there, and when the shift was over, again revert to the status of passenger and deadhead back to Friday Harbor. On occasion, we'd make arrangements so I would fly to Anacortes. MA would get a ride to the airport from the ferry terminal. Then I would fly her back to Friday Harbor. We had done this several times without incident, saving her much wasted time.

One day when I went over to pick her up, I arrived before she did and to avoid shutting the engine down (which involved hand-propping to start again) I sat and waited with the engine idling. My regular mechanic, Elton Hannaman from Friday Harbor, was then working at the Anacortes airfield. He saw me, came out of a hangar and asked me if I would be willing to take a young man around the pattern once just for the experience in a vintage airplane. This young man was a sailor at Whidbey Island Naval Air Station working as an aircraft mechanic, and he had been coming to the Anacortes Airport, working for nothing, just to learn more of the trade in his free time. Elton stuck him into the front cockpit and off we went. It was my plan to take off, make a circuit, 'buzz' the airstrip, which means flying low and fast down the runway, then making another circuit and landing. About the time I taxied out, MA showed up at the terminal and watched me depart.

I took off and turned to the right. Normally, I would go straight out over the water and then make my turn to the right toward Friday Harbor, making less noise for the residents along the waterfront. Continuing my turn so that I was nearly 180 degrees, I heard a loud explosion and saw a blur of parts departing up and to the left. The engine stopped immediately. I didn't know what caused this until later. A counterweight had come off the crankshaft and had torn a cylinder off. When the engine siezed, the torque was diminished to zero, and the energy was applied to the airframe, giving me a violent roll. With all the weight gone from the exploding parts departing, the aircraft was tail heavy and the nose went up. I was almost inverted at that time. I looked down at the shoreline and noticed that the tide was out and said to myself, "That's where I'm going." However, allowing the nose to come down to the horizon (forcing it might precipitate a stall) and rolling the wings level, I could no longer see the beach. Ahead was a residential street, but I couldn't get aligned with it because of tall fir

A good bird gone west

trees on my right. Not wanting to bank to the left to gain alignment, and thereby having to lower the left wing, which might collide with the ground first, I tried skidding the aircraft for the best alignment I could achieve.

My right landing gear touched down on the grass covered 12-foot shoulder on the left side of the street. (The whole terrain in this area is terraced to give residents unimpeded marine views.) There was no house where I touched down, perhaps because it was too steep on which to build. My left gear touched down about three feet downhill of the west edge of the shoulder and ploughed a furrow up through the sod. The left gear collapsed and the left wing broke, and I slid down the street about 100 feet and came to a stop by the opposite curb.

In the process of sliding down the street, the carburetor broke on the pavement. When we came to a stop, I rolled out of the cockpit to the left and since the gear had collapsed on that side I was fairly close to the ground. I had pain in my back and couldn't stand up straight. The broken wing was hinged up over the front cockpit, and at that moment I wondered how I was going to get my passenger out of there. I asked him if he was all right and he said he was okay. I told him to get out of there because we were going to have a fire. He managed to push the wing out of the way easily. We went a few feet and sat down on the curb. There was a black, oily fire and we moved further

A good landing is one you get to walk away from.

away as the gas from the broken carburetor ignited. The heat from the friction of metal sliding on the street caused the ignition. We moved down and across the street, sat there and watched. A car came by and a young woman stopped, looked at me, and asked if my name was Brewer. Being a little dazed, I asked her, "Who in Hell wants to know." It turned out she was a deck hand on the ferries and she lived nearby. She drove down to the ferry and brought my daughter back up. The police and the fire department arrived.

In the meantime, MA was waiting for me to come back from my circuit. She saw me make my turn and make what she thought was a hammerhead acrobatic maneuver, and wondered why I was doing that. About that time, she heard the explosion and then she heard another when we hit the ground. My passenger told me that we had eight seconds between the time the engine blew and the time I hit the street. Whether he was looking at his watch or counting to himself, I don't know. When MA saw the pall of black smoke, she went into the hangar and told Elton. They jumped into his vehicle and headed in our direction. In the process of leaving the airport, a ferry captain was approaching the airport because he had an airplane there. He knew both Elton and MA and flagged Elton down. The captain said an airplane was down and both people were out and okay. MA asked him how he knew, and he said he'd heard it on his scanner radio. MA arrived on the scene and Elton proceeded to pick up parts that had blown off the airplane. One woman was guarding the cylinder, stuck in her front yard. Elton had to take a piece of the wreckage away from one of the policemen. He had picked it up and had it on the seat in his patrol car. No one is supposed to touch anything like that until the National Transportation Safety Board determines the cause the accident. Debris is evidence.

An ambulance arrived and they insisted that I lie down on a piece of plywood. They carted my passenger and me off to Anacortes hospital. X-rays of my back determined there was a compression fracture of 'T-11,' the eleventh thoracic vertebra. The impact was considerable, and I also incurred a hernia. I already had had two of these so I didn't think too much about it. My passenger was not hurt. My back bothered me for a week or so, and later the hernia was operated on and it healed just fine. The airplane was almost a 'total.' I managed to salvage a number of parts which I later sold to a Ryan enthusiast in California (about 600 pounds). The National Transportation Safety Board wanted my crankshaft from my engine in order to determine what caused the engine failure. Elton and I dismantled the engine and I took the crankshaft down to Seattle so the NTSB could ship it to Washington for analysis. This was returned later since it belonged to me, however worthless it was. The cause was 'cyclic fatigue.'

What is 'cyclic fatigue?' If you take a piece of wire and bend it and then bend it back the other way and keep doing this, sooner or later the molecular structure gets 'tired,' and it breaks. Apparently this happened to one of the machine screws that held the counterweights to the crankshaft.

So, the National Transportation Safety Board said the reason my engine blew up was due to cyclic fatigue. Let's go back in time a bit and see how this happened. Ever since I bought the Ryan, I found oil on the left side of the airplane, coming from number four cylinder. This could have been due to faulty valves or faulty piston rings, among other things. The engine in the Ryan was a Kinner. It had five cylinders and was a radial engine. Generally, radial engines have an odd number of cylinders. This is because one of those cylinders has a master rod to which all the other rods are attached. The attached connecting rods are in equal numbers for balancing purposes.

It seemed to me that the oil leak was getting worse, so I called this to the attention of Elton, my mechanic. He suggested taking number four cylinder off and sending it out to be overhauled. He did this and reinstalled it after the overhaul. The first time I went to fly after this work, during the run up before takeoff, I noticed oil still collecting where it had before. Something was wrong. I aborted my flight and returned to the hangar. Draining some oil out of a sump on the front of the crankcase, I found a small piece of shiny metal shaped like a lengthened football, about 3/8-inch long. Draining a second small sump, I found bronze colored powder in the oil. I showed these to Elton and he said we should overhaul the engine. I helped him remove it from the airplane and put it in his van. He intended to take it home to Anacortes and work on it there. We had put the engine down with the propeller shaft up. When he went to work on the engine, he found he could not turn the shaft. Tearing it down, he found out why it would not turn.

The rods connecting the pistons to the master rod are held in place by things called link-pins. The link-pins were about the diameter of a nickel and about 3 inches long. Each of these had a spring-loaded tit that fell into a hole when assembled. This kept the link-pin from slipping in or out, in other words, it locked the pin in place. Elton found that the link-pin for number four rod was broken in two. Apparently, when we put the engine in his van with the shaft up, the link-pin took the opportunity to fall out of position. The portion with the locking tit stayed in place; the other piece had fallen down and blocked the crank cheek from turning. Apparently, while the engine was running, this broken piece would try to migrate out of position, banging against the crank cheek which caused the rod to jump a bit, which in turn caused the piston to rock and pump oil out of the exhaust of number four cylinder. The tiny metal football-shaped piece I found fit nicely between the two broken pieces of the link-pin.

To balance the crankshaft, two counterweights are attached to it to offset the master rod and its associated mass. These are about an inch thick, half-moon in shape and weigh about 12 pounds apiece. Each is held in position by two special machine screws. The repeated (or cyclic) vibration caused by the link-pin banging against the crank cheek had fatigued one of the machine screws and it failed. In turn, this caused the second screw to fail, setting the weight free to become a missile and tear off number four cylinder plus ripping a hole in the crankcase.

During overhaul, we consulted the engine manual, which said not to touch the counterweights, but to contact the factory for guidance. There had been no factory since the end of WW II. So we called Al Ball in California, the expert on Kinner engines. He also said not to touch them. The probable reason for leaving them alone was because the special machine screws were torqued in place, then a hole bored through them and the counterweight and a pin inserted into that hole to keep the screw from backing out. If the screws were removed, it would hardly be possible to achieve the proper torque and align the holes for the locking pin again.

The NTSB wanted to see my logbooks, too. Two were burnt up in the airplane but the third and most current was legible. This logbook was returned to me, charred and water-soaked in a plastic bag. They didn't question me at all, probably because about two weeks earlier I had a ramp-check. A ramp check is when an FAA inspector walks up to your airplane after he's seen you operate it and checks to see that the pilot and the airplane have all their papers in order. However, I did have a telephone call from Oklahoma City from an FAA official asking how I ever recovered from a spin or a stall at such low altitude. I told him there was neither a spin nor a stall. Apparently satisfied with that, the conversation ended. Later I learned that if I had admitted spinning or stalling, he would have written me up for losing control of the airplane and perhaps taken my license from me. Was he baiting me? Perhaps he was.

The date I lost my airplane, the Ryan PT-22, was May 22nd, 1992. A week or so after this date, Whidbey Island Naval Air Station was to have an air show. Ken Morley and myself were invited to bring our vintage aircraft to this event; however, they insisted that we show proof of insurance. Neither of us had any insurance. Ken had been doing research and had found a good source, but we had not yet applied for this insurance. When I lost the Ryan, it was a total loss for me (outside of the sum I received for 600 lbs. of parts).

So, I was without an airplane. My mechanic friend, Elton Hanaman, had the bones of a home built aircraft in his hangar. The airplane was a 1929 parasol design, called a Pietenpol Air Camper. The fuselage framework was mostly finished and some other work had been done, including the wing ribs. I did a little work on it, and bought a 1930 Model A Ford four-cylinder engine from Elton to power the machine. I took this engine to Vancouver, Washington and had it overhauled. I made the wing spars and that was about it. I lost interest in the project, perhaps because someone else had done the work. Later, I sold this project.

As a temporary substitute for being grounded, I bought a vintage motorcycle, a 1942, 45 cubic inch flat head Harley Davidson from a fellow in Spokane, Washington. I brought the bike back to the island in my pickup truck and rode it a bit, but had some trouble with the magneto system, so I modified it to operate with a battery and distributor system, which it originally had.

Next, I looked for a new airplane, I should say 'different,' rather than 'new', because what I had in mind was a biplane. Why a biplane? Well, that's what airplanes looked like when I was a kid.

Many pilots contract the disease of 'one-up-manship', where there is an urge to buy something faster and bigger as time goes on. I have no desire to go in that direction. One might hold in esteem an airplane that would fly 140 miles an hour when used to flying just 100 miles an hour. After flying 900 miles an hour in jet fighters, I don't succumb to this disease. In fact, I tend to go in the opposite direction. The Cessna I had would fly about 105 miles an hour; the Ryan would do well at 90. Now, biplanes have a great deal of lift because of the large wing surface; however, they also have a good deal of drag and don't go very fast. This appealed to me, so I started looking around for a biplane. Although they are uncomfortable, noisy, sometimes oily and demanding to fly, they are real airplanes.

Pilot-author Richard Bach wrote a little piece called, "Why be an Antiquer?" I quote him here for his insight relative to flying vintage aircraft: "The modern airplane driver [notice he doesn't even call him a pilot], has been described as a man with a sincere interest in aviation, but a fear of flying. On the day he decides to overcome that fear, he learns from a soaring pilot how to ride the great sea of air. He learns from the homebuilder about aircraft anatomy and the many ways an airborne machine can fit together. And he learns from an antiquer how to control a winged personality that has a life and a will as strong as his own. Until he has some of this learning tucked away, he remains a man with a paper license."

I checked out a few biplanes that were for sale. None of them rang my bell until I found a 1937 British de Havilland Tiger Moth for sale nearby in Canada. I hired Elton to go with me and take a look, making what one would call a mechanic's survey. The owner was reluctant to sell his airplane, but he could no longer fly solo because of heart trouble. He let me know that he was picky about the person who he would sell it to. I suppose my previous military experience and having flown in another vintage aircraft might have convinced him to let me have it. He was attached to this airplane, having spent 6 years rebuilding it; in fact, he named it after his father, who had been a pilot in the South African Air Force during the twenties. During WW I, his father had been in the English Royal Air Force as well. This man's name was Harry Teague. The seller had put his father's name on the nose of the Tiger Moth calling it, "Old Harry." I asked the seller if it would be all right with him if I left the name "Old Harry" on it; he was delighted and somewhat emotional about this idea. I gave up the idea of calling it "The Orange Crate" (because of its color).

Let's take a look at Old Harry. The correct identification for Old Harry is de Havilland 82A Tiger Moth. Its predecessor was called a Gipsy Moth. After WW I, de Havilland was producing Gipsy Moths using surplus French Renault engines. They would modify these and call them Cirrus engines. This supply dried up, so de Havilland designed their own engine called the Gipsy Major. The basic design was made in 1925.

Old Harry's serial number is 3621. It was built at Hatfield, England and shipped directly to Australia on the nineteenth of November, 1937.

It was registered as VH-UYR, the property of the Royal Victorian Aero Club at Essendon Airport, Melbourne, Australia. In September of 1940, it was impressed into the Royal Australian Air Force as A 17-685. I have some photographs of Old Harry showing these markings.

After the war, Old Harry was on the island of Tasmania where

(above) VH-UYR airborn over Melbourne, Australia, owned by the Royal Victorian Aero Club, 21 November, 1937

A very forlorn looking Tiger in South Africa, registered ZS-CMC. Pietersburg Airfield. Departed S.A. 1975

Old Harry about to depart its Canadian home. 1994

My painting of Old Harry and 'Friend'

it had served as a trainer for Australian pilots during the war; I have the logs of this service. Many of these aircraft were declared surplus and sold by Crown Assets. On the 31st of May, 1946, Old Harry was bought by a Mr. Rafferty at Western Junction, Tasmania, for 125 pounds. It was never re-entered into the Australian civil register. Mr. Rafferty sold it to a Sydney businessman who shipped a batch

(above) 'Old Harry' Tiger Moth while in military service. April, 1941, serial number 3621
A 17-685, in formation

of them to South Africa. On the eighth of June, 1959, Old Harry was registered as ZS-CMC to the South African Air Force Defense Flying Club at Swartkops. I have the logs of its life in the South African Air Force. In 1960, the airplane was bought by a Mr. Levy and based at Pietersburg, in the Northern Transvaal. In 1974, Bill Teague bought this airplane and flew it from Pietersburg to Baragwanath Airfield near Johannesburg. In 1975, he shipped it to Sidney on Vancouver Island via the ship M. V. Nedloyd Kembla. Over the next six years, the airplane underwent spare time restoration. On the 31st of May, 1981, the airplane was test flown from the Victoria Airport. On the thirtieth of July it was registered in Canada as C-GWET. On the 23rd of April, 1994, I bought Old Harry and imported it into the United States, registering it as N-1937D.

Bill and his brother had learned how to fly in Tiger Moths in South Africa. When their father died in South Africa, the country had a policy of not letting anyone take any money out of the country. With the sum they inherited from their father, who was 'Old Harry', they elected to the buy an airplane and ship it out of the country rather than buying a tombstone for their father, who would be buried in South Africa where no one would ever see the tombstone.

Like many antique airplanes, Old Harry never had brakes nor a tail wheel. This configuration is satisfactory for operations off unpaved surfaces. The skid acts as a brake on the grass or dirt from friction. Many modern aircraft have tail wheels that are steerable. The skid on Old Harry was steerable within narrow limits, the steering being made principally by the rudder, using the air stream made by the propeller or the wind. I checked out in the Tiger on a grass field in Canada, then flew it to Friday Harbor, which has a paved runway. As long as an airplane is operated off unpaved surfaces, a tail wheel is redundant.

I planned to land on the last hundred feet or so of the runway and run off into the grass in order to use the skid for directional control and as a brake. Some observers at the airport got little excited because they thought that I had accidentally run off the runway. With no brakes, one could maintain directional control if taxiing against the wind by using the rudder; however, taxiing downwind on a hard surface, there would be no directional control at all.

Old Harry needed inspection by an FAA examiner in order to be licensed in the United States. The local examiner had to go to Alaska in short order and had no time to come to Friday Harbor. He did have time to come to the Bayview Airport, about 20 miles away, so I was to bring the airplane over there. Landing upwind on a paved runway and coming to a stop, I decided to taxi on the wide grass shoulder. Reaching the end of the runway and turning downwind, I stayed on the shoulder, the skid providing directional control on the grass until the shoulder narrowed to the point where I was forced to get back on the pavement. Then there was no direction control, so I shut the engine down. My mechanic Elton Hanneman was there to help me. We restarted the engine and he provided directional control by leaning against the wing. We put the airplane in a hangar, and the next morning when I flew as a passenger to Bayview, the inspector had done his work already and Old Harry was free to go. So I flew back to Friday Harbor, and again landed on the end of the runway and ran out into the grass for control.

There was a man in California who had been working on Tiger Moths for many years who had developed a brake system for the airplane. To market such a modification, the developer must show that it is safe and reliable to the FAA and obtain what is called a Supplementary Type Certificate (STC). To offset the development costs, the inventor sells the STC to users. So, I bought this and installed brakes on Old Harry. I also added a tail wheel to the airplane. It was very simple to substitute a wheel for the skid. So, Old Harry was now modernized to operate off paved surfaces as well as unpaved surfaces.

Actually, the old fashioned way of operating without brakes and a tail wheel had its advantages. Airplanes operated off large open fields, so there was no such thing as a crosswind. One could orient the airplane into the wind regardless of the wind's direction. However, with a paved runway you don't always find the wind aligned with the runway, so you have to compensate for crosswinds. Landing: this is accomplished two different ways. One is where you 'crab' into the wind, looking like you're flying a bit sideways to an observer on the ground. However, touching down in this attitude, one must straighten out the plane at the last second, otherwise there is a tendency for the airplane to ground loop or shear the gear off. The second method, which is the best, is to slip the airplane, that is, lower the wing into the wind and apply opposite rudder. This allows the airplane to slip to the side and kill the drift caused by the crosswind, and it allows the airplane to stay aligned with the runway. You can touch down this way, allowing the upwind wheel to contact the runway first. Since Old Harry was designed to operate off large open fields, the airplane could be pointed into the wind no matter what its direction, thus, no consideration was made for slipping on landing. The lower wings on the airplane were not designed to be very high off the ground, and slipping the airplane requires lowering the wing, thus, there is a limit to the amount of slip one can use with this airplane before the wing will touch the ground.

Since a Tiger Moth can take off in a couple of hundred feet (less if there's a wind), flying off larger, wider runways, it is possible at times to take off on an angle across the width of the runway, and actually taking off across a runway if the wind is right and the runway is wide enough. I have done this at Whidbey Island Naval Air Station.

An FAA Regulation requires an annual inspection of an airplane to insure that it remains airworthy. This must be done, in most cases, by an FAA licensed mechanic. So an old airplane is no less airworthy than a new one. The same general thing applies to the pilot. He must have a current medical certificate and a current biennial flight review given by an FAA licensed instructor pilot. So, old pilots aren't necessarily less competent than new ones.

Here is Bill Teague's own story about how he acquired Old Harry: "In the early nineteen seventies I was flying helicopters in the Arctic at a little town on the McKenzie River, about 340 miles north of the Arctic Circle. In September 1973, I received word that my father had died in Durban, South Africa. Sometime later, when my brother John and I were settling my father's estate, I was amazed to find that he had left me an unexpected small inheritance. At the time, South African exchange rules made it impossible to get any money out of the country. I'm not sure what gave me the idea, but it occurred to me a way to circumvent this, was to purchase an aircraft and ship it out of the country. My brother and I had owned a Tiger Moth in the late nineteen forties in which we'd both learned to fly. So it was a pretty natural progression to try and find a Tiger Moth. This was easier said than done in the limited time I had available. Nevertheless, I scoured the country and found one, almost derelict, in the back of a hangar in a small northern town. A deal was quickly struck and I illegally ferried it to an airfield outside of Johannesburg. Suffice it to say, I then had it shipped to Vancouver Island where I completely renovated it over a six-year period to the condition it is in today. At the time, my brother John and I agreed that there was little point in putting a memorial headstone on my father's grave in South Africa where it would seldom be seen by anybody, so I decided to name it, "Old Harry," in memory of my dad. I had the name, "Old Harry" painted on the nose. When Lee Brewer bought the airplane and I related the story, he quietly asked if it would be all right for him to retain it. I was deeply touched and still am. Of course, I readily agreed. What could be a more fitting tribute? And now it appears that it might be in perpetuity. Whoever thought? Edward Teague, born in January 1896 in Shropshire, England, and died in Durban, South Africa, in September 1973. He served in the Royal Flying Corps in World War One as a rigger. He served in the South African Air Force as a pilot from 1924 to 1929."

Here is some more about Tiger Moths. If you look at a Tiger Moth, you'll notice that the wings are not mounted square with the fuselage, but swept back. Originally, they were not swept back, and it was difficult to get into the front cockpit because the cabane struts that held the upper wing were partially blocking ingress and egress. When the airplane was sold to the military, (which required wearing parachutes) it was almost impossible for a person to get into the front cockpit, or get out of it for that matter. So the designers sat down and decided to move the wings further forward and, in order to keep the center of lift of the wings where it belonged, the wings were swept back. Now, if it had been an original design feature, the ribs in the wings would be parallel to the relative wind. Looking at the wings on a Tiger Moth, you'll notice that the ribs are square with the leading edge of the wing. Thus, the sweep back modified the airfoil a bit, but apparently it was considered a minor thing.

Another feature that the Tiger Moth has are things called slats on the leading edge of the upper wing extremities. These metal devices, at cruising speeds, are flush with the leading edge of the wing. As the speed of the airplane decreases, the angle of the attack, that is, the angle of the chord (a line from the leading edge to the trailing edge of the wing) is tilted up more and more as speed decreases in order to keep flying. There is a point at which that angle is too steep, and the air, instead of following the curvature of the airfoil, begins to burble and break loose from the upper surface of the wing, destroying lift. Slats are designed to deploy at this point, delaying the burbling, which, if ignored, would precipitate a stall and the plane would not be flying anymore. Slats, when deployed redirect the air stream over the leading edge again and smooth out the airflow over the wing, allowing the airplane to stall at a slower speed. Deployment of slats is automatic, but there are control cables to lock them in the retracted positions. These are to be locked into the retracted position when doing acrobatics. In some maneuvers, whether they are in or not would make no difference. But there are others where they would interfere with a maneuver because one would be extended and the other retracted.

From the cockpit, American engines turn clockwise; British engines, counter clockwise. Both engines, of course, produce a thing called torque. The engine shaft rotates one way, and the airplane wants to rotate the other. (Newton's Law of Action and Reaction.) You can demonstrate this phenomenon for yourself: sit in your car at idle, press the accelerator abruptly, and you'll notice that your automobile wants to rock to the side, opposite to engine shaft rotation. Normally, an aircraft is rigged so this torque is compensated for at power settings for cruising speed. However, at takeoff, with higher power settings, the torque bugaboo requires the pilot to compensate manually for the increased torque by applying rudder deflection to keep the aircraft straight. Operating American engines, right rudder must be applied. Tiger Moths have British engines, so left rudder must be used. Torque rears its ugly head again when power is decreased, as when approaching to land. Since the machine is rigged to compensate for torque at cruising power, any change of power requires compensatory adjustment by the pilot (some right rudder in the Tiger Moth).

More sophisticated airplanes have remotely operated trim tabs on the control surfaces to take care of torque, but Tiger Moths don't have these. So they rely on the pilot to use his controls to keep the Tiger flying properly. The experienced pilot makes these compensations quite automatically, but to a novice or to one used to flying American engines, the Tiger will fly the pilot for a while until he gets the Tiger tamed.

The Tiger Moth does have one control to alleviate different stick pressures in pitch (up and down). There is a lever with spring tension which can be adjusted to neutralize pitch forces on the control stick.

Here are some other Tiger Moth characteristics and idiosyncrasies: Most aircraft engines have a mixture control. This is to regulate the proportion of air to fuel; full 'rich' is used for takeoff and landing. While cruising, the mixture may be leaned out to improve fuel consumption. The degree of leaning depends upon altitude. There's less air the higher you go, so the amount of fuel is lessened accordingly. The fuel control lever is advanced to enrich the mixture, retarding it leans the mixture, and in some aircraft, retarding it fully stops the engine. In a Tiger Moth, this process is reversed. Retarding the mixture control lever enriches the mixture. To land, you want the mixture full rich in case engine power is applied for an aborted landing. The extra step of enriching the mixture is not necessary in a Tiger Moth because it has already been done. In a Tiger Moth there's a simple device to ensure that the mixture is full rich before touchdown. The device is a small tab attached to the throttle lever, and as the throttle is retarded to land, the tab engages the mixture control lever and pulls it back to the full rich position. Below 5000 feet, the Gipsy Major engine is not leaned out at all.

In banking an airplane, there is an undesirable effect caused by an aileron. The aileron that is deflected downward causes the airplane to roll, (as well as the other aileron being deflected upward.) An unwanted effect is caused by the drag of the down aileron, whose area is exposed to the air stream. This drag causes the airplane to yaw in the opposite direction of the desired turn. This is called 'adverse yaw.' The Tiger Moth is rigged so as you move the control stick to roll right, it will cause the left aileron to come down, but only partially. Then, with continued stick movement to the right, the left aileron will return to the streamlined position, so there is no adverse yaw. The same applies to a left turn with the right aileron starting down and then becoming streamlined.

Airplanes sometime develop ice in their carburetors, and if it gets bad enough, power is reduced or worse, the engine quits because it isn't getting enough air. To keep ice from forming, or to get rid of it if it is already there, heated air is introduced. More sophisticated airplanes have a control that admits this heat to the carburetor to forestall icing. The Tiger Moth carburetor gets its air from alongside the hot crankcase, so heated air is automatically fed into the carburetor. This may reduce the efficiency of the engine a bit, but apparently it is a lesser worry than having ice.

The Tiger Moth has no electrical system, therefore, it has no battery, no generator or alternator, no lights nor a starter. Thus, it is restricted to daylight operations and visual conditions. The engine must be cranked by hand, sometimes referred to as an 'Arm Strong' starter. If a radio or interphone between the cockpits is used, batteries must power them. Because the ignition system is not shielded, radios are limited in their use in a Tiger Moth; however, there is an STC for sale that rectifies this problem.

More Tiger Moth stuff: The ignition system on the Gipsy Major engine is similar to most small aircraft engines and embraces redundancy. There are two magnetos, in case one fails; and there are two spark plugs for each cylinder. The ignition switches are located on the outside of the fuselage, one set within reach of each cockpit. The outside location is handy for hand propping.

The fuel system on a Tiger Moth is quite simple. A 23 U.S. gallon fuel tank is mounted between the upper wings over the center of gravity. There's no fuel pump; fuel flows by gravity to a filter and to the carburetor. The engine has four cylinders that produce 130 horsepower. The engine is inverted; this puts the propeller shaft higher off the ground, thus the landing gear legs need not be so long. The engine uses about seven and a half or eight gallons per hour, giving about two-and-a-half hours of flight time with a full tank. This is rather a short endurance; however, it originally was designed as a trainer and most flying lessons last half this time. The short endurance is sometimes welcomed on cross-country flights because if it were any longer, you'd need to have a spare derriere. The lubrication system is the dry sump type as it is on a Harley Davidson motorcycle. Oil is contained in a tank and a pump delivers it to the engine; another pump returns it to the tank. Oil consumption is considerable, about a quart an hour. This rate of oil use is designed to help cool the engine's valves. An STC involves putting different rings on the pistons, diminishing this rate.

Besides an ordinary airspeed indicator in each cockpit, there's a third airspeed indicator that can be seen from both cockpits. It's mounted on the wing struts on the left side of the airplane. This is called a 'windy.' A small flat plate is mounted on a spring, and the force of the relative wind deflects this plate As this flat plate is moved, a pointer shows the airspeed on a calibrated scale. This is handy in the traffic pattern (of which most are left-handed) so one can keep their eyes out of the cockpit and, with a glance, one can see the airspeed. There is a red painted area below the number 45 (miles an hour) which indicates that if the pointer is in this area, the plane is not flying.

Sometimes pilots are surprised at some of the features of this 1932 design: inverted engine, slats, automatic carburetor heat, automatic rich mixture and ailerons designed to eliminate adverse yaw. Originally, the airplane had a system of communication between the cockpits. Leather helmets were fitted with small brass tubes, one for each ear, to which hoses were attached coming from the other cockpit where a funnel shaped speaking cone was attached. One could hear what was spoken from the other cockpit this way. These were called gosports.

There are some other airplanes that I either flew or flew in that I haven't mentioned before. I took navigator training in Lockheed AT-18s, and sometimes in the transport version of the same aircraft, C-60s. The British called these 'Bostons.'

In flexible gunnery school in Florida, we flew in B-17s. This was one of the two principal four engine bombers used throughout the world during the war; the other was the B-24. In radar school at Victorville, California, we flew in both the B-17 and B-24.

During my five-and-a-half years at Nellis Air Force Base in Nevada, besides the F-86, the F-100, T-33 and L-20, I flew a little bit towing targets with the B-26, mentioned elsewhere in my text. While at Nellis, I had a neighbor who flew several different aircraft on the base. He proposed that I checkout in some of these so that I could fly low and slow occasionally in contrast to the high altitude, high-speed jet fighters I was flying. He checked me out in the L-20, later called the U-6. This was a de Havilland aircraft called a Beaver. For a number of years, each Air Force Base had two or more of these aircraft for light duties. I flew them at Nellis, in Europe and in Montana. I also checked out in the Beech C-45, known as the D-18 in its civil capacity.

I have already mentioned the C-47, or DC-3, elsewhere in my text as well as the U-3A, or Cessna 310.

During my time on San Juan Island, I was in two Hollywood films. The first was *Practical Magic*, a concocted story about modern day witches. I was an 'extra' appearing as a Pilgrim, among others, who was witnessing the hanging of a witch in early Massachusetts. The filming was 'cut' three different times during the scene in which I appeared. The first time was when the director saw some whitish object in the distance on the ground. It turned out to be a bleached cow-pie. The second 'cut' was when a cow wandered between the gallows and the Pilgrim crowd. The third 'cut' was made when it was discovered that the noose had not been put around the witch's neck. This was an interesting experience.

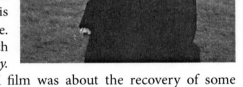

Another movie in which I appeared was *Birds of Prey*. The message in this IMAX film was about the recovery of some endangered raptors after DDT was banned from the environment.

National Geographic came to San Juan Island earlier and had done some research to determine how fast the Peregrine falcon could go. They used the birds of a local falconer and pilot, Kenny Franklin in this test. Incidentally, the speed was 242 miles an hour in a stoop (dive).These flights with the falcon were not part of the film.

Apparently Roy Disney, also a falconer, saw this National Geographic clip and saw fit to make the IMAX film, *Birds of Prey*.

Kenny was contacted to see if he would be interested in being in the film with his birds. He had trained his birds to fly alongside his ultra-light aircraft and also to 'fly' with him while parachuting. He fastened a piece of plastic pipe on the wing struts of his ultra-light and strung a fishing line through it from front to rear. The line was wound on a fishing reel in the cockpit. The bitter end of the line at the aft end of the pipe had a 'bait-ball' attached. This was a small leather sack, weighted, and embellished with some feathers and a piece of rabbit meat. He would climb to altitude and reel out his line and bait. The falcon was on a perch in the cockpit with a hood over its head. Kenny would then remove the hood, pick up the bird and throw it out of the cockpit. The bird would recover, spot the bait and pursue. Kenny would reel in his line bringing the bird alongside and then cut the line. The falcon would siezed the bait and take it to the ground.

The movie director was looking for a beautiful old biplane for scenes in the film, so Kenny contacted me to see if I wanted to participate in the movie making. I fit the bill with my 1937 de Havilland Tiger Moth biplane.

Kenny, thinking perhaps the movie makers might want the routine described above somewhere in the film, asked me if I was willing to practice what he did with his ultra-light. He wanted to see if the bird would perform the same way relative to my biplane. So, with Kenny and the hooded falcon in my front cockpit, I took off and climbed to 2500 feet. Cruising at 50 miles an hour, Kenny reeled out his line and bait, took the hood off the falcon and threw the bird overboard. The next thing I saw was Kenny throwing his reel and line overboard. Why?

On a previous occasion using his ultra-light, the bird had recovered and struck the bait so quickly that it made a roll around the aircraft before Kenny could reel the line in and cut the bait free. Once the bird siezed the bait, it would not release it. The danger was that the bird might hit the propeller or airframe. This quick recovery happened again with my airplane, so Kenny threw his reel and line overboard. The bird was found seven feet from Kenny's front door, having dragged the line and reel some distance.

We made a second flight of this sort. This time all went as planned. Kenny didn't use the line and reel this time but held the bait ball in his hand, wiggling it. The falcon flew alongside and for a few fleeting seconds it looked me in the eye. Kenny then threw the bait ball overboard. The bird struck it and took it to the ground. Not many pilots have flown formation with such a beautiful animal.

The opening scene of the film shows a close-up view of snow covered Mount Baker and the faint sound of an aircraft engine. The sound gradually increases and I fly into view until my airplane is framed in its actual size on the screen. The IMAX screen is huge. Other scenes are showing the airplane taking off, landing and making odd and gentle maneuvers to simulate a student pilot making flying errors. I have never seen this film; I don't believe it has ever been released. Why? I don't know. I do know that the CEO of Disney is now a man named Eisner. Roy Disney has been replaced. Occasionally the director calls Ken or his wife and chats with them but gives no further news about the film's disposition. Perhaps one day I will enjoy my 15 minutes of fame on the silver screen with Old Harry, my airplane.

If this film is ever released, you may not recognize me flying in it. I was a 'stand-in' for Kenny in the flying scenes. Kenny does not sport a beard, let alone a gray one, so I had to shave mine off . Helmet and goggles hide the rest of my features. Part of the story has Kenny teaching his young son how to fly, so a small person in my front cockpit was a 'stand-in' for him in some scenes. Twice it was the assistant director and another time it was a young woman. Fun, fun, fun!

Collision With Hangar

On June 2, 2006, Old Harry had just completed its annual inspection and I was taxiing out to fly. I was zig-zagging back and forth which is necessary for forward clearance. Leaving my hangar, I made a 90 degree left turn using my heel brakes. On turning back to the right, the brake failed.

I tried to continue the turn with the rudder only, but a hangar got in the way. A dent in the left slat and a wasted wood propeller resulted.

Old Harry has a new prop now and the dent is fixed, plus, taking advantage of the down time, some dents in the engine cowling have been removed and some vibration cracks welded. Old Harry awaits paint and then it will be hot to trot. Why did the brake fail? A cotter pin (split pin, since the airplane is British) was missing from the brake linkage.

In preparing for the annual, I was on my hands and knees in the front cockpit lubricating the rudder linkage, using a spray can (the only way to reach the linkage). I had used part of an old sweat shirt to wipe up the excess lube. I noticed that it had caught on something, but I pulled it loose. I believe that was how the cotter pin was removed.

An article in a recent issue of Smithsonian's "Air and Space" magazine told of a 'club,' recognizing those who had the misfortune of 'bending' a prop. I applied and now have a certificate showing that I have had four of these misfortunes: Old Harry, my Ryan PT-22, number three prop (and half the engine) on my B-29 and number four prop (which was struck by number three engine and prop when it tore off). This was on June first, 1945, over Osaka, Japan.

Chapter Fourteen

Building A Log Cabin

After retirement in 1968, there was another hiatus relative to flying for a while. Again, it was first things first. I busied myself for the first two years building a house. During the time I lived in the house, I looked for other things to occupy my time. One of these was building a car. I looked into the kit-car market and found that the kits were expensive and offered very little for my money. So I went to the drug store and bought a model kit, took a pair of dividers and scaled-up the dimensions of the model to that of a small car. I took a Volkswagen frame from one source and a VW engine from another and started with those bare bones. To make the body, I built it somewhat like a model airplane, using plywood as formers and wood and metal (welded thin wall tubing) for stringers to give it some shape. Next I applied a layer of polyurethane foam and then four layers of fiberglass (two of mat and two of cloth). I moved the gas tank from the front to the rear. The

Replica of a 1927 Bugatti

steering column was extended two feet. as were the clutch, brake and accelerator pedals. I had a friend paint it gray, with black fenders. I painted 1928 model A Ford wire wheels yellow. A few years later, after I finished it and tried to license it, the State of Washington balked for reasons that are too long to explain here. The model I used was a 1927 French, Model 35-B Bugatti. This is as cute as a bug's ear, but has sat unlicensed for about twenty years.

I met a young woman on Lopez Island twenty-five years my junior in 1973. She had lost her job and intended to go back home to Spokane. I offered her a place to live in my house in Friday Harbor and helped her get a job there. This association would last about 30 years. After a while she was unhappy living in my house and found a place to rent, at the same time, inviting me to come along. I did this, not once, but at three different rentals. She wasn't happy with this arrangement, so I encouraged her to buy some property. She did this, then she wanted to build a log cabin on this property and wanted to know if I would help her. I did this, and the agreement, (as a jest) was that I would be paid 10 cents an hour. I would have no claim on the property because I didn't need it. Next, she wanted a pond, primarily to attract wildlife. Periodically, she stocked it with trout. I helped to build this pond clearing timber and doing some work with a small bulldozer I had. We built the cabin, but it had no plumbing. I built an outhouse and a smokehouse for the salmon we caught. A shallow well was dug and I built a crude pump house, as well as a wood shed, and a shed for a generator I bought (the first of four generators.) Later, she bought a horse, which needed a paddock and a shed for it and hay storage. I built these.

Most of the lumber that was used to build a shelter for her horse was cut with my chain saw mill. Later, windstorms blew down 40 or 50 trees. I bucked these up into sixteen-foot lengths and skidded them out of the woods with my little bulldozer. I stacked these up for future use.

The cabin was built using concrete pier blocks on which creosoted posts were erected. These posts were salvaged from the beach, having been set adrift as waste by pile drivers. We dragged logs off the beach using a winch on a pickup truck. A logging truck brought them to the building site. The only tools we had to assemble the logs were hand winches (called come-a-longs), a peavey, an ax, and a chain saw. As the walls arose, it became increasingly difficult for lack of other tools, so, after five logs in height, I framed the rest of the walls in a conventional way and these were covered with plywood sheathing, and finished with cedar shakes that I had hand split.

The roof was of tongue and grooved hemlock car decking, tar paper, then shakes that I had split by hand from cedar bolts gleaned from the beach. An interior post that supported a beam was a totem pole, which I had carved and given to her for a Christmas earlier.

I bulldozed a trail up the hill and roughly along her western property line, so she could exercise her horse there. I dug a trench from the pump house to the cabin and laid plastic pipe to a stock-watering tank of 220 gallons under the cabin. I plumbed the cabin with plastic

The log cabin I built on San Juan Island, WA

pipe. We used a 12-volt battery to pressurize the water; this wasn't too satisfactory, so I installed a pressure tank and a demand-type water pump, powered by a small generator. A toilet, sink and shower were added next to replace the outhouse. Next, I made a laundry building to facilitate washing and drying clothes.

A solar system was installed using solar panels, associated controls and large storage batteries. This system primarily provided lighting where propane had been used before. She wanted a deck on two sides of the cabin; I built these and associated staircases. I also built a staircase inside the cabin so that the loft could be used for a bedroom. Some of my artwork in the form of woodcarvings was used to decorate the ends of the barge boards on the gable ends of the roof plus a piece at the apex of the south gable.

I built a garage with the timber I had piled up. I bought a small band sawmill, moving the logs with my bulldozer, and cut them into dimension lumber. I cut enough lumber to frame a 24' X 32' garage. A neighbor had some large cedar trees that had been blown down in a storm and offered them to me. I milled these into siding for the garage. All this construction was done without power tools (except the saw mill). The roof of the garage was of steel. A few years earlier, I had bought a large quantity of steel roofing from a lumber company in town that had replaced its roof. So, this was put to good use. I paid for a concrete pad in front of the garage as well as part of a septic tank installation. I paid the last $800.00 to retire the mortgage on her land. Next, a deep well was drilled and good water found. Also about this time, electricity was brought in through the cooperation of neighbors. She wanted a water tower to improve the plumbing system; this was hired done using lumber that I had milled.

She was unsatisfied with the dark interior of the cabin so I installed two skylights. Still unsatisfied, an additional room, 16-feet square, was built; she called it the 'sun-room.' I did the framing with my milled lumber and siding with more hand-split shakes. I bought and installed six 4-foot by 4-foot windows. The underpinnings, flooring and roofing were hired. I did the dry wall work in the sunroom. The old deck was rotting, so I tore it out and replaced it plus extending it on the south side of the building.

A perennial task of mine was cutting and splitting firewood to feed a wood heating stove, (actually, three stoves over time), that I bought to heat the cabin.

She was unhappy with the cabin and over a period of a few years, became unhappier, and resolved to tear it down. Her plan was to a build a new home, retaining the sunroom. She wanted to know if I would contribute to this new enterprise. I balked because it would involve a substantial portion of my life savings and at age 80, I felt I should have the use of my savings. Because of this and probably other factors, I was told, on the 30th of January, 2004, to "Get out... go!" I got out. During these 31 years I paid no rent but I did on occasion pay half her property taxes. Upon separation, I made no claim for labor that I provided during 31 years. At the outset, I did all these things for her to help her to establish an estate with the understanding that none of it would belong to me because I didn't need it. I had provided all the furnishings for the cabin, and when I left, I didn't take everything. I left the heating stove, kitchen range, washer, drier, hot water heater and double bed, all of which allowed the cabin to be livable. Incidentally, the totem pole and mantle piece that I had carved for her were cut up into pieces by a chain saw and dumped in my yard. I asked why she had done this, but no answer was given. I have reassembled the parts of the totem pole as a monument to vindictiveness.

When I met her, she had nothing. What was the reason I did all these things for her? There must have been some attachment. I went along with all her wishes (except a hot tub). She complained that I didn't express my attachment in words. Now, we aren't all alike. Some of us show our feelings by our deeds and don't feel a need to verbalize them. If I like persons, I do things for them. There is more than one way to be romantic, but perhaps I don't fit the norm.

She was dissatisfied with me as a partner and has outlined this in detail, although it took her 30 years to voice this. My only regret is that I have lived with an alcoholic a second time in my life and its insidious effects. I don't like smoking either.

During these years, I gave up my home I built before I met her and I abandoned my dream of building a log cabin on my waterfront property on Henry Island. Apparently I've outlived my usefulness to her and was shown the door (which I had made by hand). I had essentially become little more than a handy-man.

Another activity during this period, involved Emil Olson, a 92 year old gentleman at the convalescent center. He owned an old fishing boat he had built in Alaska in 1915. It was a troller, used in commercial salmon fishing. It sat in Friday Harbor at anchor, Charlie's father caring for it. He got tired of this and told Emil, who then looked for someone to give it to. I heard of this and I went to see him; he was born in Norway, and he had shipped out in the Norwegian Navy at age fifteen. Besides sailing in the Norwegian Navy, he sailed in square-riggers. One time he told me that they had an average speed of seventeen knots from Rio to Cape Town. Well, the old gentleman said, I give it to you." So we accomplished some paperwork and I took it over. I did some work on the boat and got the engine running. It was a Sterling two cylinder gas engine, made in Tacoma in 1922. The

The boat Falcon aka: Two Bits

sound the engine made when running sounded like: two bits, two bits, two bits. Consequently, that was one of the monicers applied to the boat: "Two Bits." Another was "Chug-a Dig-a." Each time I visited Emil, he would tell me that "Falcon" was the true name of the boat because that was the name of the first ship that he sailed on in the Norwegian Navy. The engine was fascinating. To start it, one drained some gasoline from the bottom of the carburetor, poured some into each cylinder through a priming cup attached to each cylinder, put a steel bar (called a Johnson bar) in a hole in the flywheel, turned this until it was under compression,. Next, one held the fly-wheel with the left hand and extracted the Johnson bar and set it aside. One then closed a knife-switch. Current from a six volt battery would energize two model T Ford coils, (one for each cylinder) providing energy to the spark plugs. After the engine started, one would then shift the ignition to a magneto. The battery was charged by a six-volt automobile generator.

I replaced the canvas on top of the cabin and some woodwork. We fished for bottom fish with this boat, and also made trips around the islands and one time to Sidney, British Columbia. Later, when I bought Rain Bird, my schooner, Falcon was surplus to me. Two young men, who had worked at Roche Harbor during the summer, had saved their money and were looking for a boat that they could use for commercial bottom fishing. I sold it to them for what it cost me to renovate the boat, and off they went.

In October of 1972, they had the boat tied up to a piling on Stuart Island; a stiff wind arose, broke the rope and the boat went on the rocks and sank. When I learned of this, I went up to Stuart Island, thinking that I could find some of the debris on a particular beach. I was right. I salvaged some of the canvas that I had just put on the cabin top and some wood trim. Later, I used these as a frame for a painting I made of "Two-Bits." Mark and I took a small tape recorder down to the boat one time and captured all the noise that was made in starting the engine. We took the tape up to let Emit listen to it. His blue eyes sparkled and he was delighted, immediately recognizing his old friend. I have a couple of souvenirs from the Falcon: a clock that doesn't work and a small compass that I keep in a glass case with other memorabilia. We never told Emil that the boat had been destroyed.

Chapter Fourteen

Rain Bird

This month marks 37 years since I bought the schooner Rain Bird. Since this object has been a large part of my life since retirement, please allow me to relate salient features of this love affair.

While visiting my brother Bob, he told me of a tugboat he had seen from his office window where he worked in Tacoma. Knowing I had a penchant for tugboats, he suggested we take a drive and look at it. When we arrived there, it was gone. Then, having read an ad in a Seattle paper about a schooner for sale in Tacoma, we went to take a look at it. This was a boat designed and built by Bill Garden, probably the foremost yacht designer in the northwest. I was struck by its beauty and got out my wallet. Mark and I went down to Tacoma to take possession. The first day we got as far as Shilshole Marina in Seattle. The second day we got to Friday Harbor, however,

My acrylic painting of Rain Bird

the leg from Port Townsend to Friday harbor was somewhat rough. Mom had given us some sustenance to take along including some salami. Mark ate more than his share of this and became seasick. A contributing factor may have been water sloshing around on the deck inside the hull. The boat, having sat idle for some time and being made of wood, had allowed some seams above the waterline to open a bit and allowed some water to enter to the dismay of Mark. I put him to work pumping the bilge and that seemed good medicine for him. So began (to date) 37 years of hard labor.

A wooden boat requires a good deal of maintenance. Consider putting your furniture out of doors and trying to keep it looking its best. A good deal of this labor must be conducted on hands and knees, which brings me to the present time, when I have a faulty knee, and I find this work more and more demanding. I'm considering selling the boat. Years ago, a man came along dockside and asked me if I would consider selling the boat. I told him that if I got in a position where I couldn't take care of it, or couldn't sail it, I would think about it. Each spring, in the month of March, for few years, I would get a call, saying, "Brewer? How's your health?" Then one time I saw him in Victoria with his own boat and he no longer called me.

Rain Bird 'On the hard'

During the summer, my regimen was to work on the boat in the mornings and go sailing in the afternoons. To amuse myself, I would often chase other sailboats to see if I could overtake them. Then one day I saw the designer-builder, Bill Garden, and he asked me if I raced the boat. When I said no, he said I should. So, having a lengthy list of sailboats that I had overtaken amusing myself, I thought, "Why not?" So, I cast about to see if there were a sailing club or yachting club that would accept me. Racing costs the sponsor money, so one has a situation where "if you invite me to your race I'll invite you to mine." This mandates that a person belong to some club or organization that sponsors races, making it a reciprocal arrangement. Now, some races are 'open,' that is, open to anyone that wants to participate. However, the bulk of races require that you to belong to an organization as I've described. So, I cast about, looking for an organization I could join. There was a yacht club in Friday

Harbor, however, there were no sailboats in it. Then I heard there was a sailing association in Canada, called the Canadian Forces Sailing Association. This was a club allied with the military. So, I contacted them by telephone and told them who I was and my connection with the military. I asked them if they would entertain an application from a foreigner; the answer was, "Why not," so I applied. I am seldom at the facility, which is in Esquimalt Harbor which also, houses Canadian warships. I try to get over every spring for their opening day ceremony, but sometimes weather or other factors prevent this. I rationalize

Honorary Commodore. Victoria Classic Boat Festival, 1983

that I am the best member (since 1976) they have: I pay my dues and I don't use the facilities. So that started racing. I haven't raced much since about 1988 or so. I won just about every recurring race in the local area plus some down sound as well as in Canada.

A handicap system is used in most races, if it wasn't, not many would participate because the fastest boat would win most of the time. The system is designed to level the playing field so that everybody has a chance to win. There is a formula to determine a handicap. It contains many factors. A boat ends up with a number that represents the number of seconds that the particular boat may deduct from each nautical mile of the racecourse. Thus, a large number is given to the naturally slower boat and, conversely, a low number is given to a fast boat. A major factor in the formula is the waterline length of the boat (not the overall length). Longer waterlines allow greater speeds. This is because, a 'displacement hull,' (as contrasted a skimming or planing hull) can only go so fast. As it moves through the water, it forms a bow wave from the bow on back. What goes up, must come down, so water is pushed up to a crest then the water descends, forming a trough. The faster the boat goes, the longer this wave becomes until the trough is under the aft end of the boat. Now the boat hull has no support in the rear and it squats down in the trough and tries to sail uphill on the aft slope of the wave generated. It can't do this, thus there is a limit for each boat. This limit is called the 'hull speed.' It is determined by taking the square root of the waterline length times a constant of 1.34. For example, a boat with a waterline length of 25 feet (the square root of 25 is 5; 5 X 1.34 is 6.7 knots); this is its speed limit. It is easy to see that a longer waterline length would allow greater speed. Some other factors are the square footage of the raced sail area, whether the boat has a thin fin keel or a full length keel, a folding propeller (to reduce drag) or not, whether the boat will use free-flying sails or not (like a spinnaker), and other miscellaneous factors.

My boat, "Rain Bird," has a large handicap; it is possible for me to cross the finish line last and still win after the arithmetic is done. It is amusing to see sailors scratch their heads when they see an old wooden boat, single-handed (the way most of my racing has been done) awarded first place.

Odd things happen when racing. The following might be interesting. I once won a trophy for a race that I wasn't in. Annually, there was a 'Round the Island Race out of Friday Harbor. This was a two day affair, going around the island in a prescribed direction, staying overnight at Snug Harbor. I did well the first day, but didn't know that I was first. It was a beautiful day to be sailing and guests were to arrive the next morning in Friday Harbor, so I continued around the island and went home. That year, for the first time, a special trophy was offered in honor of an avid sailor who had recently died. This trophy was to be given to the boat that

My 'Rain Bird' with the lowers: main, fore and jib

had the best showing for the two days. It happened that there wasn't enough wind to allow anyone to complete the course in the allotted time the second day. Having won on the first day, that was it, and I wasn't even in the race the second day.

In another race, I had my choice of being either first or last. This was a single-handed race from Cadboro Bay on Vancouver Island to Esquimalt Harbor via Trial Island and the Quarantine Buoy. The breeze was light from the east and I had up my maximum amount of sail. After a mile or so, I was leading the fleet. Our course took us out into Baines Channel, the current there being from the east to west which essentially cancelled the light wind. I was adrift with the current and was being carried toward some rocks, and to avoid them, I started my engine and turned up wind, motoring behind the whole fleet. I shut the engine off and began sailing again. Upon arriving at the finish line and securing my boat to a float, a person came down and said, " Well, congratulations, I guess you won." I said I had started my engine, although I told him I had looked at the race instructions and there was nothing said about starting engines. In other races, I had seen the proviso that allowed engines to be used to stay off the rocks or get out of the ferry's way or other ship that had the right away, just so long as a sailor didn't gain on the course. This man said he'd seen me do what I described. I then asked him if anyone else had done the same thing. He said four others had and he added that they had withdrawn from the race. So right there, I had my choice of being first or last. I withdrew and that was that.

I was in a single-handed race from Vancouver to Nanaimo and back, a two-day race. We were told that the boat that would finish us would be the same vintage powerboat that started us. There was a southerly breeze and I had done well. As I approached the finish, some multi-hulled boats had caught up and passed me. They had started later than the mono-hulled boats, being naturally faster. Then all of a sudden, those multi-hulled boats changed course. I wondered why. I took a look through my binoculars and saw a sailboat anchored near a red buoy and I followed the multi-hulls across a finish line. There was a blue pennant flying from the anchored boat's forestay (designating a committee boat), and a person on the bow calling out the time as I passed by. I hove to and started to douse my sails, then I noticed the boat that had started us was about a half mile away anchored near a buoy. I went over there and crossed the briefed finish line, hove to, doused my sails and motored in to the moorage. There were 110 boats in the race and about 95 used only the first finish line; they actually had not completed the course. There was a lot of concern about this and the race committee people held a meeting. They had made a gross error and to attempt to rectify things, they took everyone's time across the first line and extrapolated it to the second line. How did this happen? This race was sponsored by the Royal Naval Sailing

Association of Vancouver and a young lieutenant had been tasked to go to Nanaimo and arrange for berthing for the racing boats. He had done this; then a few days later, he had been transferred to Hawaii. Another young lieutenant was appointed in his place and he thought part of his job was to arrange the finish line at Nanaimo, thus, there were two lines. The second day, I didn't do too well on the run back to Vancouver. This was an odd one.

At the start of another race, the current was running north to south and the wind was light out of the north. As the starting time approached, all the boats were trying to make their way upwind, trying to keep from drifting backwards across the starting line. I happened to be on the western extremity of the line. As the starting time approached, one by one, all the boats, except mine, drifted backwards on the wrong side of the committee boat. So I had a backward start across the starting line and was all alone. The light breeze persisted, and I never got to the finish line within the time limit. The tidal current had changed, and being a slower boat, I was hung out to dry. For some years I complained about this; boats with high handicaps (meaning they were slow) would often be caught by a change of tide which controls currents, while the faster boats would arrive at the destination prior to the tidal change. Hence, high handicapped boats were discriminated against. Also, slower boats, if the race were in the afternoon, would tend to run of out of wind as the sun went down, whereas the faster boats had a better chance to get to the finish line. I think this has been compensated for but I don't know for sure.

Well, sailboats aren't all pleasure, especially an older wooden boat, whose maintenance demands quite a bit of time and some money. There are marine organisms that attack the bottom of boats. Because of this, the boat must be hauled out of the water about once a year to prevent attack. The organisms come in two varieties: plants and animals. Seaweed likes to grow on boats; worms like to eat wood. Where I am, there are two types: one is a worm called a gribble which bores tiny holes in the wood, leaving it look like a sponge, the other is the teredo, a wood boring crustacean which bores holes sometimes big enough to stick your finger into. One can see the work of both of these by looking at the driftwood on saltwater beaches. Other animals can grow on the bottom of your boat: oysters, mussels and the ubiquitous barnacle. To form a barrier against these organisms, one paints the bottom of his boat with a poisonous paint. The poison is usually copper oxide. This paint comes in various colors and it is not unusual to pay a hundred dollars a gallon for this paint.

When a boat is removed from the water, usually at a shipyard, the staff removes most of the organisms with a pressure washer. Barnacles, mussels and other hard organisms have to be removed mechanically by scraping.

At one time, other paints contained tri-butyl-tin oxide. This was found to be too poisonous and was outlawed. Cleaning the bottom and applying the protective paint not only preserves the underwater surface, but also reduces friction, which slows the boat down. If you move your boat to fresh water, it will kill the salt-water organisms.

There is an electronic process that attacks metal submerged in saltwater. If you put more than one kind of metal in salt water, you would have a battery. In the periodic table of the elements, there is a group of metals, which are classified by their 'nobility.' The less noble metal in an electrolyte, such as saltwater, will give itself up to a more noble metal. This is called galvanic corrosion and it will cause metal parts under water to be destroyed. You can demonstrate this galvanic action by taking a lemon, insert a penny (copper) in one end of the lemon and a nickel in the other end. The lemon juice is an electrolyte and all of this will form a small battery, the nickel giving itself up to plate the copper.

Stray electrical currents can cause electronic corrosion. One current is the result of differences in the grounding of electricity on land and that in the water. When using shore power on your boat, you should be careful to keep the electrical cable out of the water. One microscopic hole in the insulation of the cable could cause the disintegration of underwater metal parts on your boat. Faulty wiring on a boat can also lead to electrolysis.

Zinc, which is on the bottom of the totem pole of nobility, is used to combat electronic and galvanic corrosion below the waterline. Various shapes of this metal are fastened to the major underwater metals on a boat's bottom. If the forces of corrosion are present, these zincs will give themselves up first, thus protecting the keel, propeller and other metal fittings.

Boat maintenance involves some costs. To haul out, normally you have to use the facilities of a shipyard. These folks charge a fee to remove your boat from the water and another fee for pressure cleaning. Of course there are labor costs if you hire help. Moorage is another cost. Most marinas usually charge by the foot of boat length, payable monthly. Most marinas don't own the bottom where they are constructed, it belongs to the State. The bottom is leased to the marina, which in turn, passes this cost on to the tenants. Insurance is another cost. This comes in the same varieties as automobile insurance. Then there are parts of the boat that need to be overhauled or replaced. One of the first things I replaced was some of the cables that support the masts, called shrouds. Originally, these were of galvanized steel. Over time, these corroded, so I replaced some of these with stainless steel shrouds. Then there are those wooden members that have to do with controlling the sails; these we call spars. The spar that held the jib sail snapped in two during a race; I replaced it with another that I made. This one also broke later. The third time, I made one of a fir four by four and was careful not to make any holes for screws that held fittings on the spar, because eventually, they'll allow water to enter, weaken the wood and cause it to fail. A major cost was replacing the foremast. I noticed a soft spot near the base of the mast inside the boat, and digging around a little bit. I found some rot, so I had a new mast made.

Checking my engine prior to using the boat one time, I noticed some engine oil in the coolant, and draining some oil from the crankcase, the first thing that came out was anti freeze. So the engine had to be overhauled. It was a four-cylinder diesel engine with only about 2,600 hours of use of a potential 10,000. However, it didn't fail because of use or misuse. My mechanic discovered an error in assembling the engine. Of a 30-year warranty, it only had a few months to go, and it was useless to make a claim. This was a major expense, and to do things right, I also had the transmission overhauled at the same time.

A lesser cost was losing the heat exchanger for the oil system, and later, the heat exchanger for the transmission. Another time, when coming back from Canada under engine power, I prepared to moor and reduced the throttle, as I did, I heard a loud clashing sound and shut the engine down. This involved replacing a thing called a damper plate, which is attached to the engine's flywheel. So, things happen. Right now, I believe my built-in battery charger is malfunctioning. It's about 40 years old, so I believe a new one is needed.

Other costs include the initial purchase price, sales tax, diesel fuel for the engine, oil, transmission fluid, grease and other lubricants. When I bought the boat, diesel fuel cost 28¢ a gallon; at this writing, it is more than $2.28 a gallon. Sails can be a major cost. They're made of 'orlon' (polyester), which deteriorates because of ultraviolet radiation.

Periodically, they need to be replaced. Other maintenance involves keeping the exterior of the boat protected using paint and varnish, pine tar and other products. One might discover a soft spot in some of the wood. This needs to be removed, new wood spliced in, made fair and finished. If the boat is brand new, you're not likely to spend much time doing this, however, I find each year I spend more time on this type of maintenance.

The person I bought Rain Bird from was an avid sailor. He entered and won many notable races, one of which was the Master Mariners' Race in San Francisco Bay. This was a race between older classical sailing vessels, mostly schooners, ketches and yawls. He outfitted Rain Bird with a 90-gallon steel tank that straddled the trunk cabin. The reason he did this was to carry enough fuel to reach San Francisco without going into the hazardous Oregon ports. I spoke to one of the crew members who was on this trip, (who used to live in Friday Harbor) and he said they arrived at San Francisco on one day, made a practice trip around the race course on the second day, then on the third day, raced and won first place. The following day they headed back for the Northwest. The former owner was a building contractor and quite busy, so he didn't waste much time on this trip.

Another feather in his cap was participating in the Victoria-Maui race from Victoria, British Columbia to Maui, Hawaii. This was in 1968, and at that time there was an organization called the Cruising Club of America that handicapped sailboats. This organization divided the boats into three classes A, B and C. Boats were assigned to one of these classes, depending upon several factors, which was an attempt to put similar vessels in the same category. Rain Bird was first in her class and third over all. On the return trip to the Northwest, the engine failed. The engine was only used to charge the batteries to provide power for making radioed position reports. Rain Bird hailed a steamer and if asked if they would relay a position report for them. When the steamer crew learned that their batteries were dead, they gave them some new ones. One day, about fifteen or twenty years ago, a man came alongside my berth and said that he recognized my boat and related that at one time he and his crew had given Rain Bird some batteries at sea.

Bill Johnson, the former owner, won other prestigious races including Barkley Sound, Vashon Island, and the Little Swiftsure three consecutive years and probably many others that I don't know about. The reason Johnson sold Rain Bird was that he had two teenage daughters and there is not a very much room below decks. He bought a larger boat in Florida and brought it to the Northwest. On one occasion, when I was out sailing, I noticed a large boat approaching; I recognized Johnson and hove to and changed a sail so I could race him up the channel toward Friday Harbor. He liked this. I beat him into the harbor and he seemed to enjoy the encounter with his old friend. Former owners of Rain Bird number six: Garden himself, two sets of partners and Bill Johnson. Since I have had the boat, I have met them all.

Over the years, while working on the boat, I have had many visitors stop by. One time, it was a former owner that lived on the East Coast. He said he had some winches that came off the boat and offered to send them to me. I now have those on the boat.

Another person said he knew the designer-builder Bill Garden when he was building Rain Bird. He said Bill didn't have much money at the time, however, one day he showed up with a nice tweed jacket, and he assumed Bill was seeing better times. Bill turned around and showed him a hole it in the jacket; this person told me that Bill said it was a bullet hole, and that he got the jacket at the morgue. Later, I asked Bill about this and he said it was not a bullet hole but a knife hole.

Over the years, there have been two different people who have come by the boat and said they had contacted Garden and asked if he would release the drawings of Rain Bird because they wanted to build a sister ship. Both of these people said that the reply from Garden was that he was not interested. Why would this be? Well, he built the boat himself and also spent his honeymoon aboard. So, there may be some sentimental attachment that is guarded by not seeing replicas.

Shortly after I bought Rain Bird, I went to Deer Harbor, on Orcas Island. An elderly gentleman helped me secure my lines, and as I stepped off the boat, he shook my hand and said that he had built the boat. Knowing that Garden had built it, I found out later that this man was Marty Monson in whose shipyard Garden had built the boat.

A few years ago, while working on the boat with my back toward the dock, I heard a voice say, "I have the original bill of sale for this boat and I find it's faulty, so I've come to pick up my boat." When I turned around, there was Bill Garden and Ernie Gann, a local resident and famed author and aviator. These two were old friends. Ernie asked Bill how much it would cost to build another Rain Bird. Bill said that he had spent 7000 hours on its construction, and at the time of their visit, shipyard labor rate was $40.00 an hour. So, that made $280,000.00

without considering the cost of materials.

Polyester plastic with reinforcing glass fibers has revolutionized the boat building industry. Probably more than 95% of the boats found in a marina now are made of plastic. A few might be of steel or even ferro-cement, but very few of wood. This is both good and bad; good because it allows many more people to enjoy being on the water and good because maintenance is not as great as it is with older wooden boats; bad because the skills and craftsmanship that built wooden boats has disappeared to a large extent.

Ernie Gann was also an artist, and in his later years, he spent quite a bit of time at this. Occasionally, when I saw him in the marina, he would say, "Come out sometime and bring your paint box." I never did this but I wish I had. I always seemed to be too busy.

One day, when I was talking to a friend by the boat, Ernie came by and said, "I thought you'd like to have this." He leaned an object up against the boat and walked away. It was one of his paintings: Rain Bird in an evening scene, coming down the bay in the moonlight. I still have this and appreciate his gesture.

Sailboats have different kinds of rigs. Most of them are sloops, which have a single mast that is tall with a somewhat small main sail foot and a large sail forward, called a jib. If it is really big, it's called a Genoa jib. Another single masted sailboat is called a cutter. At first glance, it looks like a sloop, but on closer inspection, you will see that the mast is further aft than it is on a sloop, and cutters usually have two fore stays to the sloop's one. If the vessel has more than one mast, it will be a schooner, ketch or a yawl. Ketches and yawls have the tallest mast forward and a shorter one called a mizzen, in the rear. If the mizzen is forward of the steering station, it's a ketch; if it is aft of the steering station, it's a yawl. A schooner has two or more masts. If it has only two, (as most schooners do) a shorter one will be forward of the taller main mast. If the masts are of equal lengths, it can be a schooner as well. Different rigs have their good and bad points.

Rain Bird is a schooner. Schooners excel if the wind is on the beam (a crosswind). They were developed on the East Coast to take advantage of both sea breezes and land breezes. During the day, the earth heats up more than the water along the coast, the air rises over the land, being heated, and as it does, it is replaced by cooler air coming in from the sea. Thus, you have a wind more or less perpendicular to the coast. At night, the land cools off quicker than the water does, and the process is reversed, again having a breeze perpendicular to the coast.

Schooners were developed to take advantage of this phenomenon. Square-riggers, which dominated coastal trade, were replaced by schooners. Whereas it took many men to go aloft to bend on or douse sails on a square-rigger, a schooner only required one man per mast.

In racing a schooner on a reach, it excels. If the course requires going up wind, the schooner will not point quite as high, that is, sail as close to the wind as say, a sloop, and in an archipelago like the San Juan islands, winds tend to follow the channels around the islands. Consequently, racecourses among islands find boats beating up against the wind or running downwind, but seldom finding the wind on the beam. These factors are not compensated for in a handicapping system.

There was an old gentleman, since deceased, named Arnold Sheldon who lived in Friday Harbor. He built his own sailboat and enjoyed using it. He also enjoyed using his talent of writing verse. For a while, the local newspaper would publish one of his verses each week. He eventually compiled some of these and published a book of verse, called "Ferry Tales of the San Juans... from bad to verse." I was honored when he wrote one about my schooner and me:

> Lee Brewer and his Rain Bird make a very lovely sight,
> Enchanting ferry passengers with nautical delight.
> He tacks his schooner back and forth, and with expertise,
> Does everything a crew would do with single-handed ease.
> The way he manages that gear almost makes it seem
> As though he and his boat are one, a one-man, one-boat team!
> Other yachtsmen, seeing this, have marveled at his skill.
> But some of them were jealous though they bore him no ill will.
> Brewer, getting wind of this, with self-serving humor,
> Got his friends to spread around a Doughnut Shop-type rumor
> Of how he had a crew below obeying his commands,
> Grinding winches, hauling lines, responding to demands.
> While he lounged in his cockpit putting on his show,
> They were making him look good working down below!
> Now all the town's in on his joke and everybody loves it
> Let the tourists figure out how the hell he does it!

Chapter Fifteen

Art in My Life

As I age, I can look back and see some of the factors that made me what I am. I grew up during The Great Depression when life was drab in comparison to life today. Money was close to nonexistent. Money might enlarge one's horizons, but it wasn't available. As I remember, to escape the mundane, entertainment was sought. Movies were popular and provided temporal escape as did the radio, (which was better in one respect than later TV because it required the mind to be creative in order to make images to match the narrative). Also, looking around the corner to see what the world looked like outside of one's individual confines seemed to be inviting. One way to do this was to observe, that is, look at things that seemed attractive and either take note of these or pursue some that didn't cost anything, or cost very little. What were these things? They might be labeled as 'cultural' aspects of life. In my case, early on, I seemed to be attracted to good-looking things. Nobody told me what was good-looking, or what was ugly, but unconscious observation seemed to single out the fact that some things were better looking than others. I noticed this in automobiles. Not all looked the same as they seem to today. They were easily differentiated from one another. One could tell at a glance what make a car was without looking at its logo. As a youngster, the cars that appealed mostly to me were those that have since made their way into the ranks of 'classics' over the years.

In 1951 the Museum of Modern Art in New York had an exhibit that was concerned with the esthetics of automobile design.* They showed eight of what they considered to be the most beautiful cars ever built. Not knowing what these were nor even knowing that such an exhibit took place, it is interesting that I have owned four of these: a 1937 Cord, two different models of the 1948 Lincoln Continental, a 1949 Jeep and five different Volkswagen Bugs. Although the Jeep and the Volkswagen are not beauties in my mind, they were included in the exhibit because hey are absolutely functional machines, there isn't any thing in or on them that is not functional. Who is to argue that functionality is not an element of beauty?

1948 Lincoln Continental Cabriolet

Generally, airplanes fall within the good-looking category, although there have been and are some ugly ones. Most airplanes are good-looking because they are functional in design. There isn't anything there that has no function: no frills or decorative parts (although paint jobs may detract or enhance the appearance of aircraft.) There are no 'dress-up' parts as you can find in automotive catalogs to tack on to your car, motorcycle or even to your boat. For example, musical horns, hood ornaments or even bumper stickers. Other good-looking things are tugboats or towboats. They are handsome because they don't have anything that is nonfunctional. What's there is to do its job. If any element of a design is not strictly

1942 Harley Davidson WLC, 45 cubic inch flathead

functional, it is superfluous, useless to the task under consideration. I didn't learn this in school. The appreciation of good-looking things

Both of these vehicles were included by the Museum of Modern Art as among the most beautiful cars ever made

* From the Ethetics of Motorcar Design, at the Museum of Modern Art, Autumn 1951

Mom with Cord

Some of my paintings:

An early pastel drawing from 1942

seems to have been unconsciously realized naturally. Early evidence of this seems to have come about simultaneously with a creative urge, that is, a propensity to work with my hands, thus, I made models of boats and airplanes and I liked to draw. Drawing was quite limited because of lack of materials. A stub of a pencil might be around but there was no paper to be had except scratch paper from school. I recall making a drawing of a woman's head to give to my girl friend for Christmas when I was about 13. I took a sheet of rough paper from an unused photo album and worked at it until my erasures made a hole in the paper. I was embarrassed giving it to her, but I had no money to buy a gift. The crude offering was accepted and her parents offered some suggestions and encouraged me. I started making sketches of movie stars

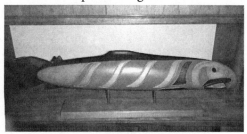

Sockeye Salmon, Western Red Cedar; carving

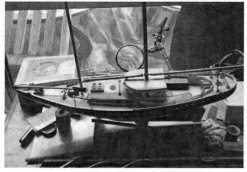

Model of Rain Bird, Yellow Cedar unfinished

from magazines and their images could be recognized. There were no art lessons; just observation, trial and error.

In grade school, some talent was discerned by the art teacher; I overheard her telling my mother this evaluation when I was ten. One likes what one does well and I enjoyed the art classes. I don't recall any art classes in junior high school although there were mechanical drawing courses. I took these and liked them. There were art classes at high school but they were to be shunned because the only boys that took them either looked like girls or had the mannerisms of girls. Perhaps my mechanical drawing experience accounts for the detail and exactitude in my painting and drawing; I don't splash on colors as some do, but 'draw with my nose.' Perhaps I am more of an illustrator than an artist.

I did well in the one engineering drawing course at the University of Washington before I went in the Army in WW-II. Then, after war's end, it was back to college. Engineering had no appeal for me so I decided to try some art courses. I did well in these, graduating "Cum Laude" in 1949. Painting has been sporadic for many years; other needs seemed to be more pressing: 'first things first.' Other creative urges have included some wood carving and some jewelry making, mostly in silver. There was a short period when I did some lapidary work.

My urge to build was creative. This manifested itself over time by my building two houses, a beach cabin, a log cabin, a flying machine, a car and a small boat.

Upon retirement, I sold several watercolors locally, mostly of boats and some landscapes. Today I work mostly in acrylics, which are much less messy than oils. I usually get my art "fix" by winning a blue ribbon annually in the County Fair and

My watercolor 'Padlocked'

once I won third place in a national competition of aviation art at The Experimental Aircraft Association annual air show in Oshkosh, Wisconsin. Another of my paintings has been accepted for exhibition recently at this event. Over 200 entries are submitted annually for this competition and a jury selects about 40 to hang in their gallery for a year. The gallery is located in the EAA's museum.

So, you have seen some scenes of my life as an aviator, sailor and artist. I trust some of them have been either interesting or entertaining. I could perhaps do better as an author, but I would have to be more creative and make up things, invent stories. I have tried to be factual and tell it like it was. I consider myself a survivor from some of my 'close ones' and appreciate having been somewhat adventurous in my 85 years. I still have the urge to get out my paint box, hoist my sails and kick the tire and light the fire!

FINI